MOUNTAIN BIKE!
Southern Utah

A GUIDE TO THE CLASSIC TRAILS

FIRST EDITION

D1322360

MICHAEL McCOY

Menasha
Ridge
Press

© 2000 by Michael McCoy
All Rights Reserved
Published by Menasha Ridge Press
First Edition

Library of Congress Cataloging-in-Publication Data:
McCoy, Michael, 1951-
Mountain bike southern Utah: a guide to the classic trails /
Michael McCoy. —1st ed.
p.   cm.
includes index
ISBN 0-89732-314-9 (pbk.)
1. All terrain cycling—Utah—Guidebooks.
2. Bicycle trails—Utah—Guidebooks.
GV1045.5.U8 M33 2000
796.6'3'09792—dc21   00-039444
CIP

Photos by the author unless otherwise credited
Maps by Ink Spot, a design company™
Production by Manuscript Ink™
Cover photo by Dennis Coello
Cover and text design by Suzanne Holt

Menasha Ridge Press
P.O. Box 43673
Birmingham, Alabama 35243
Distributed by The Globe Pequot Press

All trails described in this book are legal for mountain bikes. But rules can change—especially for off-road bicycles, the new kid on the outdoor recreation block. Land-access issues and conflicts between cyclists, hikers, equestrians, and other users can cause the rewriting of recreation regulations on public lands, sometimes resulting in a ban of mountain bike use on specific trails. That's why it's the responsibility of each rider to check and make sure that he or she rides only on trails where mountain biking is permitted.

CAUTION

Outdoor recreational activities are by their very nature potentially hazardous. All participants in such activities must assume the responsibility for their own actions and safety. The information contained in this guidebook cannot replace sound judgment and good decision-making skills, which help reduce risk exposure, nor does the scope of this book allow for disclosure of all the potential hazards and risks involved in such activities.

Learn as much as possible about the outdoor recreational activities in which you participate, prepare for the unexpected, and be cautious. The reward will be a safer and more enjoyable experience.

MOUNTAIN BIKE!
Southern Utah

CONTENTS

PANORAMALAND

COLOR COUNTRY

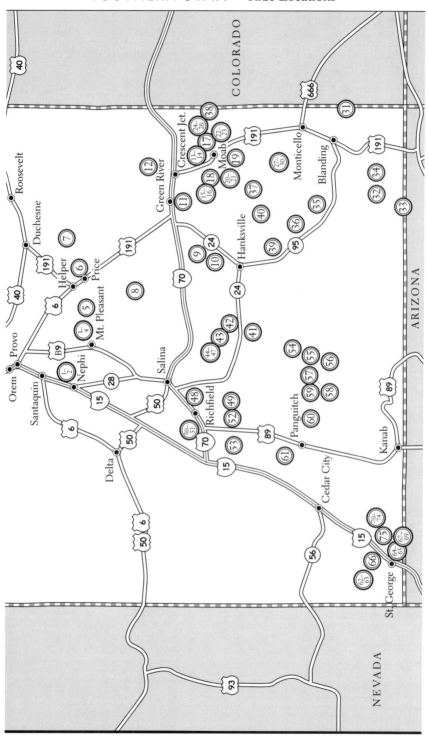

AMERICA BY MOUNTAIN BIKE! · Map Legend

Ride trailhead

Primary bike trail	Direction of travel	Optional bike trail and trailhead	Other trail	Hiking-only trail

Interstate highways	US routes	State routes	County or local roads	Unpaved roads (may be 4WD only)

Scale	True north	Cities and towns	Forest Service roads	State border

Public lands*	Ski Trails	Ski Lift	River or stream

✈ Airport

♥ Archaeological or historical site

Boat ramp

▲ Campground (CG)

Cattle guard

† Cemetery or gravesite

♠ Church

Drinking water

Telephone

Golf Course

Fire tower or lookout

Falls or rapids

Food

Gate

House or cabin

Lodging

Mountain pass

△ Mountain summit
3312 (elevation in feet)

Mine or quarry

Mountain or Butte

P Parking

Park office or ranger station

Picnic area

Power line or pipeline

Rest rooms

Spring

Stable, corral, or ranch

Fire Station

Observatory

Tunnel or bridge

Beach/Swimming Area

Cliff, Bluff or Outcropping

* Remember, private property exists in and around our national forests.

ACKNOWLEDGMENTS

This book has been more than three years in the making. I quietly cursed series editor Dennis Coello repeatedly over the course of those three years for talking me into this immense project. Now that the book is in the bag, though, I'm ready to thank him for the opportunity. Thanks, Dennis, it's been fun—really!

I also want to express gratitude to the dozens of cyclists and agency personnel who recommended rides for inclusion in this guide. Jan Wilking and Paul Oelerich at Bicycle Utah were particularly helpful in suggesting rides for several areas, and Glenn Ames at Red Rock Bicycle Co. in St. George offered terrific routing assistance for that part of the state. The crew that puts on the annual "Fish Lake in the Fall" Mountain Bike Festival were great, too, as were the dozen of good folks I pedaled with there, but whose names I don't recall. Bureau of Land Management and Forest Service personnel in every corner of southern Utah helped immensely.

Although he may be surprised to learn that he helped, my colleague Kurt Repanshek in Park City provided good information by way of an article he wrote (and which I edited) covering the Grand Staircase–Escalante National Monument for *Adventure Cyclist* magazine. Speaking of, *muchas gracias* to my editor and confidant at *Adventure Cyclist*, Daniel D'Ambrosio, who time and again permitted me to be late with materials for him because I was so wrapped up in research for this guide. Adventure Cycling member Paul Koenig of Boulder, Colorado, contributed a multi-day ride that unfortunately did not make it into this first cut, but which I hope to add to the guide in a future edition.

Also helpful in ways they may not know were my friends Tim Blumenthal, executive director of the International Mountain Bicycling Association in Boulder, and Bill Harris of the Colorado Plateau Mountain-Bike Trail Association in Montrose. And Penny Shelley, executive director of the Washington County Travel & Convention Bureau in St. George, was most accommodating during my visits to Utah's Dixie.

A special brand of thanks goes to the Teton Valley "Moab group" of which I'm a member (although recently we've been acting more like a "St. George group"): Celia Howarth, Rick and Joanne LaBelle, Dave Stein and Allison

Wilde, Paul Howarth, and Nancy McCullough-McCoy. Through all the plinky, Frisbee throwing (and related broken windows), golfing, and eating, we still somehow manage to find the time and energy to ride our bikes.

Others who accompanied me on featured rides include my brother Roger McCoy of Denver and Ramsey Bentley of Fort Collins. "Ramon," as he is known, was my roommate at the University of Wyoming many moons ago. In the ensuing years, he has permitted me to drag him along on all sorts of exploratory outings. (As long as I don't forget to bring the tequila, he's happy.)

The final and biggest thank you goes to my wife Nancy, who suffered, almost all of the time smilingly, through my longest bout of deadline stress to date.

FOREWORD

Welcome to *North America by Mountain Bike*, a series of more than 20 books designed to provide all-terrain bikers with the information they need to find and ride the very best trails everywhere. Whether you're new to the sport and don't know where to pedal, or an experienced mountain biker who wants to learn the classic trails in another region, this series is for you. Drop a few bucks for the book, spend an hour with the detailed maps and route descriptions, and you're prepared for the finest in off-road cycling.

My role as editor of this series was simple: First, find a mountain biker who knows the area and loves to ride. Second, ask that person to spend a year researching the most popular and very best rides around. And third, have that rider describe each trail in terms of difficulty, scenery, condition, elevation change, and all other categories of information that are important to trail riders. "Pretend you've just completed a ride and met up with fellow mountain bikers at the trailhead," I told each author. "Imagine their questions, be clear in your answers."

As I said, the editorial process—that of sending out riders and reading the submitted chapters—is a snap. But the work involved in finding, riding, and writing about each trail is enormous. In some instances our authors' tasks are made easier by the information contributed by local bike shops or cycling clubs, or even by the writers of local "where-to" guides. Credit for these contributions is provided, when appropriate, in each chapter, and our sincere thanks go to all who have helped.

But the overwhelming majority of trails are discovered and pedaled by our authors themselves, then compared with dozens of other routes to determine if they qualify as "classic"—that area's best in scenery and cycling fun. If you've ever had the experience of pioneering a route from outdated topographic maps, or entering a bike shop to request information from local riders who would much prefer to keep their favorite trails secret, or know how it is to double- and triple-check data to be positive your trail information is correct, then you have an idea of how each of our authors has labored to bring about these books. You and I, and all mountain bikers, are the richer for their efforts.

You'll get more out of this book if you take a moment to read the Introduction explaining how to read the trail listings. The "Topographic Maps" section will help you understand how useful topos will be on a ride, and will also tell you where to get them. And though this is a "where-to," not a "how-to," guide, those of you who have not traveled the backcountry might find "Hitting the Trail" of particular value.

In addition to the material above, newcomers to mountain biking might want to spend a minute with the glossary (see page 217) so that terms like hardpack, single-track, and waterbars won't confuse you when you come across them in the text.

All the best.

Dennis Coello
St. Louis

PREFACE

Beginning at desert elevation, you bang down stairstep ledges and muscle up impossible slickrock pitches. Knobby tires go from purring across smooth, compacted sediments to bogging down in bottomless sand. Dig deep; climb a little longer; push a little harder. Higher up now, Indian paintbrush splashes drab green hillsides with bright scarlet relief, the scents of sage and juniper mingle, and you're not sure if that rasping raven overhead is cheering or jeering. Ah, the top. Way high at last, you can't believe how far you can see. Intense, hot sun; chilly breeze. Have a drink, gobble a snack, laugh with your companions. Then get back to it.

Submit to gravity and lean into that turn. Dive headlong through that shimmering stand of aspen. Mud, sweat, and gears; champagne air and stunning views . . . these are some of what mountain biking in southern Utah is about. I probably don't need to tell you this, since you're reading this book, but mountain biking is infectious, irresistible — it *feels* right. To borrow from the Lovin' Spoonful, it gives you a smile that won't wipe off no matter how hard you try. The sport combines the two-wheeled independence we discovered as kids with the liberating joy we find as adults in the timbered mountains and red rock deserts.

Like the kayak, the sailboard, and fatboy powder skis, the mountain bike is a ticket to silent freedom. Deciding where to set oneself free, though, can present a real dilemma — particularly in the western United States, where so much of the land is publicly owned. Nowhere is this more true than in southern Utah. Millions and millions of acres managed by the state, the U.S. Forest Service, the Bureau of Land Management, and the National Park Service hold more potential routes than ten gnarly dudes or gnarliosa dudettes could cover cumulatively in two lifetimes. That's no lie, and that's where I come in.

It was early spring 1997 — incredibly, more than three years ago — when the former editor of the *Mountain Bike!* series, Dennis Coello, first asked if I would author this guide. I had just finished an intensive, three-year labor of love planning, plotting, and researching the Great Divide Mountain Bike Route, a 2,470-mile bike-packing route running through the Rocky Mountains from Canada to Mexico. Backing up even further, I'd been researching mountain bike and road bike routes for over 20 years, beginning with the TransAmerica Bicycle Trail and including a pair of mountain bike guides I wrote for The Mountaineers (*Mountain Bike Adventures in the Four Corners Region* was one of them). So—although some readers may have little sympathy for my plight—the last thing I wanted to do was jump into another huge fat-tire research project. I needed a break. I felt the urge to learn to surf; or go to Arkansas, buy a little outfit, and take up bass fishing—*something* other than mountain biking. The conversation, spread out over several weeks, went something like this:

Dennis: "Mac, I'd like you to author the Menasha Ridge Press guide to mountain biking in southern Utah."

Me: "Dennis, I'm done writing mountain bike guides. *Finito. No más.* The end. People think it's a romantic way to make a living, but I *know* how much work those things are, and so do you. Been there, done that. Find another sucker."

A few weeks pass.

Dennis: "Have you thought about it some, Mac? Southern Utah is the plum of the country, you know."

Me: "But there's already half a dozen guides to that part of the country. Why do we need another one?"

Dennis: "We don't have one written by you."

Me (my stroked ego causing me to soften a bit): "Well, I guess there could be worse things than spending a few months in the canyon country. But I don't think so."

I don't know how Dennis knew we still had four feet of snow in our yard in mid-March, but I'm convinced he did and that he was playing off my cabin fever. A few more weeks pass. Mid-April, still two feet of snow on the ground.

Dennis: "Whaddaya think, Mac?"

Me: "Okay. I admit it. I'm hooked. I love what I do. Take me to the desert."

In hindsight, it truly was a privilege to travel through country so fine, so surprising, so spectacular, by a mode as fun the bicycle, all under the guise of work. Now that it's done, though, I have to tell you, it *was* a lot of work. Hundreds of hours spent in the pickup truck and on the bike were only the beginning, the prelude to countless more hours at the computer, on the telephone and on the floor, poring over maps and photos. And I still don't consider the project completed. I'd like to invite you to join me in considering this book as phase one of a work in progress. I had hoped the guide would include at least 100 rides, but 75 will have to do this time around. (For one thing, for a state that's so "dry," I was foiled numerous times by heavy rains that made roads and trails impassable.) But I'll keep working on it. I promise. And please, if you run across any gems that you feel should be in future editions, let me know about them. Send the information to:

Michael McCoy
c/o Menasha Ridge Press
P.O. Box 43673
Birmingham, AL 35243

Southern Utah is big, big, big. It's also colorful, drab, high, low, hot, cold, lushly forested, and void of vegetation. In certain instances, those prone to such maladies could suffer claustrophobia and agoraphobia on the same ride and within minutes of one another. There's a certain comfort to the homogeneity or consistency of landscape in a place like, say, Iowa. Southern Utah is the antithesis of the endless, rolling corn and soybean fields of Iowa. You never know what you're going to find when you set out. Southern Utah is confounding and confusing; it's a conundrum. Its landscapes defy logic. Even after all the time I've spent beating around its outback, I still can't quite grasp it. It can be exasperating. You can get lost, dehydrated, burned by the sun, and then freezing cold when that sun goes down. But more often, fortunately, mountain biking through southern Utah is energizing, exciting, and a downright spectacular way to spend time.

Have I come up with the best 75 rides in that part of the world? Probably not. Some of the rides in this book are indisputably among the best, but others are ones I just happened to happen across. They're in the book because, when the spirit moved me, I pulled off the road, pulled the bike out of the truck, and started riding, just to find what lay hidden around the bend and the one after that. While on reconnaissance missions I spotted dozens of other trailheads and diverging roads going places I would love to have explored, but lack of time and/or energy (or too much rain) precluded it. I guarantee that you can stumble across rides every bit as good as many of those included here by using this book as your locator for "adventuring areas." In my view, a guidebook such as this is successful if people buy it and follow the featured rides. But I consider it *wildly* successful if it tempts and persuades readers to further explore a given area on their own after trying out a highlighted sampler or two.

Many guidebooks, in my opinion, contain too many difficult rides. Neophytes and intermediate-level riders typically are the ones who really need guidance, whereas advanced mountain bikers tend to find their own rides through word of mouth and not to rely as heavily on guidebooks. So, I've attempted to err toward the intermediate, but I'm not sure I was successful; doing so within the constraints of southern Utah's radical terrain is a tall order. Moreover, there are quite a few classic expert rides that just couldn't be left out.

Regarding organization of the book, I've borrowed the regions into which the Utah Travel Council divides southern Utah; although, for logistics' sake, I've moved a corner of their Panoramaland into my Castle Country. Beginning in the north-central part of southern Utah, the book leads you in serpentine fashion from Castle Country to Canyonlands to Panoramaland and, finally, to Color Country.

I'm a history, natural history, and archaeology nut, but from the outset I resolved to restrain myself and not go overboard including information of that sort. As I see it, my main job here is to tell you (1) how to get to the trailhead, (2) what to expect when riding the trail, and (3) how not to get lost while pedaling from point A to point B. Excellent books on my favorite subjects, written by individuals far more knowledgeable than I, are widely available and highly recommended as companions to this guide.

By the way, I urge you camp out for at least part of the time you spend in southern Utah, whether to you "camping" means sagebrushing it or traveling in a 32-foot Runnamucka. Particularly in the desert, it is in the early morning and evening when things really come alive, and you won't get the full desert (or mountain) experience if you're holed up in a motel room at those times of day. Impressions I keep with me from the desert, which help me get through the six months of winter common in the Tetons, include the bats of summer darting about at twilight (if a red-tailed hawk is a Cadillac, then a bat is a Mazda Miata). The light—of morning, of evening, of night . . . different in every direction you look and always changing throughout the day. Shadows reflecting off clouds; clouds casting their own shadows on rimrock walls; the heat; the cold; the solitude of most of the rides, except for the fat-tire fellowship of the Slickrock Bike Trail and other Moab-area trails. The dryness; and just how wet water looks when you see it in such arid country. The redness of rock and cliffs; a rampaging red river where ten minutes ago only sand filled the wash.

While riding what for me was one of those previously mentioned classic hard rides—the Mytoge Mountain Loop (Ride 46)—I had a funny experience; unique, but at the same time representative of the sorts of serendipitous things that can happen when you're pedaling through the backcountry. It was during the Fish Lake in the Fall Mountain Bike Festival, a fun and highly recommended get-together that happens each September. We were a large group, but by the time I was about 12 miles into it we were well spread out. Some riders were behind me, some were ahead, and I was alone at the moment. I was dying—out of water, hungry, tired, thirsty, close to seeing double. Suddenly, I thought I *was* seeing double: Ahead a couple hundred yards were two horsemen, wearing identical dusters and white Stetsons, astride similar-looking horses. As I pulled up close, I stopped to talk to the riders, whom by then I recognized as two distinct individuals.

"Howdy!" I said.

"You look like you could use a cold beer, friend," the bigger man said.

"You know, as a matter of fact I could," I said, not even trying to hide my excitement at the thought (and conveniently forgetting to remember things I've read about not mixing exercise and alcohol).

He reached down into his saddlebag and pulled out a frosty Coors Light. "Here you go pardner," he said, grinning.

What I said next just popped out. Call it exercise-induced insanity, endorphin euphoria, or whatever, but I couldn't help myself. Glancing up, I said, "I ride 12 tough, grueling miles, climb 2,500 vertical feet over stumps and rocks and roots, sweat and freeze, and then sweat some more . . . and you give me a *light* beer?"

My new friend just looked dumbfounded, but his companion burst out laughing, obviously remembering the old Coors Light ad campaign I was parroting.

"Uh, just kidding," I said. "This is perfect. Thanks."

Funny things happen in the outback, yes they do. On another occasion I was driving south over drenched gumbo clay from Kodachrome State Park toward Grosvener Arch, in the Grand Staircase–Escalante National Monument. It had been raining for three days, but still a newly posted sign informed me that the road was open as far as Grosvener. Not far past that sign, though, I topped a rise to look down on a Bureau of Land Management rig mired in a low spot, its right rear tire hanging precariously off the edge of the road. There was 10 to 15 feet of nothing but air between it and the bottom of the wash. The truck obviously wasn't going anywhere soon. Not wanting to get stuck myself, I pulled over and walked the 100 yards down to the situation. The young BLM employee in charge of the vehicle was perplexed and agitated, wondering how the heck to get out of the predicament. "Damn," he told me, "there was a road there yesterday." A torrent of water had taken out a good four feet from the right-hand side of the road, and he'd driven right into the void. I helped him out as best I could by standing there and scratching my head, too.

Suddenly a gnarly old desert rat, a specter straight out of "The Monkey Wrench Gang," gray-bearded, gray-headed, and odiferous, materialized on the far side of the road mess. "Young man," he said, "why in God's name did the government send you out in this country with tires like that on your rig?" Said river rat, who lived nearby and had tractor-worthy tires on his beat-up four-wheel-drive Dodge, grabbed a chain out of the bed and proceeded to pull the young BLMer out of the quagmire. It is the way of the wild to help those in need.

ETIQUETTE AND ETHICS

A few years back I read a travel article in *The Missoulian* (Missoula, Montana) by Page Stegner, son of Wallace Stegner, the late, great chronicler and novelist of the Rocky Mountain West. In it he wrote—apparently in an uncontrolled fit of arrogance—that "an infestation of mountain-biker blight recently discovered in the Moab area is rapidly spreading throughout the Colorado Plateau."

Let's vow to prove Mr. Stegner wrong. It may not be your job to make people like you, but it is incumbent on you and me to act on behalf of, and not to the detriment of, others who enjoy mountain biking. Make peace, not turmoil, for those who will follow in your tracks. Always abide by the International Mountain Bicycling Association's Rules of the Trail (detailed in the Introduction), but also know that there are additional considerations to be aware of in the exceedingly dry deserts of the Southwest:

> Avoid riding or walking through gardens of cryptobiotic soil. These living crusts, found only in arid regions like southern Utah, are self-sustaining biological units, composed of a mix of mosses, algae, fungi, and lichens. They're extremely fragile and take decades to form or to heal.

> When camping, try to find previously used sites rather than creating a new one.

> Pack out your garbage, organic as well as inorganic. An apple core, for example, can take more than two years to break down in the desert.

> For human waste disposal, use the "cat hole" technique by digging a hole four to six inches deep and at least 300 feet from any water source. Pack out toilet paper in a resealable plastic bag. If you're camping at an undeveloped site along a river or stream— as counterintuitive as it may sound—the National Park Service recommends urinating in the river rather than along the beach or bushes, where odor will build up.

PERSONAL SAFETY

There are certain safety matters you also need to be aware of, which may not be concerns in your part of the country:

Lightning, a potential killer, is very common in southern Utah, particularly in the mountains. (It recently hit close to home in my case: One of the many companions I rode with while researching this book was Dave Malinowski. He and his girlfriend, both professional adventure racers, were killed by lightning in Wyoming's Medicine Bow Mountains in the summer of 1999.) Avoid peaks and ridges when conditions are right for the build-up of thunderheads. Thuderstorms can also cause flash flooding in arroyos and creekbeds; watch closely for these phenomena and *never* camp in a water course.

Various sorts of creepy-crawlies are found at the lower elevations of southern Utah, including rattlesnakes. The Arizona Strip, for instance, south of St. George, is home to five species of rattlers: the sidewinder, mojave green, speckled, western, and black-tailed rattlesnakes. Generally, snakes will not be a hazard when you're biking, but do watch where you're stepping and putting your hands when climbing in rocky areas or walking through brush.

Hantavirus, a serious respiratory illness spread by rodents—in particular, deer mice—was first diagnosed in the Four Corners in 1993. Since then it has killed several dozen people in the region. Infected rodents carry the virus in their feces, urine, and saliva; infection can occur in humans if dust from the dry saliva or excreta is inhaled. Avoid disturbing rodent burrows and visiting places that are likely to be frequented by rodents, such as vacant cabins and other dwellings, barns, outbuildings, caves, and rock overhangs.

PAST AND PRESENT CULTURES

Southern Utah is home to literally hundreds of thousands of prehistoric Native American sites, many of which have been thoughtlessly or maliciously vandalized over the years. Keep an eye out for the brochure entitled "Archaeological Heritage of Utah," produced in partnership by the National Park Service, the Bureau of Land Management, and several other agencies. The publication, widely available throughout the region, includes the locations of more than 30 major sites. It also features tips on treading lightly to protect yourself as well as the ruins you visit. Among the pointers:

Watch for rattlesnakes.
Do not climb on ruins or lean on ruin walls.
Feel free to photograph rock art, but don't touch it.
Respect other visitors, some of whom may consider the ruins sacred.

Also, you should *never* remove an artifact from a site, regardless of how inconsequential it may seem. That includes stone chippings and potsherds.

Today, the Native American cultures of Utah have been largely displaced by that of the Mormons. The state's population is roughly 66 percent Mormon, which often translates to a rather staid atmosphere of God-fearing reverence and family values. New Orleans it ain't, but these are good people. Moreover, although the percentage of Mormons is high, this also means that fully one-third of the state's inhabitants are non-Mormon. In fact, Utah today is more ethnically diverse than it ever has been. The minority population grew by 50 percent in the 1990s, resulting from a booming economy and from doors that have swung open

wider than they've been since the Mormons moved in 150 years ago. Look for these trends to continue and intensify as the 2002 Winter Olympic Games approach as well as in the aftermath of the games.

Just as you would do when visiting an Indian reservation or a foreign country, you should show respect for the Mormon culture when you're in Utah. The mere fact that Mormons settled and prospered in a land so harsh and unfriendly should be reason enough to elicit that respect, along with no small amount of awe.

That's it; lecture's over. Let's go have some fun!

Michael McCoy

Wildlife Viewing

7 Nine-Mile Canyon
24 Onion Creek–Kokopelli
27 Dancing with Cottonwood Creek
51 Clear Creek–Fish Creek
61 Big John Flat
66 Live at Leeds

Climbers' Delights

1 Pole–Summit Pull
47 UM Pass
49 Sevier Grunt
53 Marysvale Not-So-Flat
57 Alan Canyon–Water Canyon Loop

Short and Sweet

2 Oak to Aspen
8 Wedge Overlook
11 Crystal Geyser
12 Sego Canyon
13 Willow Flats
35 Natural Bridges National Monument
50 Lott Creek Trials and Piñon–Juniper Hillclimb
58 Panorama Trail
70 Grafton Ghost Town

Entry-Level Single-Track

16 Gemini Bridges
45 Lakeshore Trail West
60 Casto Canyon
65 Green Valley Toboggan Run

Family

4 Res to Des
10 Wild Horse Escape
14 Salt Valley Road
15 Hurrah Pass
28 Hart's Draw
29 Colorado River Rim
31 Hovenweep
39 Burr Point

Family (continued)

41 Capitol Reef Scenic Drive
44 Sevenmile Cruise
48 Glenwood Getaway
62 Gunlock Loop
71 Gooseberry Cruiser

Technical Single-Track

5 Castle Valley Ridge Trail System
23 Porcupine Rim
46 Mytoge Mountain Loop
67 Race Course Loop
73 Gooseberry Gander

Slickrock City

17 Klondike Bluffs
18 Bartlett Wash
20 Poison Spider Mesa
21 Amasa Back
22 Slickrock Bike Trail
30 Elephant Hill–Confluence Overlook
72 Gooseberry Slickrock Trail
74 Rockville Bench

What a View!

3 Skyline Drive–Miller Flat Loop
25 Dewey–Koko 1
32 Valley of the Gods
33 Monument Valley
34 Comb Ridge
40 Panorama Point
56 Grand Staircase–Escalante National Monument
59 Powell Point
73 Gooseberry Gander

Multiday Epics

37 White Rim Road
38 Kokopelli's Trail
42 Cathedral Valley
55 Hole-in-the-Rock Road

INTRODUCTION

TRAIL DESCRIPTION OUTLINE

Each trail in this book begins with key information that includes length, configuration, aerobic and technical difficulty, trail conditions, scenery, and special comments. Additional description is contained in 11 individual categories. The following will help you to understand all of the information provided.

Trail name: In some instances, trails are named by the author. In others, trail names are as designated on United States Geological Survey (USGS) or Forest Service or other maps, and/or by local custom.

At a Glance Information

Length/configuration: The overall length of a trail is described in miles, unless stated otherwise. The configuration is a description of the shape of each trail—whether the trail is a loop, out-and-back (that is, along the same route), figure eight, trapezoid, isosceles triangle, decahedron . . . (just kidding), or if it connects with another trail described in the book. See the Glossary for definitions of *point-to-point* and *combination.*

Aerobic difficulty: This provides a description of the degree of physical exertion required to complete the ride.

Technical difficulty: This provides a description of the technical skill required to pedal a ride. Trails are often described here in terms of being paved, unpaved, sandy, hard-packed, washboarded, two- or four-wheel-drive, single-track or double-track. All terms that might be unfamiliar to the first-time mountain biker are defined in the Glossary.

Note: For both the aerobic and technical difficulty categories, authors were asked to keep in mind the fact that all riders are not equal, and thus to gauge the trail in terms of how the middle-of-the-road rider—someone between the newcomer and Ned Overend—could handle the route. Comments about the trail's length, condition, and elevation change will also assist you in determining the difficulty of any trail relative to your own abilities.

Scenery: Here you will find a general description of the natural surroundings during the seasons most riders pedal the trail and a suggestion of what is to be found at special times (like great fall foliage or cactus in bloom).

Special comments: Unique elements of the ride are mentioned.

Category Information

General location: This category describes where the trail is located in reference to a nearby town or other landmark.

Elevation change: Unless stated otherwise, the figure provided is the total change in elevation as measured from high point to low point. Total gain, that is, the cumulative total feet in which the trail ascends, is difficult to measure accurately, but suffice it to say that it generally exceeds the simple difference between high and low points. In an effort to give you a sense of how much climbing is involved in a particular ride, brief but general descriptive phrases are used in conjunction with elevation change.

Season: This is the best time of year to pedal the route, taking into account trail conditions (for example, when it will not be muddy), riding comfort (when the weather is too hot, cold, or wet), and local hunting seasons.

Note: Because the opening and closing dates of deer, elk, moose, and antelope seasons often change from year to year, riders should check with the local Fish and Wildlife Department or call a sporting goods store (or any place that sells hunting licenses) in a nearby town before heading out. Wear bright clothes in the fall, and don't wear suede jackets while in the saddle. Hunter's-orange tape on the helmet is also a good idea.

Services: This category is of primary importance in guides for paved-road tourers and is far less crucial to most mountain bike trail descriptions because there are usually no services whatsoever to be found. Authors have noted when water is available on desert or long mountain routes and have listed the availability of food, lodging, campgrounds, and bike shops. If all these services are present, you will find only the words, "All services available in . . ."

Hazards: Special hazards like hunting season, rattlesnakes, mountain lions, bears, ticks, poison oak, earthquake, lightning, other trail users, and vehicular traffic are noted here. Other hazards which are considered a regular part of a ride, such as steep cliffs, boulder stair-steps, or scree on steep downhill sections are discussed in the "Notes on the trail" section.

Rescue index: Determining how far one is from help on a particular trail can be difficult due to the backcountry nature of most mountain bike rides. Authors therefore state the proximity of homes or Forest Service outposts, nearby roads where one might hitch a ride, or the likelihood of other bikers being encountered on the trail. Phone numbers of local sheriff departments or hospitals have not been provided because phones are almost never available. If you are able to reach a phone, the local operator will connect you with emergency services.

Land status: This category provides information regarding whether the trail crosses land operated by the Forest Service, the Bureau of Land Management, or a city, state, or national park; whether it crosses private land whose owner (at the time the author did the research) has allowed mountain bikers right of passage; and so on. A note regarding fees for land usage: There is no standard by which use-fees are charged. Some land agencies charge a fee to park within designated areas, others charge a fee regardless of where you park your car. Some areas are free year-round, others only during the off-season or during the week. Some parks charge a day-use fee, regardless of whether you park a car or not. Most national forests do not charge a day-use fee, nor do most BLM districts. State parks almost always charge a day-use fee at the very least.

Note: Authors have been extremely careful to offer only those routes that are open to bikers and are legal to ride. However, because land ownership changes over time, and because the land-use controversy created by mountain bikes still has not completely subsided, it is the duty of each cyclist to look for and heed signs warning against trail use. Don't expect this book to get you off the hook when you're facing some small-town judge for pedaling past a "Biking Prohibited" sign erected the day before you arrived. Look for these signs, read them, and heed the advice. And remember, there's always another trail.

Maps: The maps in this book have been produced with great care and, in conjunction with the trail-following suggestions, will help you stay on course. But as every experienced mountain biker knows, things can get tricky in the backcountry. It is therefore strongly suggested that you avail yourself of the detailed information found in the USGS (United States Geological Survey) 7.5 minute series topographic maps. In some cases, authors have found that specific Forest Service or other maps may be more useful than the USGS quads, and they tell how to obtain them.

Finding the trail: Detailed information on how to reach the trailhead and where to park your car is provided here.

Sources of additional information: Here you will find the address and/or phone number of a bike shop, governmental agency, or other source from which trail information can be obtained.

Notes on the trail: This is where you are guided carefully through any portions of the trail that are particularly difficult to follow. The author also may add information about the route that does not fit easily in the other categories. This category will not be present for those rides where the route is easy to follow.

ABBREVIATIONS

The following road-designation abbreviations are used in the *Mountain Bike!* series:

CR	County Road	I-	Interstate
FR	Farm Route	IR	Indian Route
FS	Forest Service road	US	United States highway

State highways are designated with the appropriate two-letter state abbreviation, followed by the road number. Example: UT 89 = Utah State Highway 89.

RIDE CONFIGURATIONS

Combination: This type of route may combine two or more configurations. For example, a point-to-point route may integrate a scenic loop or an out-and-back spur midway through the ride. Likewise, an out-and-back may have a loop at its farthest point (this configuration looks like a cherry with a stem attached; the stem is the out-and-back, the fruit is the terminus loop). Or a loop route may have multiple out-and-back spurs and/or loops to the side. Mileage for a combination route is for the total distance to complete the ride.

Loop: This route configuration is characterized by riding from the designated trailhead to a distant point, then returning to the trailhead via a different route (or simply continuing on the same in a circle route) without doubling back. You always move forward across new terrain but return to the starting point when finished. Mileage is for the entire loop from the trailhead back to trailhead.

Out-and-back: A ride where you will return on the same trail you pedaled out. While this might sound far more boring than a loop route, many trails look very different when pedaled in the opposite direction.

Point-to-point: A vehicle shuttle (or similar assistance) is required for this type of route, which is ridden from the designated trailhead to a distant location, or endpoint, where the route ends. Total mileage is for the one-way trip from the trailhead to endpoint.

Spur: A road or trail that intersects the main trail you're following.

Ride Configurations contributed by Gregg Bromka

TOPOGRAPHIC MAPS

The maps in this book, when used in conjunction with the route directions present in each chapter, will in most instances be sufficient to get you to the trail and keep you on it. However, you will find superior detail and valuable information in the USGS 7.5 minute series topographic maps. Recognizing how indispensable these are to bikers and hikers alike, many bike shops and sporting goods stores now carry topos of the local area.

If you're brand new to mountain biking you might be wondering, "What's a topographic map?" In short, these differ from standard "flat" maps in that they indicate not only linear distance but elevation as well. One glance at a topo will show you the difference, for contour lines are spread across the map like dozens of intricate spider webs. Each contour line represents a particular elevation, and at the base of each topo a particular contour interval designation is given. Yes, it sounds confusing if you're new to the lingo, but it truly is a simple and wonderfully helpful system. Keep reading.

Let's assume that the 7.5 minute series topo before us says "Contour Interval 40 feet," that the short trail we'll be pedaling is two inches in length on the map, and that it crosses five contour lines from its beginning to end. What do we know? Well, because the linear scale of this series is 2,000 feet to the inch (roughly 2 3/4 inches representing 1 mile), we know our trail is approximately 1/5 of a mile long (2 inches × 2,000 feet). But we also know we'll be climbing or descending 200 vertical feet (5 contour lines × 40 feet each) over that distance. And the elevation designations written on occasional contour lines will tell us if we're heading up or down.

The authors of this series warn their readers of upcoming terrain, but only a detailed topo gives you the information you need to pinpoint your position on a map, steer yourself toward optional trails and roads nearby, and see at a glance if you'll be pedaling hard to take them. It's a lot of information for a very low cost. In fact, the only drawback with topos is their size—several feet square. I've tried rolling them into tubes, folding them carefully, even cutting them into blocks and photocopying the pieces. Any of these systems is a pain, but no matter how you pack the maps you'll be happy they're along. And you'll be even happier if you pack a compass as well.

In addition to local bike shops and sporting goods stores, you'll find topos at major universities and some public libraries, where you might try photocopying the ones you need to avoid the cost of buying them. But if you want your own and can't find them locally, contact:

USGS Map Sales
Box 25286
Denver, CO 80225
(888) ASK-USGS (275-8747)
http://mapping.usgs.gov/esic/to_order.html/

VISA and MasterCard are accepted. Ask for an index while you're at it, plus a price list and a copy of the booklet *Topographic Maps*. In minutes you'll be reading them like a pro.

A second excellent series of maps available to mountain bikers is that put out by the United States Forest Service. If your trail runs through an area designated as a national forest, look in the phone book (white pages) under the United States Government listings, find the Department of Agriculture heading, and run your finger down that section until you find the Forest Service. Give them a call, and they'll provide the address of the regional Forest Service office, from which you can obtain the appropriate map.

TRAIL ETIQUETTE

Pick up almost any mountain bike magazine these days and you'll find articles and letters to the editor about trail conflict. For example, you'll find hikers' tales of being blindsided by speeding mountain bikers, complaints from mountain bikers about being blamed for trail damage that was really caused by horse or cattle traffic, and cries from bikers about those "kamikaze" riders who through their antics threaten to close even more trails to all of us.

The authors of this series have been very careful to guide you to only those trails that are open to mountain biking (or at least were open at the time of their research), and without exception have warned of the damage done to our sport through injudicious riding. We can all benefit from glancing over the following International Mountain Bicycling Association (IMBA) Rules of the Trail before saddling up.

1. *Ride on open trails only.* Respect trail and road closures (ask if not sure), avoid possible trespass on private land, obtain permits and authorization as may be required. Federal and state wilderness areas are closed to cycling.

2. *Leave no trace.* Be sensitive to the dirt beneath you. Even on open trails, you should not ride under conditions where you will leave evidence of your passing, such as on certain soils shortly after rain. Observe the different types of soils and trail construction; practice low-impact cycling. This also means staying on the trail and not creating any new ones. Be sure to pack out at least as much as you pack in.

3. *Control your bicycle!* Inattention for even a second can cause disaster. Excessive speed can maim and threaten people; there is no excuse for it!

4. *Always yield the trail.* Make known your approach well in advance. A friendly greeting (or a bell) is considerate and works well; startling someone may cause loss

of trail access. Show your respect when passing others by slowing to a walk or even stopping. Anticipate that other trail users may be around corners or in blind spots.

5. *Never spook animals.* All animals are startled by an unannounced approach, a sudden movement, or a loud noise. This can be dangerous for you, for others, and for the animals. Give animals extra room and time to adjust to you. In passing, use special care and follow the directions of horseback riders (ask if uncertain). Running cattle and disturbing wild animals is a serious offense. Leave gates as you found them or as marked.

6. *Plan ahead.* Know your equipment, your ability, and the area in which you are riding—and prepare accordingly. Be self-sufficient at all times. Wear a helmet, keep your machine in good condition, and carry necessary supplies for changes in weather or other conditions. A well-executed trip is a satisfaction to you and not a burden or offense to others.

For more information, contact IMBA, P.O. Box 7578, Boulder, CO 80306, (303) 545-9011.

Additionally, the following Code of Ethics by the National Off-Road Biking Association (NORBA) is worthy of your attention.

1. I will yield the right of way to other non-motorized recreationists. I realize that people judge all cyclists by my actions.

2. I will slow down and use caution when approaching or overtaking another and will make my presence known well in advance.

3. I will maintain control of my speed at all times and will approach turns in anticipation of someone around the bend.

4. I will stay on designated trails to avoid trampling native vegetation and minimize potential erosion to trails by not using muddy trails or shortcutting switchbacks.

5. I will not disturb wildlife or livestock.

6. I will not litter. I will pack out what I pack in, and pack out more than my share if possible.

7. I will respect public and private property, including trail use and no trespassing signs; I will leave gates as I found them.

8. I will always be self-sufficient and my destination and travel speed will be determined by my ability, my equipment, the terrain, and present and potential weather conditions.

9. I will not travel solo when bike-packing in remote areas.

10. I will leave word of my destination and when I plan to return.

11. I will practice minimum impact bicycling by "taking only pictures and memories and leaving only waffle prints."

12. I will always wear a helmet when I ride.

Worthy of mention are the following suggestions based on a list by Utah's Wasatch-Cache National Forest and the *Tread Lightly!* program advocated by the U.S. Forest Service and Bureau of Land Management.

1. *Study a forest map before you ride.* Currently, bicycles are permitted on roads and developed trails which are designated bikes permitted. If your route crosses

private land, it is your responsibility to obtain right-of-way permission from the landowner.

2. *Stay out of designated wilderness areas.* By law, all vehicles, including mountain bikes are not allowed.

3. *Stay off of roads and trails "put to bed."* These may be resource roads no longer used for logging or mining, or they may be steep trails being replaced by easier ones. So that the path returns to its natural state, they're usually blocked or signed closed to protect new vegetation.

4. *Keep groups small.* Riding in large groups degrades the outdoor experience for others, can disturb wildlife, and usually leads to greater resource damage.

5. *Avoid riding on wet trails.* Bicycle tires leave ruts in wet trails. These ruts concentrate runoff and accelerate erosion. Postponing a ride when the trails are wet will preserve the trails for future use.

6. *Stay on roads and trails.* Riding cross-country destroys vegetation and damages the soil. Resist the urge to pioneer a new road or trail, or to cut across a switchback. Avoid riding through meadows, on steep hillsides, or along stream banks and lakeshores because the terrain is easily scarred by churning wheels.

7. *Always yield to others.* Trails are shared by hikers, horses, and bicycles. Move off the trail to allow horses to pass and stop to allow hikers adequate room to share the trail. Simply yelling "Bicycle!" is not acceptable.

8. *Control your speed.* Excessive speed endangers yourself and other forest users.

9. *Avoid wheel lock-up and spin-out.* Steep terrain is especially vulnerable to trail wear. Locking brakes on steep descents or when stopping needlessly damages trails. If a slope is steep enough to require locking wheels and skidding, dismount and walk your bicycle. Likewise, if an ascent is so steep that your rear wheel slips and spins, dismount and walk your bicycle.

10. *Protect waterbars and switchbacks.* Waterbars, the rock and log drains built to direct water off trails, protect trails from erosion. When you encounter a waterbar, ride directly over the top or dismount and walk your bicycle. Riding around the ends of waterbars destroys their effectiveness and speeds erosion. Skidding around switchback corners shortens trail life. Slow down for switchback corners and keep your wheels rolling.

11. *If you abuse it, you lose it.* Mountain bikers are relative newcomers to the forest and must prove themselves responsible trail users. By following the guidelines above, and by participating in trail maintenance service projects, bicyclists can help avoid closures that would prevent them from using trails.

12. *Know your bicycle handling limitations.*

You get the drift. So that everyone can continue riding our bikes through some of our country's most beautiful places, I urge you to follow the codes above and not be the "one bad apple" that spoils it for the rest of us.

HITTING THE TRAIL

Once again, because this is a "where-to," not a "how-to" guide, the following will be brief. If you're a veteran trail rider, these suggestions might serve to remind you of something you've forgotten to pack. If you're a newcomer, they might convince you to think twice before hitting the backcountry unprepared.

Water: I've heard the questions dozens of times. "How much is enough? One bottle? Two? Three?! But think of all that extra weight!" Well, one simple physiological fact should convince you to err on the side of excess when it comes to deciding how much water to pack: A human working hard in 90-degree temperature needs approximately ten quarts of fluids every day. Ten quarts. That's two and a half gallons— 12 large water bottles or 16 small ones. And, with water weighing in at approximately 8 pounds per gallon, a one-day supply comes to a whopping 20 pounds.

In other words, pack along two or three bottles even for short rides. And make sure you can purify the water found along the trail on longer routes. When writing of those routes where this could be of critical importance, each author has provided information on where water can be found near the trail—if it can be found at all. But drink it untreated and you run the risk of disease. (See *giardia* in the Glossary.)

One sure way to kill the protozoans, bacteria, and viruses in water is to boil it. Right. That's just how you want to spend your time on a bike ride. Besides, who wants to carry a stove or denude the countryside stoking bonfires to boil water?

Luckily, there is a better way. Many riders pack along the inexpensive and only slightly distasteful tetraglycine hydroperiodide tablets (sold under the names Potable Aqua, Globaline, and Coughlan's, among others). Some invest in portable, lightweight purifiers that filter out the crud. Unfortunately, both iodine *and* filtering are now required to be absolutely sure you've killed all the nasties you can't see. Tablets or iodine drops by themselves will knock off the well-known *giardia*, once called "beaver fever" for its transmission to the water through the feces of infected beavers. One to four weeks after ingestion, giardia will have you bloated, vomiting, shivering with chills, and living in the bathroom. (Though you won't care while you're suffering, beavers are getting a bum rap, for other animals are carriers also.)

But now there's another parasite we must worry about—*cryptosporidium*. "Crypto" brings on symptoms very similar to *giardia*, but unlike that fellow protozoan it's equipped with a shell sufficiently strong to protect it against the chemical killers that stop giardia cold. This means we're either back to boiling or on to using a water filter to screen out both *giardia* and crypto, plus the iodine to knock off viruses. All of which sounds like a time-consuming pain, but really isn't. Some water filters come equipped with an iodine chamber to guarantee full protection. Or you can simply add a pill or drops to the water you've just filtered (if you aren't allergic to iodine, of course). The pleasures of backcountry biking—and the displeasure of getting sick— make this relatively minor effort worth every one of the few minutes involved.

Tools: Ever since my first cross-country tour in 1965 I've been kidded about the number of tools I pack on the trail. And so I will exit entirely from this discussion by providing a list compiled by two mechanic (and mountain biker) friends of mine. After all, since they make their livings fixing bikes, and get their kicks by riding them, who could be a better source?

These two suggest the following as an absolute minimum:

tire levers	spare tube and patch kit
air pump	Allen wrenches (3, 4, 5, and 6 mm)
spoke wrench	six-inch crescent (adjustable-end) wrench
chain rivet tool	small flat-blade screwdriver

On the trail, their personal tool pouches contain these additional items:

channel locks (small)
air gauge
tire valve cap (the metal kind, with a valve-stem remover)
baling wire (ten or so inches, for temporary repairs)
duct tape (small roll for temporary repairs or tire boot)
boot material (small piece of old tire or a large tube patch)
spare chain link
rear derailleur pulley
spare nuts and bolts
paper towel and tube of waterless hand cleaner

First-Aid kit: My personal kit contains the following, sealed inside double Ziploc bags:

sunscreen
aspirin
butterfly-closure bandages
Band-Aids
snakebite kit
gauze (one roll)
gauze compress pads (a half-dozen 4" × 4")
ace bandages or Spenco joint wraps
Benadryl (an antihistamine, in case of allergic reactions)
water purification tablets/water filter (on long rides)
Moleskin/Spenco "Second Skin"
hydrogen peroxide, iodine, or Mercurochrome (some kind of antiseptic)
matches or pocket cigarette lighter
whistle (more effective in signaling rescuers than your voice)

Final considerations: The authors of this series have done a good job suggesting that specific items be packed for certain trails—rain gear in particular seasons, a hat and gloves for mountain passes, or shades for desert jaunts. Heed their warnings, and think ahead. Good luck.

Dennis Coello

AND NOW, A WORD ABOUT CELLULAR PHONES . . .

Thinking of bringing the Flip-Fone along on your next off-road ride? Before you do, ask yourself the following questions:

- Do I know where I'm going? Do I have an adequate map? Can I use a compass effectively? Do I know the shortest way to civilization if I need to bail out early and find some help?

- If I'm on the trail for longer than planned, am I ready for it? Do I have adequate water? Have I packed something to eat? Will I be warm enough if I'm still out there after dark?

- Am I prepared for possible injuries? Do I have a first-aid kit? Do I know what to do in case of a cut, fracture, snakebite, or heat exhaustion?

- Is my tool kit adequate for likely mechanical problems? Can I fix a flat? Can I untangle a chain? Am I prepared to walk out if the bike is unridable?

If you answered "yes" to *every* question above, you may pack the phone, but consider a good whistle instead. It's lighter, cheaper, and nearly as effective.

If they start searching for you, but dusk is only two hours away, and you have no signaling device and your throat is too dry to shout, and meanwhile you can't get the bleeding stopped, you are out of luck. I mean *really* out of luck.

And when the battery goes dead, you're on your own again. Enough said.

Jeff Faust
Author of Mountain Bike! New Hampshire

CASTLE COUNTRY

Castle Country, the smallest of the four travel regions covered in this book, encompasses such an astounding array of landscapes that it is like the rest of southern Utah in microcosm. Because it is relatively small compared with the other three regions, I have cheated a bit and included three rides (1, 2, and 3) that are technically within Panoramaland. Not only does this give the Castle Country ride count a boost, but it also makes more sense in terms of the book's flow and the meandering manner in which the reader is encouraged to travel through southern Utah.

The "Castle" in the name Castle Country no doubt refers to such features as the cliffs outside Green River and the turretlike Castle Gate formation north of Price. But plenty of rock formations in the region resemble castles less than they do hobbits and goblins, natural outlaw hideouts, and rimrock cattle corrals. Castle Country's foremost treasure for backcountry explorers is the San Rafael Swell, a monolithic dome of uplifted sandstone whose sloping eastern flank, the San Rafael Reef, is interrupted by a maze of intriguing slot canyons. The term *reef*, also applied to the Capitol Reef and other folds on the Colorado Plateau, was used by early travelers who found expanses of rock like these to be serious hindrances to getting from here to there.

Hundreds, even thousands of mountain bikers from the Salt Lake Valley and beyond, in their determined quest to get to their mecca (a.k.a. Moab) as fast as possible, zip past and scarcely notice the San Rafael Reef as they drive south from Price toward Green River. Little do they know what an amazing abundance of riding lies hidden behind that inclined buttress of sandstone. The San Rafael Swell remains relatively void of cyclists; even the rides featured in this guide merely hint at the opportunities. A great way to delve deeper is to sign up for the annual San Rafael Swell Mountain Bike Festival in May (call the Emery County Travel Council at (888) 564-3600 or (435) 381-5620 to learn more).

Castle Country is also noted for its Fremont Indian rock art, most notably that found in Nine-Mile Canyon, aptly nicknamed "the world's longest art gallery." Meanwhile, over on the western edge of the region, cliffs and castles give way to the forested slopes and meadows of the Wasatch Plateau, where some of Utah's best high-elevation rides await your oversized rubber tires.

Castle Country does indeed surrender to Canyonlands, the most heralded and sought-after mountain-biking destination in Utah, perhaps in the world. But if you consider Castle Country as nothing but miles of desolate country that must be covered before reaching paradise, the loss is yours. Some of the state's best riding is found here, but you have to get off the beaten track and work a little harder to find it. Just remember—the looking is half the fun!

RIDE 1 · Pole–Summit Pull

AT A GLANCE

Length/configuration: 19.5-mile combination, consisting of a short, 1-mile out-and-back (0.5 mile each way) connecting to an 18.5-mile loop

Aerobic difficulty: Tough, beginning with a 2,000-foot climb over 5 miles of pavement

Technical difficulty: Challenging, with 6.5 miles of single-track that is sometimes smooth, sometimes very rocky, and sometimes extremely cow-hoof-pocked Other surfaces include pavement and smooth dirt road

Scenery: Tremendous views of 11,877-foot Mount Nebo, the highest peak of the Wasatch Range

Special comments: Watch your distances carefully on the single-track portion, as route finding is a bit of a challenge

This 19.5-mile ride (18.5-mile loop with a short spur leaving and returning to the campground) is rated aerobically tough, primarily because of the gruelling, 5-mile climb faced at the outset. Amid a redrock setting embellished with pine, fir, and aspen you'll look up at the bare alpine world of Mount Nebo looming to your left. Its cooling beauty might help take your mind off the broiling climb. (Note: You can avoid the tough climb by doing this as a 12.5-mile point-to-point—from mile 5.5 to mile 18—if you have a shuttle vehicle or don't mind hitching a ride back to your car.) The aerobic demands are followed by a technical challenge as you begin negotiating the often rocky and/or cattle-battered, 6.5-mile-long Summit Trail single-track. Once you get on the trail, however, you never lose or gain as much elevation as it appears you might, because it snakes along the ridge top, offering outstanding views as it goes. Try to get an early start, as the ride will probably take a good four hours and the initial climb can get very hot.

General location: Eight miles northeast of Nephi.

Elevation change: Approximately 6,200 to 8,200 feet.

Season: May through October.

Services: All services are available in Nephi; there's also a KOA campground at the junction of Nebo Loop Road and UT 132. Water is available at Ponderosa Campground, the trailhead.

Hazards: Car traffic on the Nebo Loop Road, and tough, rocky stretches of single-track.

Rescue index: You probably will not run into anyone on the 6.5 miles of single-track. (The only fellow I encountered was a coyote.) Help can be summoned back at Ponderosa Campground or by flagging down a motorist on Nebo Loop Road.

Land status: Uinta National Forest.

Maps: Uinta National Forest visitor map or DeLorme *Utah Atlas & Gazetteer*, page 45.

RIDE 1 · Pole–Summit Pull
RIDE 2 · Oak to Aspen

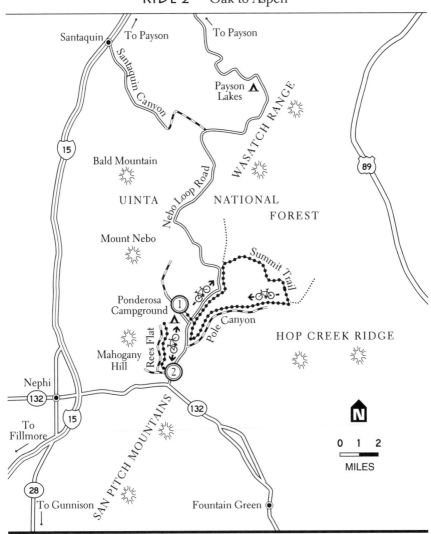

Finding the trail: From Nephi (32 miles south of Spanish Fork on Interstate 15), drive about 5 miles east on UT 132, then turn left onto Nebo Loop Road. After 3 miles-plus, turn left and proceed 0.5 mile to Ponderosa Campground. The ride starts there.

Source of additional information:

Uinta National Forest
44 West 400 North
Spanish Fork, UT 84660
(801) 342-5260

Notes on the trail: Leave Ponderosa Campground, riding the 0.5 mile back to Nebo Loop Road then turning left/north onto the blacktop/chipseal surface. Shift into low and start grinding away. At 5.5 miles, you'll cross a cattleguard, more than likely take a breather, and go right onto the signed Summit Trail, which begins pleasantly enough as it sidehills through coniferous forest. After 0.5 mile you'll arrive at a trail junction and bear straight ahead (Trail 130 goes left). A little less than a mile farther along you'll encounter a tough, quarter-mile uphill followed by an equally tough downhill of similar duration. At 7.5 miles cumulative is another gnarly downhill skirting a fence line. A mile past that you'll pass through a gate and bear right along the fence line. Approximately 0.25 mile from there is a junction where you'll want to go straight (Page Fork Trail 088 goes left), continuing through the sage- and shrub-filled saddle. Soon you'll see a Carsonite post marking where the trail enters an aspen forest. At about 10 miles cumulative there's a big rock cairn atop the knife-edge ridge, from which you can see far down to the left and the right. In another mile, after a rocky downhill, pass another Carsonite post; 30 yards past that post, turn right downhill. (Another, less maintained trail continues uphill—that's the wrong way.) In 0.5 mile you'll see a cattle trough and small corral, then arrive at a junction with Trail 114, where you'll continue down toward "Pole Canyon Road—1." (The trail also goes left, toward Spencer Canyon.) The next 0.5 mile of trail is smooth and sweet, as it flirts occasionally with the creek. At 12 miles empty onto Pole Canyon Road, a delightfully pitched two-wheel-drive road of packed sediments. Let 'er fly for the next 6 miles, then turn right onto Nebo Loop Road and follow it for a little more than a mile, returning to Ponderosa Campground at 19.5 miles.

RIDE 2 · Oak to Aspen

AT A GLANCE

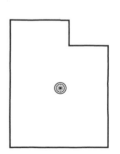

Length/configuration: 9-mile out-and-back (4.5 miles each way)

Aerobic difficulty: Moderate

Technical difficulty: Easy, over graded two-wheel-drive road, sandy and rock-embedded two-wheel/four-wheel-drive road, and a short stretch of smooth single-track (possibly downfall-strewn)

Scenery: Coming out, the view of the San Pitch Mountains to the south is stupendous

Special comments: Primarily a workout ride, but with an intriguing desert-meets-the-mountains feel and a nice single-track payoff at the top

This nine-mile ride, though it may not inspire you to write home, is definitely worth doing if you're in the area. It's a straightforward 4.5 miles up and 4.5 miles back, over graded two-wheel-drive road, as well as some sandy/rocky semi-four-wheel-drive road and a short stretch of single-track. It's moderately difficult aerobically, due to the extended uphill on which you gain 1,200 vertical feet, but technically it's quite

Midway between oak and aspen stands.

easy. Beginning amid a dry setting of scrub oak and juniper—that rustle you hear in the brush is an acorn-gathering squirrel, not a cougar . . . you hope—by the final stretches you're riding in shimmering aspen forest. At the turnaround point, Salt Spring Creek, you may note a Carsonite marker on the other side of the creek marking a trail going both left and right. Feel free to explore by foot to the left, up toward Mahogany Hill; in addition or instead, if you're feeling adventurous and still have plenty of water, you may choose to investigate by bike going down to the right, just to see where you end up.

General location: Six miles east of Nephi.

Elevation change: Approximately 5,800 to 7,000 feet.

Season: April through November.

Services: All services are available in Nephi; there's also a KOA campground at the junction of Nebo Loop Road and UT 132. Water is available at Ponderosa Campground, 3 miles north of the trailhead.

Hazards: Ride carefully on the old closed road portion and through the aspen forest, where the trail can be obscured by downfall.

Rescue index: Help can be summoned by flagging down a motorist on the Nebo Loop Road or by going to Ponderosa Campground (3 miles north of the trailhead).

Land status: Uinta National Forest.

Maps: Uinta National Forest visitor map or DeLorme *Utah Atlas & Gazetteer*, page 45.

Finding the trail: From Nephi (32 miles south of Spanish Fork on I-15), drive about 5 miles east on UT 132, then turn left onto Nebo Loop Road. In approximately 0.75 mile, just inside the forest boundary, pull off to the right and park near the information kiosk.

Source of additional information:

Uinta National Forest
44 West 400 North
Spanish Fork, UT 84660
(801) 342-5260

Notes on the trail: Ride onto gravel Forest Service Road 163, located just up and on the opposite side of the road from the trailhead. Bear right across the cattle guard adjacent to a cattle-loading area. The road soon turns sandy, with rocks embedded in the surface, as you climb quite steeply amid a setting of oak and juniper. At 1 mile, bear straight where a four-wheel-drive road goes left. At just past 2.5 miles, at the head of Salt Cave Hollow, drop down into Maple Spring Hollow, starting up toward Mahogany Hill at 3 miles cumulative. At 3.5 miles (0.1 mile before the road dead ends), bear right steeply uphill onto a faint track cut by erosion. This bumps up to an old road bed containing bulldozed humps and boulders, obviously put there to preclude travel by motorized vehicles. At just over 4 miles the road devolves into single-track and winds through an aspen forest. At 4.5 miles you'll arrive at Salt Springs Creek, the turnaround.

RIDE 3 · Skyline Drive–Miller Flat Loop

AT A GLANCE

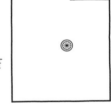

Length/configuration: 34-mile loop

Aerobic difficulty: Difficult, with a total of some 3,000 feet of climbing

Technical difficulty: Easy, except for a stretch of moderately difficult four-wheel-drive road dropping off the plateau. Other riding surfaces include pavement, graded gravel, and compacted sediment (with mud holes likely).

Scenery: Top-of-the-world views in every direction

Special comments: On this ride you'll sample a 12-mile stretch of Skyline Drive, a ribbon of dirt that roller-coasters through the central Utah highlands for approximately 100 miles

This 34-mile loop is aerobically exhausting but technically easy, except for a stretch of rocky four-wheel-drive track dropping off the Wasatch Plateau. Other riding surfaces include pavement, graded gravel, and compacted sediment that's typically smooth, with a high cruisability quotient (although occasional mud holes are likely). You'll begin by following 12 miles of Skyline Drive, a treasure of a track topping the Wasatch Plateau that offers a great opportunity for a multiday bike-packing trip. At the north end, it leaves Highway 6 west of Soldier Summit and ascends Clear Creek Ridge to the Wasatch Plateau, following it for mile after undulating mile before dropping to I-70 at a point east of Salina. Because of the high elevation, the

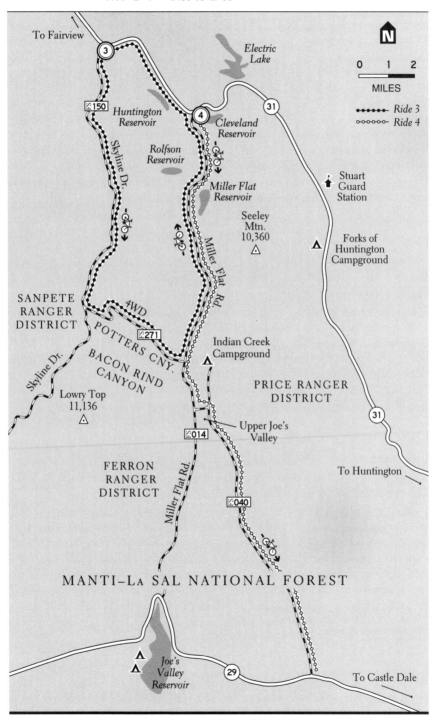

To Fairview

3

Electric
Lake

0   1   2
MILES

•••••• *Ride 3*
ooooooo *Ride 4*

150

*Huntington
Reservoir*

4

31

*Cleveland
Reservoir*

*Rolfson
Reservoir*

Skyline Dr.

*Miller Flat
Reservoir*

Stuart
Guard
Station

Seeley
Mtn.
10,360

Forks of
Huntington
Campground

SANPETE
RANGER
DISTRICT

4WD

POTTERS CNY.

Miller Flat Rd.

271

Indian Creek
Campground

PRICE RANGER
DISTRICT

Skyline Dr.

BACON RIND
CANYON

Lowry Top
11,136

014

Upper Joe's
Valley

31

FERRON
RANGER
DISTRICT

Miller Flat Rd.

040

To Huntington

MANTI–LA SAL NATIONAL FOREST

Joe's
Valley
Reservoir

29

To Castle Dale

season on Skyline Drive is short; last winter is never far away and neither is the next, and, in fact, the two can collide. I rode the loop on Labor Day weekend and still encountered snow patches remaining from the previous winter. Up, down, up, and down you will go—if the season is right—through a wonderful ground cover of lupine, Indian paintbrush, and other brilliantly hued wildflowers. Stretching away in the distance is a repetition of west-trending ridges repeatedly cut by deep, aspen-choked drainages; to the east, you'll skirt open tundra holding thick pockets of fir. On leaving the high plateau you'll drop easterly to the Miller Flat Road, which dishes up a trio of testy climbs each 1.5 to 2 miles in length. On the final five miles over UT 31 you'll gain another 800 feet of elevation; by the time you return to the beginning point you'll know you been doing something other than couching out and watching *Seinfeld* reruns. If you'd like to overnight in the vicinity, good dispersed camping—provided it's not already overrun with ATVers—can be found in the vicinity of Potters Ponds (mile 18), where you could just as readily begin the loop. Just be sure to do it in a counterclockwise direction, as described here.

General location: 14 miles east of Fairview.

Elevation change: Approximately 8,600 to 10,600 feet.

Season: July through September.

Services: All services are available below to the west in the Sanpete Valley towns of Fairview and Mount Pleasant.

Hazards: Skyline Drive can range from ugly to impassable during and after rains, so avoid it if the weather is bad or recently has been. Lightning is a serious concern on the lofty plateau as well. UT 31, which you'll follow for 5 miles, has a good shoulder, but ride defensively nevertheless. (When I rode the loop I was chased by a sheep-herder's dog on Skyline Drive, but he didn't catch me. Being pursued by a snarling hound at 10,500 feet is a breathtaking experience.)

Rescue index: Because you're on a segment of the Great Western Trail, and because the Miller Flat area is popular for camping, you'll probably encounter ATVers on the loop, who could provide assistance in a pinch.

Land status: Manti–La Sal National Forest.

Maps: Manti–La Sal National Forest visitor map or DeLorme *Utah Atlas & Gazetteer*, page 46.

Finding the trail: From Fairview, drive east on UT 31, making the steep pull through gorgeous Fairview Canyon. At the top of the pass, at 9 miles, you'll see Sky-line Drive North going left. Continue on the highway for another 5 miles, motoring through open parks embellished with aspen stands and private cabins, then pull off to the right toward Skyline Drive South (also signed as the Great Western Trail). Park in the big parking area beside the road.

Source of additional information:

Sanpete Ranger District
540 North Main 32-14
Ephraim, UT 84627
(435) 283-4151

Notes on the trail: From the parking area, ride south on Skyline Drive South, look-ing far down on the Sanpete Valley. Smooth gravel quickly devolves into a surface of compacted sediment. At 2.5 miles you'll pass a spur dropping left. You can see the town of Fairview below to the right and, ahead, the awesome sight of a series of westerly running drainages cutting into the innards of the plateau. At 8.5 miles FS 37 drops right toward Mount Pleasant. At 12 miles you'll leave Skyline Drive, dropping left onto FS 271 into Bacon Rind Canyon. The road starts out as a very rocky four-wheel-drive track. At 13.5 miles, switchback left around the toe of the ridge into Potters Canyon; then, in another mile, cross Potters Creek. Stick to the "main" road as you zip past numerous slop-camp spurs, soon coming in alongside a big power line. Just after the road quality improves at about 17.5 miles, you'll pass Potters Ponds on the right. It's a smooth half-mile downhill from there to Miller Flat Road (FS 14), onto which you'll turn left. Proceed climbing to the watershed divide at 20 miles, then enjoy a couple of free miles before commencing another 2-mile climb. From 24 miles you'll coast down to Miller Flat Reservoir, then at 27 miles pass the upper end of Huntington Creek National Recreation Trail on the right (no bikes permitted). Climb from there to UT 31, turning left onto it at about 29 miles. Ride along the good shoulder for 5 miles, returning to the beginning point at 34 miles.

RIDE 4 · Res to Des

AT A GLANCE

Length/configuration: 25-mile point-to-point

Aerobic difficulty: Moderate

Technical difficulty: Easy, over graded gravel, along with a couple of miles of unsurfaced road and 3 miles of pavement

Scenery: You descend from mid-elevation sagebrush basin/timberlands to what begins to feel a lot like canyon country

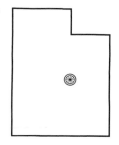

Special comments: This makes a good ride unless you happen to hit the area during a wet spell, when the unsurfaced roads can be mucky

The first 11 miles of this 25-mile point-to-point are coincidental with miles 18 through 29 of Ride 3, only here you're going in the opposite direction. With a progression of longish climbs and descents over the first 15 miles followed by a memorable multimile descent along Cottonwood Creek, the ride is rated aerobically moderate in difficulty. Mostly well-surfaced roads, along with two miles of unsurfaced road and three miles of pavement, earn it an easy technical rating. Numerous intriguing spurs branch off here and there along the way—so many, in fact, that this would make a good ride to do fully loaded, allowing you to set up camp where you choose and then explore the tougher side trails unencumbered. Plenty of opportunities for dispersed camping lie along the early stretches of the route, in a setting of sagebrush flats rimmed with sloping islands of aspen and fir.

General location: The beginning point is 19 miles southeast of Fairview; ride's end is about 10 miles northwest of Castle Dale.

Creating "aspen art"
is a popular pastime
for sheepherders.

Elevation change: A high of around 9,250 feet and a low of 6,600.

Season: June through October.

Services: All services are availble in the Fairview–Mount Pleasant area and in Castle Dale.

Hazards: A fair amount of vehicle traffic is common along the northern portions of Miller Flat Road.

Rescue index: Summoning help from a passing motorist or going to the Trail Mountain Mine (22 miles into the ride) will be your best bets.

Land status: Manti–La Sal National Forest, BLM.

Maps: Manti–La Sal National Forest visitor map or DeLorme *Utah Atlas & Gazetteer*, pages 46 and 38.

Finding the trail: From Fairview, drive east on UT 31, making the steep pull up scenic Fairview Canyon. At the top of the pass, at 9 miles, pass Skyline Drive North and then, 5 miles later, Skyline Drive South. Continue on the highway for another 5 miles, turning right just past Huntington Reservoir toward Joe's Valley Reservoir onto FS 014/Miller Flat Road. Park in the big parking area on the right, adjacent to the junction.

Source of additional information:

Sanpete Ranger District
540 North Main 32-14
Ephraim, UT 84627
(435) 283-4151

Notes on the trail: Ride south on FS 014/Miller Flat Road, passing many dispersed camping areas over the first few miles. At 2 miles you'll cross Rolfson Creek, then come in alongside Miller Flat Reservoir a mile later. At 11 miles pass FS 271 going right (it inches up onto the Wasatch Plateau), then soon drop into a tightening canyon. At the junction at 13 miles, turn left onto FS 040 toward Cottonwood Creek and Indian Creek Campground; FS 014 continues straight toward Joe's Valley Reservoir. In 0.75 mile, turn right toward Cottonwood Canyon (Indian Creek Campground is a couple of miles to the left), commencing a climb of nearly 2 miles over an unsurfaced road. Gravel resumes at the top, where you'll begin descending through a stunning, aspen-filled canyon (note the single-track paralleling the road in many places). It's a tight, timbered setting a world apart from where you just came. At 18 miles things start getting rockier, more badlands-like. At 22 miles, amid the activity of the Trail Mountain Mine, you'll hit pavement. A mile from there you'll leave the national forest for Bureau of Land Management lands, then arrive at UT 29 in another couple of miles, at 25 miles total.

RIDE 5 · Castle Valley Ridge Trail System

AT A GLANCE

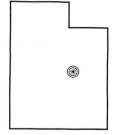

Length/configuration: Several loops and out-and-backs of various lengths can be made on this network comprising some 30 miles of trails and dirt roads suitable for biking

Aerobic difficulty: Moderate to difficult

Technical difficulty: Moderate to difficult

Scenery: Tremendous long-range vistas from the high ridge tops

Special comments: Rather than leading you on a specific ride, the entire trail system is described here in general terms

The Castle Valley Ridge Non-Motorized Trail System was developed by the Manti–La Sal National Forest and several cooperating partners, including the Cyprus-Plateau and Genwal coal companies, Carbon and Emery Counties, and the Utah Division of Parks and Recreation. The work, performed between 1992 and 1994, entailed rebuilding 14 miles of trashed and/or forgotten trail, as well as constructing 10 miles of new trails. In addition to single-track trails, the system includes several miles of rustic dirt road. Of the system's five trails, only three are recommended for mountain

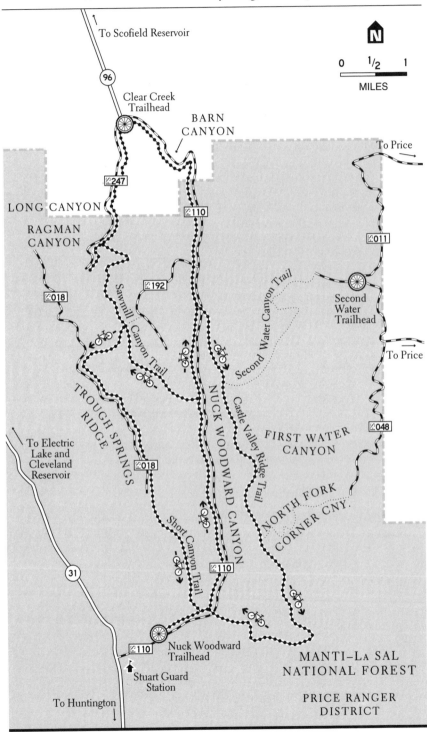

N

0   1/2   1
MILES

To Scofield Reservoir

96

Clear Creek
Trailhead

BARN
CANYON

To Price

247

LONG CANYON

110

RAGMAN
CANYON

011

018

192

Sawmill Canyon Trail

Second Water Canyon Trail

Second
Water
Trailhead

To Price

TROUGH SPRINGS RIDGE

NUCK WOODWARD CANYON

Castle Valley Ridge Trail

FIRST WATER
CANYON

048

To Electric
Lake and
Cleveland
Reservoir

018

Short Canyon Trail

NORTH FORK
CORNER CNY.

31

110

110

Nuck Woodward
Trailhead

Stuart Guard
Station

MANTI–La SAL
NATIONAL FOREST

To Huntington

PRICE RANGER
DISTRICT

An hour ago, before the rainstorm hit, this was a dry streambed.

biking: Castle Valley Ridge Trail (rated moderately difficult), Short Canyon Trail (most difficult), and Sawmill Canyon Trail (moderately difficult). Two others—Second Water Canyon and Corner Canyon, both located on the east side of the system—are not recommended for mountain biking because of their exceedingly steep and sustained grades. (A third trailhead, Second Water, accesses these trails; however, directions to it have not been provided here because the trails aren't recommended.)

En route to the Nuck Woodward Trailhead be sure to swing into the interesting old Stuart Guard Station, where, among other information, you can pick up a copy of the pamphlet mentioned under "Maps." Camping is not permitted at the trailheads, but there's plenty of camping close to both Nuck Woodward Trailhead (Forks of Huntington, Old Folks' Flat) and Clear Creek Trailhead (Scofield Lake State Recreation Area).

General location: 20 miles west of Price.

Elevation change: Approximately 7,500 to 10,000 feet.

Season: June through October.

Services: The closest full-service town to the Nuck Woodward Trailhead is Huntington, 20 miles southeast. If you're setting out from the Clear Creek Trailhead, Fairview is about 26 miles west.

Hazards: Some portions of the trails are very rocky and technical. Beware of getting caught in a thunderstorm, both out of respect for the associated lightning and because the dirt roads of the system can become impassable when wet.

Rescue index: You may encounter other cyclists on the trails, as well as equestrians and hikers. Don't count on it, however, and go prepared for anything. The historic

Stuart Guard Station, located about a mile from the Nuck Woodward Trailhead, will probably have Forest Service personnel on duty or at least on the grounds.

Land status: Manti–La Sal National Forest.

Maps: Manti–La Sal National Forest visitor map; Castle Valley Ridge Trail System map/brochure.

Finding the trail: To get to the Nuck Woodward Trailhead, located at the southern end of the system, from Huntington travel approximately 20 miles northwest on UT 31. At a point 2 miles past Forks of Huntington Campground, turn right at the recently renovated Stuart Guard Station onto FS 110. You'll come to the trailhead in just under a mile. To access the Clear Creek Trailhead, situated at the trail system's northern end, simply go 6 miles south on UT 96 from Scofield (located a mile south of Scofield Reservoir). Both trailheads have plenty of room for parking.

Source of additional information:

Manti–La Sal National Forest
Price Ranger District
599 West Price River Drive
Price, UT 84501
(435) 637-2817

Notes on the trail: As you can see by the map, several variations on the loop or out-and-back themes are possible here. A couple of recommendations include the 15-mile loop made by riding 6 miles up Nuck Woodward Canyon on FS 110 from Nuck Woodward Trailhead, then returning on the 9-mile Castle Valley Ridge Trail; and the 11-mile loop similarly composed of first heading north on FS 110, but then turning northwest onto the Sawmill Canyon Trail and returning to the trailhead by way of FS 018 and Short Canyon Trail. For relatively short mileages, these rides gain a great deal of elevation — in the vicinity of 2,000 feet each — but the views earned are worth the efforts spent.

RIDE 6 · Mesa to Mesa Loop

AT A GLANCE

Length/configuration: 16-mile loop

Aerobic difficulty: Moderate; 1,000 feet of elevation gain

Technical difficulty: Easy, over pavement, sandy double-track with some embedded cobbles, packed sediment, and graded gravel

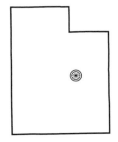

Scenery: The moody Book Cliffs, snow-capped in spring, dominate the views

Special comments: Be advised that the road situation is subject to constant change, owing to ongoing mineral exploration and development

RIDE 6 · Mesa to Mesa Loop

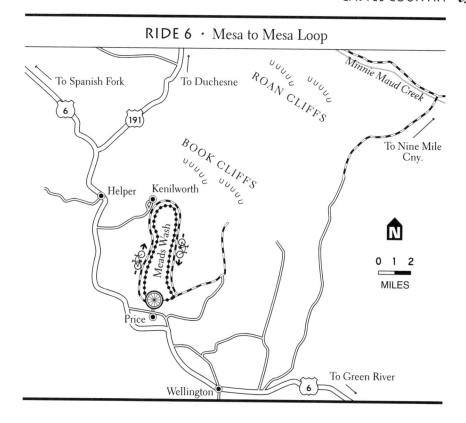

This ride conveniently begins and ends right in the agreeable, full-service town of Price. It alternately climbs and descends the pair of 1,000-foot-high ridges sandwiching Meads Wash, which runs between Price and Kenilworth, an intriguing mining camp nestled against the base of the Book Cliffs. The 16-mile loop is rated aerobically moderate and technically easy, as it follows a mix of pavement, sandy double-track, and packed-sediment and graded-gravel roads. Much of the route can turn extremely yucky when wet, so avoid it during and immediately after rains. Also know that, simply because you're close to civilization and because the ride appears rather straightforward on the map, these things don't mean that the route finding is easy. There are, in fact, a lot of places to go wrong on this ride, which explains the lengthy passage under "Notes on the trail."

While in Price (Utah's coal capital for more than a century) don't miss the College of Eastern Utah's excellent Prehistoric Museum. It holds displays of Native American artifacts and critter fossils, including ones taken from the Cleveland-Lloyd Dinosaur Quarry south of town. The museum is at 155 East Main, on the north side of the Price Municipal Building, a legacy of the Works Project Administration days of the late 1930s.

General location: The ride begins and ends in the town of Price.

Elevation change: Approximately 5,600 to 6,600 feet.

Season: Spring and fall; go in early morning or in the evening if you do it in summer.

Services: All services, including bike shops, are found in Price.

Hazards: There's a chance of encountering motorized traffic on much of the route.

Rescue index: Except for miles 3.5 through 7.5, you'll be riding graded roads possibly shared with oil-company trucks.

Land status: City of Price, state land, BLM.

Maps: DeLorme *Utah Atlas & Gazetteer*, pages 46 and 47.

Finding the trail: Drive north on 300 East to 500 North. Turn left/west and park in front of buildings that are part of the College of Eastern Utah.

Sources of additional information:

Bureau of Land Management
125 South 600 West
Price, UT 84501
(435) 636-3600

CEU Prehistoric Museum
155 East Main
Price, UT 84501
(435) 637-5060

Notes on the trail: Ride west on 500 North for 0.1 mile, then turn right onto 100 East. Stay on the flats, avoiding the big hill and skirting a town park on its east side. At just over 0.75 mile, turn left at the T onto 900 North. Shortly this feeds onto a dirt road that curves right and begins up a steep hill toward a mesa holding radio towers. At the apex, at 1.5 miles, continue north rather than veering left toward the radio towers, on a wide, hard-packed dirt road. Ignore the numerous tracks going left and right here and there. At 2 miles, at a main junction, continue north toward the cliffs (a road of similar surface goes east). Soon you'll pass under a power line; continue straight where a good road forks left toward an oil well. At 3.5 miles cross a cattle guard, pass under the high wire and bear right onto a fainter four-wheel-drive road, continuing north up the plateau on this nice, sandy double-track through the junipers and piñons. Keep the rustic juniper-and-barbed-wire fence line on your right as the road turns quite rocky. At 5.5 miles bear straight/left downhill (the track going right comes to a good viewpoint in 0.25 mile). After the short, rocky downhill, you'll ascend gradually northeastward to the head of a draw, through a sagebrush-filled meadow. At just beyond 6 miles, begin dropping toward Kenilworth. In another mile, you'll arrive at a highway junction and make a hard right onto the dirt road rather than riding onto the highway. (Leave the route here to explore the interesting old mining town of Kenilworth.) After swinging east/southeast, go left at the fork, continuing to aim for the cliff to the east. At 7.5 miles you'll cross an old cinder-covered railbed and then another. Continue straight toward the cliffs, heading uphill on the better road—a good, wide dirt road that bends right as it climbs directly along the cliff base. After topping out at a high point at 8.5 miles, you'll cross a cattle guard and stay right rather than going left, entering a new drainage. In about 0.25 mile go left, keeping the oil well on your right, rather than heading up to the right on an equally good road. (It leads to some interesting mesa top exploring, where I spent about 2 hours trying to convince myself I was somewhere that I wasn't.) Start a long downhill cruiser, staying straight on the main road whenever confronted with a choice. At just under 11 miles, continue straight rather than heading left toward the obvious gap. A mile from there, where there's a road going left and on the right is a big pond and other developments, continue straight on what turns into an even better gravel road. At about 13.5 miles you'll drop steeply off the ridge, skirting some water tanks, into Price. Toward the bottom, before the road curves left and just before coming to some houses, turn right at a gas pipeline sign. After curving left, this becomes a residential street. Turn right onto 8th North; then, in a little over a mile, go left onto 3rd East. At 16 miles you'll be back at 500 North and the ride's beginning point.

RIDE 7 · Nine-Mile Canyon

AT A GLANCE

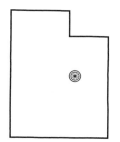

Length/configuration: Out-and-backs of up to 60 miles (30 miles each way) can be made on the main road, while numerous canyon spurs and loops are also possible

Aerobic difficulty: Easy to difficult

Technical difficulty: Easy to difficult, ranging from the well-graded main road to very steep ascents and descents to and from the high West Tavaputs Plateau and the Bad Land Cliffs

Scenery: Miles and miles of sandstone walls cutting through the Book Cliffs, Roan Cliffs, and West Tavaputs Plateau

Special comments: Nine-Mile Canyon has been referred to as "the world's longest art gallery," for its rich abundance of prehistoric pictographs and petroglyphs

Nine-Mile Canyon is an unexpected name for a canyon that's actually closer to 40 miles in length. The name dates back to the first survey of the area made by John Wesley Powell and party, and it refers to mouth of the creek's distance from a certain waypoint. If you're feeling laidback, you can do a simple out-and-back of nearly any length along the graded-dirt main road (up to 60 miles round-trip); or, if you're feeling spunky, you can delve into something technically and physically much tougher, such as the Harmon Canyon to Prickly Pear Canyon loop or the Gate Canyon–Wrinkle Road–Franks Canyon–Nine-Mile Canyon loop. Nine-Mile Canyon makes a great place to head—after loading up bikes, camping gear, food, and water—and just explore for a couple of days, by car, by foot, and by mountain bike. A visit here makes one realize how truly isolated some areas of the United States remain even today. Much of the land bordering the road is private; however, by driving a short way up one of the side canyons you'll typically be able to find good dispersed camping on BLM lands. From the Minnie Maud Creek bridge, it's about 30 miles to the end of public access, where the road is gated at a private-property boundary just past Franks Canyon.

In the late 1880s a regiment of the U.S. Army's black "buffalo soldiers" improved an existing primitive trail through here, transforming it into a designated federal highway. Some of the 9th Cavalry's work can still be seen in places, such as along the foot trail leading to Smith's Well (the trail begins up Gate Canyon at a point several miles from Nine-Mile Canyon). Before being supplanted by US 40 and US 191, the road carried hundreds of travelers and tons of goods and supplies, as it served as the

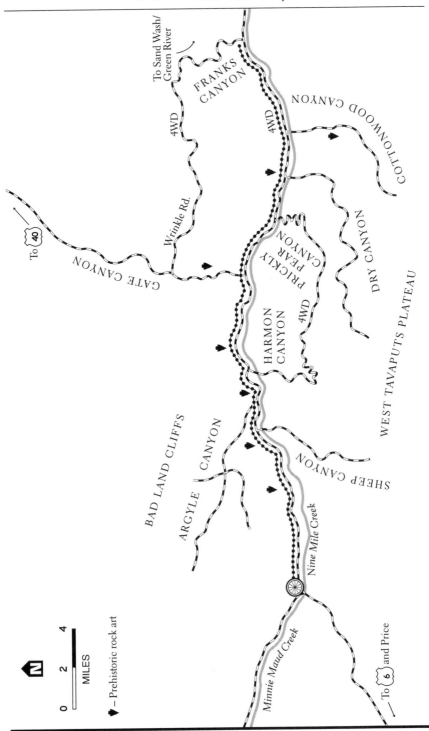

vital link between the communities of the Uinta Basin and the railhead at Price. Farther back in time, the canyon was a seasonal home to millennia of prehistoric Americans, from Paleo Indians of more than 10,000 years ago to the relatively recent Fremont culture, whose artists found the smooth sandstone panels of the canyon ideal as palettes. Although you have to get up close—literally or with binoculars—and look hard to find the rock art in many cases, this canyon holds what is widely regarded as the largest concentration of pictographs and petroglyphs in North America. Remains of Fremont granaries and shelters can also be spotted.

General location: Twenty-four miles northeast of Wellington.

Elevation change: The road loses about 1,000 feet over its 30-mile length; to do the canyon-to-ridge-top loops, you'll gain between 1,500 and 2,000 feet.

Season: April through May and September through October are best. Summers can be very hot.

Services: No services are found along the route. Stock up on supplies in Price. In a pinch, water can be taken and filtered from Nine-Mile Creek.

Hazards: Dehydration is the probably the biggest concern, along with the possibility of getting lost and/or stranded in a side canyon. If you're caught in a rainstorm, you might have to sit it out for a while to allow the slick, gumbo-mucked road to dry.

Rescue index: The area is very remote. You may be able to summon help from a motorist on the road or at a ranch in the valley bottom; however, you likely won't encounter anyone else up the side canyons.

Land status: Bureau of Land Management.

Maps: DeLorme *Utah Atlas & Gazetteer*, pages 46 and 47. You can also obtain Nine-Mile Canyon maps/informational brochures, some of which include locations and descriptions of rock art, at the BLM office or at the CEU Prehistoric Museum in Price.

Finding the trail: From 3 miles east of Wellington on US 6, turn north onto Nine-Mile Canyon Road. After about 12 miles of pavement and 9 miles of unpaved road, you'll come to the Minnie Maud Creek bridge. You can park a little farther along near the BLM informational sign, and start your ride there; or you can continue driving on the good road until the spirit moves you to pull over and start riding.

Sources of additional information: See sources of additional information for Ride 6.

Notes on the trail: For an out-and-back on the main road as long as 60 miles (30 miles each way), park just past the Minnie Maud Creek bridge. Alternatively, continue a few miles to Sheep Creek, where you can do up to a 50-mile out-and-back (25 miles each way) and/or take the spur of several miles up Sheep Creek Canyon to a panel of petroglyphs. Back on the main road, by continuing to Gate Canyon, where the road splits (Gate Canyon is the continuation of the historic route to the Uinta Basin town of Myton), you'll still have a potential 30-mile out-and-back (15 miles each way) in Nine-Mile Canyon. Just about any of the side canyons passed—Argyle, Dry, Cottonwood, Franks, and others—offer intriguing fat-tire challenges. The 23-mile Harmon Canyon to Prickly Pear Canyon loop, which uses a stretch of the Nine-Mile Canyon Road, is a navigational and physical challenge not to be taken lightly. Ditto the longer Gate Canyon–Wrinkle Road–Franks Canyon–Nine-Mile Canyon loop.

RIDE 8 · Wedge Overlook

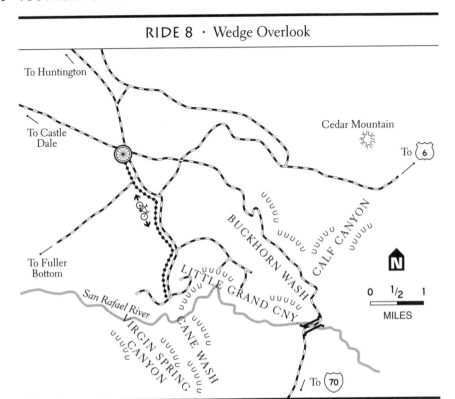

To Huntington

To Castle Dale

Cedar Mountain

To (6)

To Fuller Bottom

BUCKHORN WASH

CALF CANYON

LITTLE GRAND CNY

San Rafael River

VIRGIN SPRING CANYON

CANE WASH

To (70)

N

0   1/2   1
MILES

RIDE 8 · Wedge Overlook

AT A GLANCE

Length/configuration: 13-mile out-and-back (6.5 miles each way)

Aerobic difficulty: Easy

Technical difficulty: Easy, over graded gravel/dirt road

Scenery: Most of the ride is across juniper-studded plateau offering superb horizon views, with the real visual payoff at the turnaround

Special comments: Provides an easy and auspicious introduction to the San Rafael Swell country

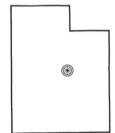

This 13-mile out-and-back ride (6.5 miles each way) is easy both physically and technically. It traverses a flat desert plateau en route to the Wedge Overlook, a spectacular vista looking several hundred feet down on the canyon of the San Rafael River, where rock, colored in various hues of red, has been sculpted into a labyrinth of sheer walls and buttes. The road you take from Castle Dale to the trailhead is the first stretch

The real visual treat comes at this ride's turnaround.

of the byway that drops down Buckhorn Wash to a bridge crossing of the San Rafael River, then continues to I-70—and keeps going south from there, as well, through the Swell's Sinbad Country and points beyond. In fact, the intrepid driver with high clearance and a full tank of gas can go all the way from Castle Dale to Caineville, located just east of Capitol Reef National Park, without setting tires on pavement, passing a wealth of Swell mountain-biking opportunties along the way. (Before leaving Castle Dale, by the way, you should take in the interesting Museum of the San Rafael.)

General location: 14 miles east of Castle Dale.

Elevation change: Negligible. Pretty darn flat.

Season: March through May and September through November are best. Summers are extremely hot.

Services: All services are available in Castle Dale.

Hazards: There may be some vehicle traffic on the route. Other than that, don't get too close to the rim at the turnaround.

Rescue index: Cars or trucks may be encountered on the route. If not, Castle Dale is the closest place to obtain help.

Land status: Bureau of Land Management.

Maps: DeLorme *Utah Atlas & Gazetteer*, pages 38 and 39. Additionally, good maps of the San Rafael Swell are available at the sources listed below.

Finding the trail: From Castle Dale, go 1.5 miles north on UT 10, then turn east toward "San Rafael Swell National Heritage/Conservation Area." Continue 12.5 miles to the junction with the Wedge Overlook spur road, parking to the side of the road.

Sources of additional information: See sources of additional information for Ride 6.

Notes on the trail: Ride south toward the Wedge Overlook on a wide gravel road. At 0.5 mile you'll pass a spur going right toward Fuller Bottom; then at 2 miles a road going left toward Gypsum Mine Junction. At 4 miles the road turns a bit more meandering and interesting as it twists through piñon-juniper tablelands. You'll reach the end of the route at 6.5 miles at the canyon rim, where you'll enjoy an amazing look down on the San Rafael River canyon.

RIDE 9 · Temple Mountain Loop

AT A GLANCE

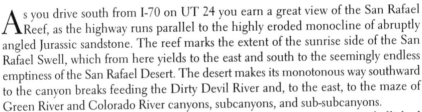

Length/configuration: 18.5-mile loop

Aerobic difficulty: Moderate, with more than 1,500 feet of elevation gain

Technical difficulty: Easy to moderate, with surfaces of pavement, packed gravel, rocky double-track, and soft wash sand

Scenery: The ride encircles distinctive Temple Mountain, while providing long-range views of Capitol Reef and the La Sal, Abajo, and Henry mountains

Special comments: A good sampler showing off the San Rafael Swell's diversity, from timber-peppered mesas to bare-rock slot canyons

As you drive south from I-70 on UT 24 you earn a great view of the San Rafael Reef, as the highway runs parallel to the highly eroded monocline of abruptly angled Jurassic sandstone. The reef marks the extent of the sunrise side of the San Rafael Swell, which from here yields to the east and south to the seemingly endless emptiness of the San Rafael Desert. The desert makes its monotonous way southward to the canyon breaks feeding the Dirty Devil River and, to the east, to the maze of Green River and Colorado River canyons, subcanyons, and sub-subcanyons.

This 18.5-mile loop circumnavigates Temple Mountain, a spire-embellished butte rising above the San Rafael Reef whose name derives from its silhouette's supposed resemlance to the Latter-day Saints Temple in Salt Lake City. Temple Mountain has long been a source of uranium, and that which was used to make the world's first atomic bomb reportedly came from here. Numerous tunnels and caves (as well as mining artifacts), legacies of the 1950s uranium boom, are found on and around the mountain. Use great care if walking off the route because mine collapse is a possibility; also know that high concentrations of radon gas can collect at mine entrances. The ride is rated aerobically moderate in difficulty and technically somewhere between easy and moderate. Much of the ride is over paved and well-graveled roads; other parts, however, follow rocky double-track and the potentially soft, deep-sand surfaces of North Temple Wash.

General location: 20 miles north of Hanksville, or 35 miles southwest of Green River.

Elevation change: 5,200 to 6,750 feet.

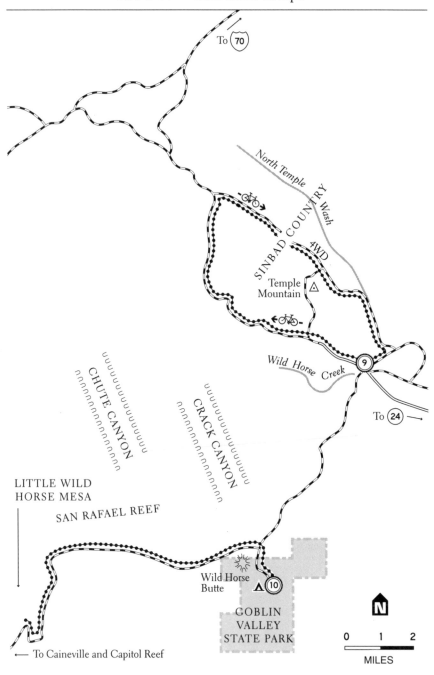

To (70)

North Temple Wash

SINBAD COUNTRY

4WD

Temple Mountain △

Wild Horse Creek (9)

To (24) →

CHUTE CANYON

CRACK CANYON

LITTLE WILD HORSE MESA

SAN RAFAEL REEF

Wild Horse Butte △ (10)

GOBLIN VALLEY STATE PARK

N

← To Caineville and Capitol Reef

0 1 2
MILES

Season: March through May and September through November are best. Summers are broiling.

Services: The closest full-service towns are Hanksville and Green River. No services are available in the immediate area, other than a campground at Goblin Valley State Park (7 miles south of the trailhead).

Hazards: You'll encounter some sharp rocks that could cause a flat tire, as well as deep wash sand that could cause a flat-out fall.

Rescue index: The ride is remote (surprise! you're in southern Utah!); the closest available help will probably be at Goblin Valley State Park, 7 miles south of the ride's beginning.

Land status: State, BLM.

Maps: San Rafael Desert 1:100,000 metric map (BLM) or DeLorme *Utah Atlas & Gazetteer*, page 39.

Finding the trail: From 15 miles northeast of Hanksville on UT 24, or 22 miles southwest of I-70, turn west onto the paved road leading toward Goblin Valley State Park. In a little over 5 miles, where a left takes aim at the state park and another road goes straight west, pull off and park.

Source of additional information:

> BLM Henry Mountains Field Station
> 406 South 100 West
> P.O. Box 99
> Hanksville, UT 84734
> (435) 542-3461

Notes on the trail: From the trailhead, ride west on the paved road bisecting the innards of the San Rafael Reef, by way of South Temple Wash. At just under 1 mile, on the right is a spur leading to a close-up view of a panel of Fremont shield-style rock art. The pavement soon ends but the uphill does not, as you continue climbing on a surface of high-grade gravel, surrounded by huge outcrops. At just under 2 miles, continue straight where another path forks right (this skirts close to Temple Mountain, rejoining the trail below at 13.5 miles). You'll then cross a draw; continue straight where Chute Canyon Road goes left. Continuing up, at 3.5 miles you'll pass through a gap to confront an altogether new view. Ascend the ridge toward Flat Top, with Capitol Reef National Park visible to the distant left. Up you'll continue, onto a high plateau bedecked with stands of piñon and juniper. Almost everything in close proximity, other than Temple Mountain, now lies below you. At 9 miles, just prior to coming to a big mesa on the right, turn hard right onto the primitive track to start down, initially through a scattering of timber and over a stretch of angular, tire-threatening rocks. At 12 miles, pass through a low gap, then, 0.5 mile later, bear right on the main track as a fainter track goes left. Cross a couple of draws, curve right to drop through a major wash, and top out at just over 13 miles, bearing left at the fork. In another 0.5 mile, after crossing the big draw, merge left onto a road coming in from above to the right (it's the other end of the one mentioned above at just under 2 miles). Pass some old foundations and structures at 14.5 miles; at just under 16 miles, continue as the road merges with North Temple Wash. Spin through the sand as best you can in low gear for the next couple of miles, curving right at 17.5 miles to leave the wash. Bear right off the main track in another mile to close the loop.

RIDE 10 · Wild Horse Escape

AT A GLANCE

Length/configuration: 21-mile out-and-back (10.5 miles each way)

Aerobic difficulty: Easy

Technical difficulty: Easy, over graded dirt road and a bit of sand

Scenery: From the uniquely animated surroundings of Goblin Valley State Park, the ride skirts the southeasternmost extension of the San Rafael Reef

Special comments: Provides good access to some inviting canyon hiking

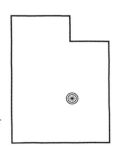

To paraphrase and contradict the Rolling Stones, wild horses *could* drag you away—Wild Horse and Little Wild Horse Creeks, that is, the drainages you fly through and flirt with on this ride. The views are pretty enough to steal your heart, and, I suppose, the creeks could literally drag you away with raging waters if you happened through at precisely the wrong time. The 21-mile out-and-back (10.5 miles each way) is easy both aerobically and technically. For the most part you'll pedal at moderate grades along a road of graded dirt, as well as through some splashes of dry wash sand. It's a cruiser of a ride, conveniently beginning and ending at the campground in Goblin Valley State Park. This park, the residence of hundreds of comically eroded characters of Entrada Sandstone, is a place you definitely should visit if you're anywhere in the vicinity. At the suggested turnaround, you'll want to take a good, long look in every direction: The infinite vista encompasses the Capitol Reef, Thousand Lake Mountain, Boulder Top, Factory Butte, the Henry Mountains, and a lot more. If you're feeling spunky, hoof it up onto adjacent Little Wild Horse Mesa for an even better look at your impressive surroundings.

General location: 27 miles north of Hanksville, or 42 miles southwest of Green River.

Elevation change: 4,750 to 5,000 feet.

Season: March through May and September through November are best. In summer you could fry an egg on your helmet.

Services: The closest full-service towns are Hanksville and Green River. No services are available in the immediate area.

Hazards: Dehydration is probably your biggest concern; it's a dry, wide open, and potentially hot ride.

Rescue index: The closest available help will probably be at Goblin Valley State Park, the trailhead.

Land status: State, BLM.

Maps: San Rafael Desert 1:100,000 metric map (BLM) or DeLorme *Utah Atlas & Gazetteer,* page 29.

Finding the trail: From 15 miles northeast of Hanksville on UT 24, or 22 miles southwest of I-70, turn west onto the paved road leading toward Goblin Valley State

Giving Little Wild Horse a whirl, the San Rafael Reef is a constant companion.

Park. In a little over 5 miles, turn left and continue 7 miles to the state park. Find a campsite and get ready to rock and roll.

Source of additional information:

BLM Henry Mountains Field Station
406 South 100 West
P.O. Box 99
Hanksville, UT 84734
(435) 542-3461

Notes on the trail: From the campground, spin north for a mile, then turn left onto the dirt road toward Wild Horse Butte, the high mesa on your left. After a 2-mile descent you'll cross a cattle guard at 2.5 miles, then bear right at the fork. At just over 3 miles ride through the more-than-likely dry wash of Wild Horse Creek, then descend toward the San Rafael Reef. At about 5 miles you'll pass through a fence line and climb for 0.5 mile, with the reef to your right. At 6.5 miles ride into the wash of Little Wild Horse Creek. (At 0.5 mile north of the road from this point, Bell and Little Wild Horse Canyons split going left and right, each offering some potentially intriguing slot-canyon hiking.) The ensuing ride through Little Wild Horse wash teeter-totters between sandy and hard-packed. At 10 miles, after a 3.5-mile canter down Little Wild Horse, you'll climb rather steeply for 0.5 mile to a high point and the recommended turnaround.

CANYONLANDS

Canyonlands is the universe of mountains, rivers, and desert largely responsible for the Beehive State's reputation as a mountain-biking paradise. All of Canyonlands, along with huge hunks of the bordering states and adjacent regions within Utah, are technically part of the Colorado Plateau, a high, uplifted, radically eroded tableland. The region's huge elevation differential translates to a staggeringly broad range of terrain and habitat types, making southeast Utah arguably the world's premier destination for a fat-tire getaway—regardless of the season.

For northerners and mountain residents weary of winter, Canyonlands offers a sunny respite from the cold and snow. Conversely, for desert dwellers from nearby hot spots like Phoenix and Albuquerque it provides high-altitude places to ride that remain relatively cool even at the height of summer. In other words, you'll want to visit the red-rock deserts that are so well known and publicized, of course, but you also should make a summer visit to take some sample spins atop the region's high ridges at subalpine altitudes.

The epicenter of this fantastic wonderland, as far as the mountain biker is concerned, is Moab, a town that uranium built and mountain biking made larger. Moab has everything fat-tire travelers could want or need, including a slate of motels, campgrounds, eating establishments, and shuttle services all catering to mountain bikers. More good news, for those who enjoy a brew or two: You can actually find a place in Moab to get a beer, which in the dry climes of southern Utah's Mormon country is often easier said than done.

Like swallows to Capistrano, come spring flocks of mountain bikers land in Moab . . . in their case driven not so much by some internal clock as by the schedule of their school's spring break or by an overdose of snow and cold up north. As you come into the area from Price or from Colorado in late March or early April, you might think you're fooling yourself: It still looks like winter, after all. But soon after crossing Interstate 40 and continuing south to approach Moab, you're suddenly surrounded by masses of rock that glow with an incandescence so brilliant it competes with the sun, which by now is probably shining, too. It's magical how it happens, but happen it does in this world of sheer walls of reddish Entrada sandstone, underscored by the paler swirls and petrified cowpies of Navajo sandstone. And then there's the place names, as poetic to the ear as the landscapes they represent are beautiful to the eye: Poison Spider Mesa, Porcupine Rim, Slickrock Bike Trail.

When in Moab don't miss ducking into the newish Interagency Visitor Center, located at the southeast corner of the junction of Center and Main. (The corner of Center and Main traditionally was the site of the Latter-day Saints church in many pioneer Mormon settlements. How interesting that a tourist center has assumed that esteemed location in Moab!) Here the National Park Service, Bureau of Land Management, U.S. Forest Service, Grand County Travel Council, and Canyonlands Natural History Association have joined forces to establish one of the best, most information-packed visitor centers you'll find anywhere in the West. If it has to do with biking, hiking, four-wheeling, river running, or any other outdoor activity commonly pursued in the desert Southwest, you'll probably be able to find a whole bunch of good stuff on it here.

Another, even newer addition to town is the Moab Skyway chairlift, which opened in May 1999. The chairlift ride begins just out of town off Kane Creek Boulevard (on the way to Hurrah Pass and several other featured rides), and ends ten minutes and 1,000 vertical feet later atop the Moab Rim. The developer, Emmett Mays, dreamed for years about a lift such as this, which would offer even wheelchair-bound folks the chance to get on high and have a look down on Moab's otherworldly setting. Mountain bikers can even haul their bikes up the lift to connect with the rugged Moab Rim Trail.

Although it's true that Moab is Canyonland's most heralded destination—and deservedly so—by no means should you limit your explorations to that area. On Moab's popular rides, in the high seasons anyway, you'll frolic in the two-wheeled camaraderie of hundreds of fellow fat-tire fanatics; almost anywhere else in Canyonlands you'll relish the isolation and solitude. This chapter includes a dozen rides in close proximity to Moab, but more than a dozen that are farther afield—and these only touch on the bounty of possibilities awaiting to be prospected by the intrepid route finder. And talk about scenery—anywhere and everywhere you look. Take the fascinating little settlement of Mexican Hat (just one example of hundreds), backed by one of the maddest swirls of twisted sediments you'll ever be confounded by. If it's been raining hard, you can look down on the San Juan River here to see it running the color of its surroundings, giving you insight into the power of erosion in this sparsely vegetated universe of rock. Isn't it ironic that in an area so arid water is the chief architect in charge?

The chapter begins with a couple of easy trips up around Green River and Thompson. By southern Utah's class-of-its-own standards, these are relatively mundane rides, but they provide good warm-ups for the generally much tougher rides around Moab. Moab-area outings appear roughly in order of difficulty, from easiest—including a pair in Arches National Park—to hardest. Next comes a trio of terrific rides located upstream along the Colorado River toward Dewey Bridge. These are followed by four scenic adventures in the Needles District of Canyonlands National Park, each surprisingly different. After that the guide takes you to Indian country: Hovenweep National Monument, the Navajo Nation's Monument Valley, and the magnificently remote Valley of the Gods. After all-too-brief interludes at Natural Bridges National Monument and Glen Canyon National Recreation Area, a pair of southern Utah's—and the world's—classic multiday fat-tire adventures are described: the White Rim Road and Kokopelli's Trail.

Your Canyonlands adventure ends at the Colorado River near Hite Crossing Marina. On the other, west side of the river you enter Panoramaland, an equally intriguing and wonderful spread of real estate stretching forever beneath the big Utah sky.

RIDE 11 · Crystal Geyser

AT A GLANCE

Length/configuration: 17.5-mile combination consisting of an 8-mile loop with an out-and-back spur at the beginning/end (0.75 mile each way) and another spur beginning 5 miles into the ride. Spur number two is 4 miles long each way.

Aerobic difficulty: Gentle, steady climbing over the first few miles will get your heart rate up

Technical difficulty: Easy riding over pavement and hardened gravel

Scenery: Broad desertscape of drab pastels backed by the looming Book Cliffs

Special comments: At the turnaround point is the intermittently spouting feature known as Crystal Geyser

This 17.5-mile ride is neither distinctive nor memorable enough to justify a dedicated trip to Green River just to experience it. However, if you're passing through anyway—as many Moab-bound cyclists are—the aerobically and technically easy outing offers a good warm-up to the generally much more challenging rides surrounding the undisputed mountain biking capital of the free world. On the ride you will pedal through classic, "beautiful in its own way" surroundings; countryside that is rather desiccated and Mars-like. It's terrain that few could love other than a geologist, but it offers an agreeable introduction to Canyonlands all the same.

The outing begins and ends at the John Wesley Powell River History Museum, which *is* special enough to warrant a trip to the "Watermelon Capital of the World." The museum, overlooking the legendary Green River, focuses on Utah river lore in general and specifically on the two Green-Colorado River expeditions undertaken in 1869 and 1871 by John Wesley Powell and his crews. The River Runners Hall of Fame is also located within the attractive complex. The barren wasteland encountered on this ride is not unlike a lot of the country encompassing another town known as Green River—this one located farther north, in Wyoming, where Powell first put in the Green River.

Alternatively, if you're camping you could begin riding at Green River State Park (which has hot showers), where shaded campsites are nestled next to the park's golf course. Beginning and ending here will add a total of about three miles to the distance. Free dispersed camping is also available near Crystal Geyser, although it's not nearly as appealing as that found in the state park.

Paved and high-grade gravel roads lead to Crystal Geyser, a cold-water gusher situated along the banks of the Green River. The geyser typically shows its stuff a couple of times each day; staff at the museum information desk may be able to tell you when the next eruption is expected.

General location: Green River is located along I-70, 50 miles northwest of Moab.

RIDE 11 · Crystal Geyser

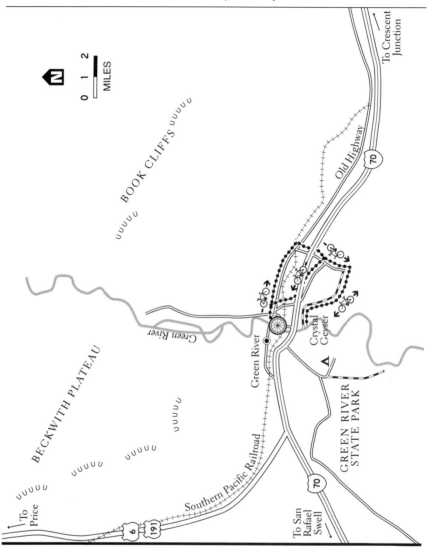

Elevation change: A climb and subsequent descent of approximately 250 feet to the geyser is about the extent of it.

Season: Year-round (weather permitting in winter). During the burn of summer, plan to ride early in the morning or in the evening.

Services: Green River has all services. Stock up on water and snacks there.

Hazards: You may encounter some car traffic on the ride, as Crystal Geyser is a popular destination for motorists.

Rescue index: Assistance, medical and otherwise, is available in Green River; passing motorists can provide emergency help if needed.

Land status: BLM, state, and private.

Maps: DeLorme *Utah Atlas & Gazetteer*, pages 39–40.

Finding the trail: Park in the lot of the John Wesley Powell River History Museum, located just east of the Green River, in the town of the same name, on the north side of East Main.

Source of additional information:

John Wesley Powell River History Museum
P.O. Box 620
885 East Main
Green River, UT 84525
(435) 564-3427

Notes on the trail: Begin by riding east on East Main. In 0.5 mile, just before milepost 4, turn left onto the paved road. After 3 additional miles you'll pass under the tracks of the Southern Pacific Railroad, then, in another 0.25 mile, turn right onto a rougher hard-surfaced road. The road widens before passing under I-70, then swings westerly to roll amid stark, brown bluffs. Soon after starting downhill, at about 5 miles cumulative, you'll cross a curious, deserted, old paved road (it is this road that you'll turn onto on the return trip) then proceed onto a winding gravel road. After descending through an intriguing jumble of rock, you'll fork right just before a power line, then curve right following the "Crystal Geyser" sign. Immediately after turning, you'll pass under the power line, then curve under it a second time. From Crystal Geyser, reached at about 9 miles, backtrack for 4 miles before turning left onto the faint, narrow paved road mentioned above. After a couple of miles the road widens; shortly beyond that point you'll turn right to cross over I-70. In another mile, close the loop and retrace your tracks for 0.75 mile to the museum.

RIDE 12 · Sego Canyon

AT A GLANCE

Length/configuration: 16-mile out-and-back (8 miles each way); longer if the spirit moves you

Aerobic difficulty: Steady climbing during the "out" portion of the ride provides a good workout

Technical difficulty: Surfaces ranging from pavement and chipseal to gravel and hard-packed dirt make for generally low technicality

Scenery: The ride pokes into the scenic Book Cliffs and Roan Cliffs, where the terrain suddenly and surprisingly turns far more scenic than that back along the interstate corridor

Special comments: Highlights include prehistoric rock art and the deserted coal-mining town of Sego

RIDE 12 · Sego Canyon

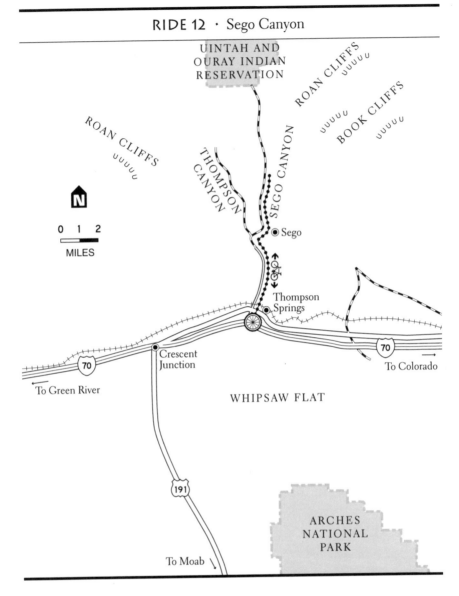

UINTAH AND
OURAY INDIAN
RESERVATION

ROAN CLIFFS

BOOK CLIFFS

ROAN CLIFFS

THOMPSON CANYON

SEGO CANYON

N

0 1 2

MILES

● Sego

Thompson
● Springs

Crescent
Junction

70

To Colorado

To Green River

70

WHIPSAW FLAT

191

ARCHES
NATIONAL
PARK

To Moab

Like the Crystal Geyser outing (Ride 11), this 16-mile out-and-back offers a nifty
opportunity to warm up to the hot and challenging rides around Moab. Technically easy (surfaces are either paved or hard-packed dirt/gravel) and—thanks to a
steady uphill—aerobically moderate, the ride passes through Thompson Canyon
before entering Sego Canyon. Both canyons are deep gashes in the rugged and
largely inaccessible Book Cliffs and Roan Cliffs. Beginning amid stark slopes and
scrub-brush flats, things turn attractive in the protected and ever-higher confines of
the canyons, where bluffs of pale sandstone prevail. The slopes near Sego ghost town
are covered in sage, and trees thrive in the bottoms. Juniper-piñon forest predomi-
nates at the higher elevations.

Some of the lonely ruins remaining at Sego.

Sights include a sandstone face adorned with Fremont Indian pictographs and petroglyphs. Sadly, they've been badly vandalized, but recent preservation efforts are in evidence. Near the mouth of Sego Canyon, just past the old cemetery, is the abandoned coal-mining settlement of Sego. In 1940 Sego had around 200 residents and reportedly at least twice that many earlier in the twentieth century. Several old rock and wood ruins remain, along with rusted car bodies, stream-support structures, and other evidence of human endeavors.

General location: North of I-70 in Thompson Springs, 6 miles east of the Moab exit.

Elevation change: Heading out you'll steadily gain elevation, a few hundred feet in all.

Season: March through November. Summers can be very hot, and the summer bugs bothersome.

Services: Thompson Springs has a service station/convenience store, where water and snacks are available. All services are found in Green River (26 miles west) and Moab (35 miles south).

Hazards: If wet, the dirt road portions can turn nasty. Conversely, during extended dry spells they can become loose and dusty. Ride with care, particularly when going downhill.

Rescue index: Auto travelers are fairly common as far as Sego. There's a pay phone at the service station/convenience store in Thompson Springs.

Land status: BLM, private.

Maps: DeLorme *Utah Atlas & Gazetteer*, page 40.

Finding the trail: The ride begins just north of I-70 in Thompson Springs, 6 miles east of the Moab exit (take Thompson Exit 185). Park at the little park just south of the service station in Thompson Springs.

Source of additional information:

Moab Multi-Agency Information Center
Center & Main
Moab, UT 84532
(435) 259-8825

Notes on the trail: From where you parked ride north on pavement toward "town," which consists of a scattering of trailers and old houses, along with what may be the tiniest post office in Utah. After crossing the railroad tracks at 0.5 mile, the main road turns to a rougher, chipseal surface. Where the canyon narrows at around 4 miles, note the small parking area on the left with picnic site and outhouse. On the cliffs adjacent to the site you can inspect Fremont Indian rock art. Beyond here the road is dirt; after 0.5 mile of it you'll take a right turn to enter Sego Canyon. (The broader Thompson Canyon, straight ahead, looks equally intriguing.) One mile after the turn, pass a cemetery on the right, then roll into the ghost town of Sego. The grade intensifies a couple of miles above Sego. This is the recommended turnaround point, although you can feel free to continue climbing for roughly another 6 miles to the boundary of the Uintah and Ouray Indian Reservation.

RIDE 13 · Willow Flats

AT A GLANCE

Length/configuration: 8-mile out-and-back (4 miles each way) on graded gravel and four-wheel-drive roads

Aerobic difficulty: A few short, moderately steep climbs, but overall quite easy

Technical difficulty: Easy, except for the occasional stretch of drift and wash sand

Scenery: Wavelike patterns of wind-blown sand, jumbles of red sandstone boulders, distant fins and arches, and an endless skyscape overhead combine to make this a particularly beautiful ride

Special comments: The drive through Arches National Park makes finding the trailhead worthwhile even if you end up nixing the ride

This four-mile out, four-mile back ride is entirely within Arches National Park on graded gravel and four-wheel-drive roads. It's easy both technically and aerobically, yet sandy stretches and short expanses of slickrock make for an illuminating, "Desert Riding 101" introductory session. The ride makes an excellent sunset outing, as it is set amid the unlikely topography of Arches National Park and the huge sky enfolding it.

Approximately one mile into the ride you'll pass a jeep trail forking right to take aim at the distant northwest. Two miles from this point the jeep trail skirts the distinctive Eye of the Whale Arch, before continuing for another seven miles to Klondike Bluffs. This potential side trip is notoriously sandy, though, and will offer reasonably fun riding only if recent rains have "set up" the sand.

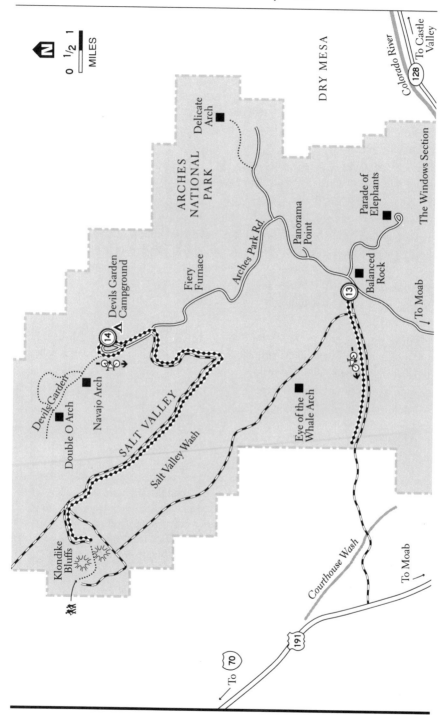

Here's another way to crank the adventure-meter up another notch: From the recommended turnaround point at the national park boundary, continue westerly across BLM lands for approximately four miles to Highway 191. En route you'll be compelled to cross Courthouse Wash, usually a wide expanse of dry, loose sand that can be a struggle to negotiate. From the highway it's 17 miles back to the beginning point, via US 191 and the Arches National Park road.

General location: Arches National Park. The park entrance station is 4 miles northwest of Moab.

Elevation change: A few short, moderately steep climbs and descents.

Season: March through mid-May and September through November. Summers in Arches are very hot.

Services: All services are available in Moab, 13 miles from the trailhead. Stock up on water and snacks there. The excellent Devils Garden Campground, the only campground in Arches, is situated 9 miles north of the trailhead along the park road.

Hazards: Too timidly hitting a patch of sand can cause a spill.

Rescue index: Park rangers occasionally patrol the Willow Flats area. Pay phones are located at the entrance station (9 miles south) and at Devils Garden Campground (9 miles north; this one is a celluar phone that requires a credit card to use).

Land status: National Park Service.

Maps: *Arches National Park Official Map and Guide* or DeLorme *Utah Atlas & Gazetteer*, page 40.

Finding the trail: From the Arches National Park entrance station, drive 9 miles north on the paved park road. Turn left and park at the picnic area opposite Balanced Rock, a feature located on the east side of the road.

Source of additional information:

Moab Multi-Agency Information Center
Center & Main
Moab, UT 84532
(435) 259-8825

Notes on the trail: From the picnic area, ride west on a high-grade gravel surface. In less than a mile, just after a gate, you'll pass the road forking right toward Eye of the Whale Arch and Klondike Bluffs. The route quickly deteriorates; from here on you'll ride on alternating surfaces of sand (sometimes rather deep) and rock through a setting of shifting dunes, sand flats, rocky washes, and gnarled junipers. The recommended turnaround point is at the national park boundary at 4 miles.

RIDE 14 · Salt Valley Road

AT A GLANCE

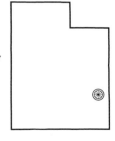

Length/configuration: 19-mile out-and-back (9.5 miles each way)

Aerobic difficulty: Easy, across terrain that is generally flat to gently pitched

Technical difficulty: Easy, with the exception of possible drift sand covering the roadway in places. Surfaces include pavement and high-grade gravel/sand, which may be extremely washboarded in places.

Scenery: A sprawling spectacle of canyon country unfolds in whatever direction you point your handlebars

Special comments: Bring a cable lock for securing your bike to a signpost at the turnaround, so that you can continue by foot to Tower Arch

This 9.5-mile one-way ride (19 miles total) approaches the area known as Klondike Bluffs (see Ride 17) from the "back," or east side. En route it pokes through the little-visited northwestern reaches of Arches National Park. The two-wheel-drive roads followed offer easy cycling, although there's a good chance of encountering substantial stretches of sand and washboard. The latter can sometimes be avoided by sticking close to the edge of the road; still, a full-suspension bike would be most useful and appreciated. It can be hot and quite dusty on the route in the middle of the day, when car traffic often picks up; therefore, this is highly recommended as a sunrise ride. At that time of day expect to hear curlews calling from the damp spots along Salt Valley Wash and to watch ravens catching early morning currents above.

The riding is rather mundane, but the setting is unforgettable. It's a big empty you'll pedal through—an empty proffering remarkably diverse, long-range vistas of the canyon country. On the way out you'll get ever closer to the castlelike Klondike Bluffs, composed of mellow, salmon-hued Entrada sandstone. On the return trip you'll gaze across the barrens at a beautiful ridge of fins, or FAAs (future arches of America), rising like sharks' teeth to the left of the La Sal Mountains. In spring these mountains add a contrasting dash of brilliant white (of unmelted snow) to the faded greens, browns, and reds more typical of the desert.

The turnaround point is the trailhead for the 1.7-mile foot trail to Tower Arch, a distinctive feature underscored with the inscription of Alexander Ringhoffer. The early 1920s prospector was key to the 1929 setting aside of 4,520 acres as Arches National Monument—a designation that was changed to national park in 1971, by which time the protected area had grown to encompass more than 70,000 acres.

General location: Arches National Park. The park entrance station is 4 miles northwest of Moab.

Elevation change: Gently graded riding alongside Salt Valley Wash with one mentionable descent (heading out) at 4 miles.

Season: March through mid-May and September through November. Summers in Arches are very hot.

Services: All services are available in Moab, 22 miles from the trailhead. Stock up on water and snacks there. The excellent Devils Garden Campground, where the ride begins, is the only campground in Arches. All of its 52 sites are available on a first-come, first-served basis only. (If you haven't read Edward Abbey's *Desert Solitaire*, do it while camping here.)

Hazards: Hitting a patch of sand while going too slow can cause a spill. The washboard common on the Salt Valley Road is more of a pain than a hazard.

Rescue index: Park rangers patrol the Salt Valley area, and other car travelers will likely be encountered. A pay phone is found at the Devils Garden Campground (it's a celluar phone requiring a credit card to use).

Land status: National Park Service.

Maps: *Arches National Park Official Map and Guide* or DeLorme *Utah Atlas & Gazetteer*, page 40.

Finding the trail: From the Arches National Park entrance station, drive 18 miles north on the paved park road to the Devils Garden Campground.

Source of additional information:

Moab Multi-Agency Information Center
Center & Main
Moab, UT 84532
(435) 259-8825

Notes on the trail: From the campground exit, loop counterclockwise through the Devils Garden parking area. Turn right after a little more than a mile onto the wide, smooth, high-grade gravel road leading toward Klondike Bluffs / Tower Arch. After approximately 4 miles total you'll begin descending (catch the distant views of the La Sals to your left!). In another mile the road swings back around to the northwest after dropping into Salt Valley Wash. On the left, a mile before the turnaround, you'll pass a four-wheel-drive road that leads 10 miles southeast to Balanced Road (it's exceedingly sandy in places and not recommended for riding). Fifty yards from there turn left off Salt Valley Road toward Klondike Bluffs and continue for another mile to the Tower Arch trailhead.

RIDE 15 · Hurrah Pass

AT A GLANCE

Length/configuration: 29-mile out-and-back (14.5 miles each way)

Aerobic difficulty: Level riding along the Colorado River, gradual uphill along Kane Creek (except for one laborious set of switchbacks) and steep uphill over the last 3 miles

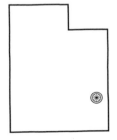

RIDE 15 · Hurrah Pass

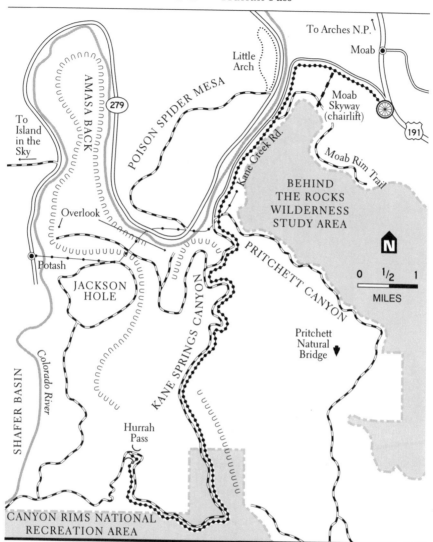

Technical difficulty: Not much challenge until the final 3 miles, where the road turns rocky and twisting. Riding surfaces include pavement, graded gravel (potentially washboarded), and rough, rock-embedded two-wheel-drive road.

Scenery: The energy spent gaining the pass reaps a visual bonanza of hard-rock desert, islands of shadowed mountains, and, far below, the Colorado River

Special comments: Ideal as a spring tune-up for getting your Moab legs, or as an interlude from all the tough stuff. Keep your eyes peeled for prehistoric rock art between miles 3 and 6.

The road to Hurrah Pass, a.k.a. No Way Pass.

The 14.5-mile spin to Hurrah Pass, unlike most Moab-area rides, is entirely on roads negotiable by two-wheel-drive vehicles (although the last three miles request high clearance). You'll begin within the Moab city limits, starting with a five-mile spin along a ribbon of pavement nestled between the Colorado River and its sheer canyon walls. Then, after seven miles of gravel that's high-grade but quite possibly washboarded, you'll commence the steep, serpentine climb to Hurrah Pass, up and over the anticline separating the canyons of Kane Creek and the Colorado River. Aerobically the ride is rated moderate; technically, easy to moderate.

As you approach the climb, you may look up at the maze of Moenkopi sediments and begin calling your supposed destination "No Way Pass," because from below it appears unlikely that a road could actually find its way to the ridge top. But it does indeed, and from the ridge the views are sublime, encompassing the Colorado River, Island in the Sky, Dead Horse Point, the slickrock sea flooding the sky above Moab, the distant La Sals rising behind the Kane Creek Canyon rim, and a whole lot more.

The intrepid and well-equipped may choose to venture on. On the far side of Hurrah Pass one track bears south and west away from the Colorado, devolving into a four-wheel-drive trail. Eventually it improves in quality as it snakes its way southward for many miles, passing through Lockhart Basin en route to an eventual juncture with State Highway 211 near the Needles District of Canyonlands National Park. Obtain more complete information from the Bureau of Land Management and/or area bike shops before undertaking this multiday adventure.

General location: The ride begins in Moab.

Elevation change: Most of the 700 feet gained are over the final 3 miles.

Season: March through mid-May and September through November are best. Summers in the Moab area are very hot, so head out at first light if your visit falls during that season.

Services: Moab has all services, including a slew of good bike shops and the all-important microbrewery. Stock up on water and food in town.

Hazards: Beware of cars, particularly along the first 5 miles of the route (paved), where traffic often moves at a good clip.

Rescue index: Motorists and other mountain bikers will likely be encountered during the ride.

Land status: BLM, state.

Maps: DeLorme *Utah Atlas & Gazetteer*, page 30, or National Geographic/Trails Illustrated's *Moab Map* (available at local bike shops).

Finding the trail: Begin riding in Moab at the corner of Main and Kane Creek Boulevard, 0.75 mile south of the intersection of Center and Main. There's plenty of parking nearby.

Source of additional information:

Moab Multi-Agency Information Center
Center & Main
Moab, UT 84532
(435) 259-8825

Notes on the trail: Ride west on Kane Creek Boulevard, veering left after 0.75 mile onto Kane Creek Road. After four additional miles of pavement you'll cross a cattle guard and ride onto gravel. After climbing, then descending a set of switchbacks, you'll pass some BLM campsites. At 11.5 miles leave the Kane Creek drainage to begin the steep, 3-mile pull to Hurrah Pass, reached at 14.5 miles. Return the way you came.

RIDE 16 · Gemini Bridges

AT A GLANCE

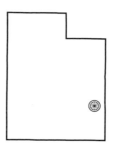

Length/configuration: 28-mile loop or 14-mile point-to-point (shuttle required)

Aerobic difficulty: 1,400 feet of elevation are gained on pavement over the first half of this long ride, then surrendered on dirt over the second half

Technical difficulty: Few technical challenges await, although occasional steep downhills are confronted. Riding surfaces include pavement, gravel, and dirt jeep trail, which dishes up occasional patches of loose rock, slickrock, and wash sand.

Scenery: Diverse, with the unique twin bridges serving as exclamation points

Special comments: You can arrange for a shuttle with a company in Moab if you'd rather avoid the 14-mile uphill ride on pavement. Route finding can be tricky over the last half of the ride, although signs and/or bike tracks usually mark the way.

Gemini Bridges is a favorite of many two-wheeled Moab pilgrims because—despite the fact that it's largely off-road—it lacks the tough technicality of many area trails. If you're addicted to the technical, you may find Gemini Bridges a bit ho-hum; contrarily, if you're intimidated by the very mention of names like Slickrock, Porcupine Rim, and Poison Spider Mesa, you'll probably like it a lot.

The off-pavement part of the route swoops down along the ridge separating the South Fork Sevenmile and Bull Canyons. On high you can look out over infinite stretches of desert bedrock sediments, interrupted only by the occasional "intrusive igneous" range of mountains, such as the isolated Henrys to the west and, to the east, the ever present La Sals. Six miles after hitting pay dirt you'll arrive at the Gemini Bridges, a pair of impressive, side-by-side natural bridges.

An abundance of side spurs branching off the main trail implore you to investigate. If you're the sort that can't resist, you'll want to save time and energy for off-route exploring by arranging for a lift over the first 14 miles of the loop. (Several commercial operators run shuttles out of Moab; inquire at one of the bike shops for a current listing of names and phone numbers.) Some of these same spurs may confound your route-finding skills, as well: Here, as elsewhere, it's all too common to have signs removed by individuals who apparently think they'll look better adorning their bedroom walls than they do out here in the wide open, doing nothing but helping keep cyclists from becoming lost.

General location: 10 miles north of Moab.

Elevation change: 1,400 feet are gained and subsequently lost.

Season: March through mid-May and September through November are best. Summers in the Moab area are very hot, so head out at first light if your visit falls during that season.

Services: Moab has all services, including several excellent bike shops. Stock up on water and food in town.

Hazards: Exercise extreme caution when riding along busy US 191, and when turning from it onto UT 313.

Rescue index: Other mountain bikers will probably be encountered during the ride.

Land status: Bureau of Land Management.

Maps: DeLorme *Utah Atlas & Gazetteer*, pages 30 and 40, or National Geographic/Trails Illustrated's *Moab Map* (available at local bike shops).

Finding the trail: Go north on US 191 from the corner of Center and Main in Moab. At just under 10 miles turn left to cross a cattle guard; park in the wide parking area adjacent to the railroad tracks.

Source of additional information:

Moab Multi-Agency Information Center
Center & Main
Moab, UT 84532
(435) 259-8825

RIDE 16 · Gemini Bridges

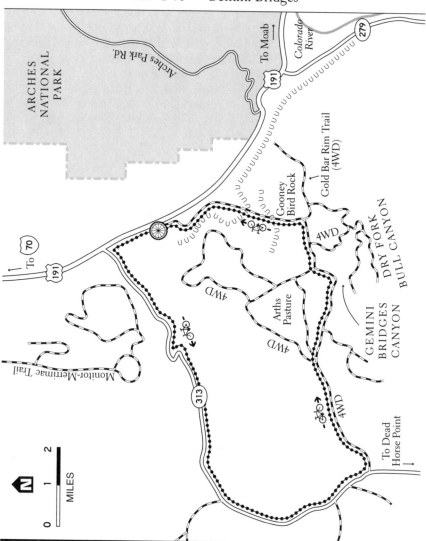

Notes on the trail: From the parking area ride north on US 191 for just over a mile, then turn left onto UT 313 toward Dead Horse Point State Park/Canyonlands National Park. Grunt uphill for mile after mile, stopping now and then to catch your breath . . . er, to survey your stupendous surroundings. At 14 miles cumulative (just under a mile past the right-hand turn to Mineral Bottom), turn left off the pavement toward Gemini Bridges. Now, most—but not *all*—of the work is over and the real fun begins. Proceed down through a scattered forest of piñon pine and juniper. Bear right off the main road toward Gemini Bridges at the Y, 4 miles after leaving the pavement. In another 0.75 mile stay left toward Gemini Bridges (right goes to Four Arch Canyon, 2 miles). A mile past there, bear right off the the main trail to follow the maze of trails leading 0.25 mile to the natural bridges. After breaking for lunch, back-track 0.25 mile to regain the main trail, which you'll continue down, soon passing a spur going right to another Gemini Bridges overlook. Half a mile from where you resumed riding on the main trail, go left to twist down an expanse of slickrock (a right here will take you eventually to the point mentioned below at 9 miles). A mile later merge right onto the better road coming in from behind left, riding straight toward the distant La Sal Mountains and the mass of sandstone fins of Behind the Rocks. One mile from that point, bear left down a steep hill, aiming at the distant gap. In 0.5 mile (9 miles cumulative since leaving the pavement), at the bottom of the downhill, turn left to begin a gradual climb of nearly 3 miles up Little Canyon. Before com-mencing the final downhill at 12 miles, take a long, hard gander into distant Arches National Park. Two miles later you'll return to your vehicle.

RIDE 17 · Klondike Bluffs

AT A GLANCE

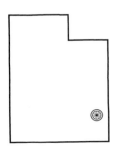

Length/configuration: 14-mile out-and-back (7 miles each way)

Aerobic difficulty: The ride out climbs gradually to begin, then provides some tougher climbing over the second half

Technical difficulty: The route encompasses broad boulevards of sandstone that should be manageable by just about any rider, yet that offer room to roam and a chance to get acquainted with free-form slickrock tricks. Other surfaces include graded road of packed sediments, occasional stretches of sand, and loose dirt and rocks.

Scenery: Broad, wide-open desert. Ends high on a plateau near the boundary of Arches National Park.

Special comments: Don't miss the dinosaur tracks located at about 5 miles — real ones, that is, not to be confused with the stenciled tracks used as route markers on parts of this ride

This 14-mile ride (7 miles each way) approaches the Klondike Bluffs from the northwest, ending just outside the boundary of Arches National Park. (If you did Ride 14, Salt Valley Road, you accessed the bluffs from their other side.) You must turn around at or before the park boundary, as mountain bikes aren't allowed on the trails within the park. Overall the outing is aerobically and technically moderate in difficulty. The riding is a breeze to begin, as you ascend the gently sloping Salt Val-ley Anticline on typically well-graded sand and clay roads. Over the second half of the ride you'll encounter a sizable stretch of slickrock, which should be negotiable by a strong novice. Tougher routes over the rock can be sniffed out, too, making this trail a good choice for riding companions possessing disparate technical skills.

Where the riding ends you can hike up onto a high point that has served as an overlook for centuries, as evidenced by the scatterings of rock chippings on the sandy ground in the open groves of piñon pine and juniper. As you look out over the endless expanse of painted desert, it's easy to imagine a prehistoric Native American doing the same as he watched for game moving below. The more distant view encompasses the uplift of the San Rafael Reef far to the northwest and, to the southeast, the nearby fins of Klondike Bluffs backed by the slickrock mounds above Moab.

General location: 16.5 miles north of Moab.

Elevation change: The ride out gains roughly 700 feet—most of it gradually, but with some semi-grunts on slickrock between 4.5 and 6 miles, along with steep pitches over rubbly dirt for the last mile.

Season: March through mid-May and September through November are best. Summers in the Moab area are very hot, so head out at first light if your visit falls during that season.

Services: All services are available in Moab. Stock up on food and water there.

Hazards: If wet, the first few miles of clay road will be greasy and slick, if not impassable. Slickrock ledges may be hazardous if approached too tentatively.

Rescue index: Other mountain bikers will probably be encountered during the entire ride and motorists over the first 3 miles.

Land status: State, BLM.

Maps: National Geographic/Trails Illustrated's *Moab Map* (available at local bike shops).

Finding the trail: From the corner of Center and Main in Moab, drive 16.5 miles north on US 191. The trailhead is 0.5 mile south of mile marker 143 (which marks the beginning of Ride 18, Bartlett Wash). Pull off and park in the wide area on the east side of the highway, adjacent to a gate in the fence line.

Source of additional information:

Moab Multi-Agency Information Center
Center & Main
Moab, UT 84532
(435) 259-8825

Notes on the trail: From the parking area, ride east through the gate onto a wide road shooting easterly through drab desert. At just under 3 miles go left, taking aim at the distant, white-tipped knobs. After passing through another gate, keep high to the left as you parallel the gash of Little Valley's wash. Immediately after riding through the wash turn right at the T, then keep an eye out for signs and cairns directing you left into a tight, relatively vegetation-rich canyon. In less than a mile from there you'll bump up onto a broad ramp of white sandstone. As you traverse it, you'll want to stay just to the right of the low, reddish bluff. Watch for more cairns, as well as stenciled dinosaur tracks, as you negotiate a potentially confounding area. (Fellow cyclists and/or the tracks of previous riders can help lead the way.) After a little more than a mile of slickrock you'll return to a rough, rocky road surface. Bear right at each of a pair of intersections in the 6-mile range, then proceed to the base of a very steep hill at 7 miles. From here you can continue by foot to the plateau's top.

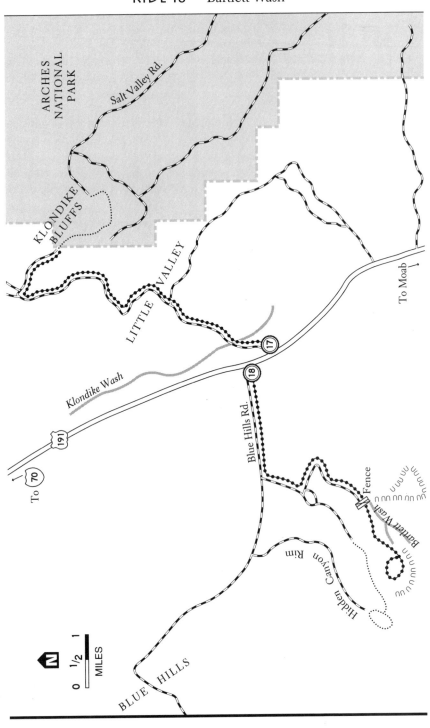

RIDE 18 · Bartlett Wash

AT A GLANCE

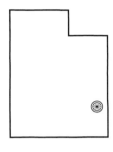

Length/configuration: 10-mile out-and-back (5 miles each way) to get to and from the slickrock; from there, you can play as long and far as you please. If a beeline were possible—which it's not—it would take you about 2 miles out and 2 miles back on the slickrock.

Aerobic difficulty: After spinning along for 5 easy miles on graded gravel and primitive sand roads, you can choose your own route on the slickrock, making this outing as tough as you desire

Technical difficulty: Straightforward to very difficult moves are possible on the slickrock

Scenery: Rising out of desert bleakness, this is a startling world of often smooth-surfaced, sometimes ledgy, multihued Entrada sandstone

Special comments: In dry conditions you can probably drive the first 5 miles of the route, as many cyclists do (weenies every one), but you'll miss a terrific warm-up spin

Once known as the private slickrock haunt of in-the-know locals, word has leaked about the playground known as Barlett Wash—and, to its northwest, the adjoining and equally entertaining Hidden Canyon. Still, owing to a less convenient location and more limited scope, you'll avoid the crazy hordes that often crowd the Slickrock Bike Trail. Neophyte to world-class slickrockers can enjoy hours of free-form riding amid a mind-numbing universe of elephant toes, monster piles of petrified prehistoric cow dung, dips and twirls of swirling bedrock, chutes and gulleys . . . and intermittent sand traps.

General location: 17 miles north of Moab.

Elevation change: You gradually climb 300 to 400 feet above the wash as you ride out. Truth is, though, you'll probably gain a lot more than that, often taken in huge gulps followed by instant elevation losses that are equal or greater.

Season: March through mid-May and September through November are best. Summers in this area are very hot, so start by first light if you ride during that season.

Services: All services are found in Moab. Stock up on food and water there. There may be water running in Bartlett Wash, but drink it only after filtering.

Hazards: Beware of getting in over your head in terms of slickrock technicality, and keep close track of where you've been so you can get back roughly the same way. It's possible to get lost and/or rimrocked out here. Patches of sand may cause sudden, radical reductions in forward momentum.

Rescue index: Hidden and Bartlett Canyons are isolated, yet other mountain bikers will likely be encountered. During the high seasons of spring and fall, you'll probably see car campers in the cottonwood groves near the slickrock trailhead.

Land status: Bureau of Land Management.

There's more than one way to get through those sand traps, as Joanne LaBelle demonstrates.

Maps: National Geographic/Trails Illustrated's *Moab Map* (available at local bike shops).

Finding the trail: From the corner of Center and Main in Moab drive 17 miles north on US 191. Immediately before mile marker 143 (0.5 mile north of the turn to the trailhead for Ride 17, Klondike Bluffs) turn west off the highway onto Blue Hills Road. Cross the railroad tracks and park in the wide area beside the road on the right.

Source of additional information:

Moab Multi-Agency Information Center
Center & Main
Moab, UT 84532
(435) 259-8825

Notes on the trail: From the parking area ride westerly for just over 2 miles on improved road, then turn left onto a more primitive road that's sandy in places. A mile after turning off the main road veer left at the Y. Go through a sandy wash bottom, then climb the short hill, passing the Hidden Canyon Road going right. A mile past the Y (4 miles cumulative) turn right toward Bartlett Wash. Just under a mile beyond, after whizzing past of string of cottonwood-protected dispersed campsites on the right, you'll pass through a metal gate. Watch closely for a sandy track climbing to the right about 200 yards past the gate. (Don't be misled by four-wheel-drive tracks heading up the sandy wash.) Push up that sandy track and arrive at slickrock nirvana, where any number of "level" options can be blazed, in addition to more challenging ones. You'll cross a considerable stretch of sand after a few hundred yards, but slickrock resumes on the other side. Not long before the turnaround you'll meet Hidden Canyon coming in on the right (where yet another universe of slickrock beckons). You'll know when you're at the turnaround—reached after a very long and meandering 2 miles—because to proceed on would mean almost certain death, without an accompanying parachute à la Evel Knievel at the Snake River Canyon. Do not despair: The ride back is every bit as fun as the ride out; maybe even more so, with the skills you've honed over the last couple of hours. An altogether fresh experience is possible within yards of your previous path.

RIDE 19 · Behind the Rocks to Pritchett Canyon

AT A GLANCE

Length/configuration: 27-mile point-to-point (shuttle required) on dirt and gravel roads, sandy double-tracks, and rugged four-wheel-drive trail, including ledges of sandstone and loose cobbles

Aerobic difficulty: Although you end up more than 1,000 feet lower than where you started, a trio of substantial climbs is tackled along the way

Technical difficulty: Tricky ledge descents in Pritchett Canyon make this outing unsuitable for beginners

Scenery: From drab sand flats to the fiery, cottonwood-lined confines of Pritchett Canyon

Special comments: Just before exiting Pritchett Canyon and riding onto pavement, you'll cross private land where a toll of $1 is levied by way of the honor system

This 27-mile point-to-point ride begins by tracing dirt double-track roads through an area webbed with old prospecting roads. Staying on the route often demands great attention to detail (although the trail does typically follow the most beaten path). Hard-packed sand, as well as soft wash sand—particularly annoying after extended dry weather—is encountered over the first 17 miles; then, from Yellow Hill on down through Pritchett Canyon, the trail turns into a rugged four-wheel-drive byway as it drops off ledge after ledge of Navajo sandstone. Loose cobbles help keep things interesting, too. It's a long one, with enough aerobic and technical challenges to please any advanced fat-tire fanatic, yet manageable by intermediate to advanced-intermediate riders. The scenery encompasses open flats, views of the orange-hued fins of Behind the Rocks, a terrific overlook on Kane Creek Canyon and the marvelous, wild beauty of Pritchett Canyon, which serves as a portion of the boundary of the Behind the Rocks Wilderness Study Area.

Alternatively, a "simple"—but tough—out-and-back ride from Kane Creek Road

RIDE 19 · Behind the Rocks to Pritchett Canyon

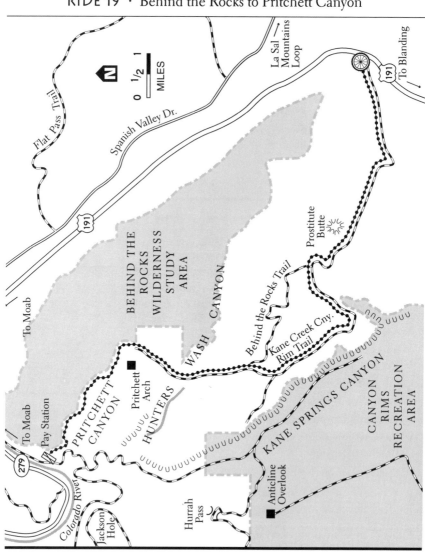

to the Pritchett Arch hiking trailhead can make for a fine outing of 12 miles round-trip, eliminating the need for a shuttle.

General location: South of Moab, between US 191 and Kane Creek Road.

Elevation change: As the altimeter goes, the ride loses approximately 1,400 feet; however, there's the small matter of 1,000 feet of uphill riding, too, so cumulative loss is closer to 2,400 feet.

Season: March through mid-May and September through November are best. Summers in the Moab area are very hot, so head out at first light if your visit falls during that season.

Services: All services are found in Moab. Stock up on food and water there.

Hazards: Big ledges and steep rocky stretches abound as you descend the dry streambed of Pritchett Canyon. Elsewhere, sand—the desert counterpart of the skier's snow snake—may rear up to grab your tires. Watch for car traffic on Kane Creek Road.

Rescue index: Other mountain bikers will likely be encountered on this ride.

Land status: Bureau of Land Management.

Maps: National Geographic/Trails Illustrated's *Moab Map* (available at local bike shops).

Finding the trail: From the corner of Center and Main in Moab, drive about 14 miles south on US 191. Turn right at the summit of Blue Hill, just past mile marker 113, and cross a cattle guard. Park in one of the many pull-outs tucked into stands of juniper.

Source of additional information:

Moab Multi-Agency Information Center
Center & Main
Moab, UT 84532
(435) 259-8825

Notes on the trail: Continue from the parking area, staying on the primary road where spurs go right. After passing some sand dunes and then crossing a wash at around 3 miles, continue on the main road as it bends right and climbs 2 miles toward Prostitute Butte. Stay left where a spur heading right goes around the butte to a pair of arches. At the four-way junction at 7 miles, go left to keep the nearby cliffs on your right. The road soon curves to parallel the eastern rim of Kane Creek Canyon for more than 2 miles, with several spurs going left to wonderful overlooks. At 12 miles cumulative, climb right away from the rim, soon commencing the rugged descent to Hunters Canyon wash, reached at a little over 15 miles. In another 0.5 mile you'll pass a hiking spur going left to Pritchett Arch. The main sandy track winds up Yellow Hill, reaching the summit at roughly 17 miles. The route finding over the next 5 miles is straightforward, although the route riding is not necessarily so. After paying your courtesy fee of $1 for the privilege of crossing private lands, turn right at 22 miles onto Kane Creek Road and pedal the remaining 5 miles to Moab.

RIDE 20 · Poison Spider Mesa

AT A GLANCE

Length/configuration: 12-mile out-and-back
(6 miles each way)

Aerobic difficulty: After a steep introductory climb up
a swtichbacking jeep road, the riding flattens some,
although you must continue humping up sandstone
ledges to gain the mesa top

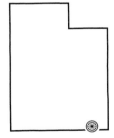

RIDE 20 · Poison Spider Mesa
RIDE 21 · Amasa Back

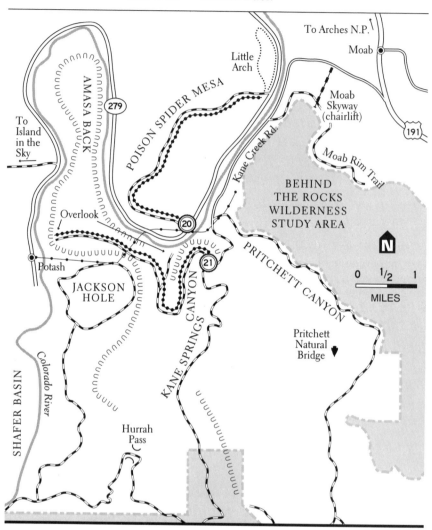

Technical difficulty: Slickrock pitches alternate with sand traps, the latter making for particularly tough riding in dry conditions. Other surfaces include hard-packed, eroded, and cobble-strewn four-wheel-drive road.

Scenery: Outstanding views of Behind the Rocks with a La Sal Mountains backdrop

Special comments: By continuing beyond the recommended turnaround, after passing through some extremely tough sandy stretches, you'll eventually arrive at the notoriously exposed, death-defying (one hopes) Portal Trail, by which you can regain Potash Road. Not recommended for the tentative rider or the faint of heart.

Makin' moves up the "Spider."

This 12-mile out-and-back (6 miles each way)—like Ride 21, Amasa Back—is a good choice to tackle if you're new to Moab riding as a hint of what's to come on legendary rides like the Slickrock and Porcupine Rim trails. Thanks largely to the inaugural climb, the ride is aerobically challenging but not a killer; meanwhile, the sand and slickrock ledges (including one that's particularly memorable) offer some real technical challenges, but they don't just keep coming at you, as is the case on some area rides. Riding surfaces include sand, slickrock, and eroded and loose-surfaced four-wheel-drive road. There's cactus, too, and the bite of the prickly pear can be severe for those who go down buns first.

Vast vistas encompass the sandstone fins of Behind the Rocks on the far side of the Colorado River to the southeast, the more distant La Sal peaks behind those, and, to the north, some of the curious formations contained in Arches National Park.

General location: Southwest of Moab on the opposite side of the Colorado River.

Elevation change: The ride out gains 1,000 feet-plus.

Season: March through mid-May and September through November are best. Summers in the Moab area are very hot, so head out at first light if your visit falls during that season.

Services: All services are found in Moab. Stock up on food and water there.

Hazards: Ledges, loose cobbles, sandtraps, and cacti.

Rescue index: Other mountain bikers will likely be encountered on this ride.

Land status: Bureau of Land Management.

Maps: National Geographic/Trails Illustrated's *Moab Map* (available at local bike shops).

Finding the trail: From the corner of Center and Main in Moab, drive 4 miles north-west on US 191, then turn left onto UT 279/Potash Road. The parking area is on the right at just under 6 miles on UT 279, immediately past the "dinosaur tracks" sign.

Source of additional information:

Moab Multi-Agency Information Center
Center & Main
Moab, UT 84532
(435) 259-8825

Notes on the trail: From the parking area, ride steeply up a switchbacking jeep road that in places is quite eroded and/or strewn with loose cobbles. After skirting (on your right) a sandstone "beehive" outcrop that could be responsible for Utah's nickname, proceed through a long expanse of sand; then, at about 3 miles, stairstep your way up onto the mesa. White stenciled jeep and/or bicycle symbols, as well as the occasional Carsonite post, mark the side-spur-abundant, potentially confusing route. (Note that the jeep stencils don't always mark the most sensible way from point A to point B— leading one to believe that the trail was laid out to provide jeepsters with thrills, rather than cyclists with a relatively easy route.) At 5 miles-plus, where the trail splits, follow the stenciled jeeps to the right. A stretch of slickrock, interrupted by islands of timber, delivers you to the hiking spur to Little Arch, the recommended lunch stop, ooh-ahh scenic overlook, and turnaround. The arch is roughly 100 yards from where you'll want to leave your bikes.

RIDE 21 · Amasa Back

AT A GLANCE

Length/configuration: 12-mile out-and-back (6 miles each way), with an optional side spur of less than 1 mile each way

Aerobic difficulty: Moderate, with a little more than 1,000 feet of elevation gain

Technical difficulty: Advanced intermediate. The ride begins on the graded Kane Creek Road but quickly dives down a difficult rocky descent to the Kane Springs Creek crossing (which, not surprisingly, becomes a difficult uphill on the way out). Beyond that point, the riding involves sandy double-track, rocky ledges, and slickrock.

Scenery: Outstanding views of the La Sals, Poison Spider Mesa, the Colorado River corridor, Dead Horse Point, and points beyond

Special comments: Of all the view rides in the Moab area, Amasa Back arguably tops them all

Amasa Back is a three-mile-long, 1,000-foot-high peninsula of land wrapped on the east, north, and south by the Colorado River. The ride to get to Amasa Back's

Of all the "best view" rides surrounding Moab, Amasa Back may top them all.

southwestern rim begins on Kane Creek Road, but you quickly leave that mellow byway to struggle down to the Kane Springs Creek bottoms, over ledges of bedrock and through rocky rubble. It is by far the ugliest part of the entire ride, so don't let it scare you off. Fording Kane Springs Creek is typically a breeze, except during and immediately after heavy rains. The riding on the other side of the creek turns easier, with portions of the old mining path following a slickrock "road" that approximates any good engineer's requirements for width and grade. On top, sandy double-track precedes the final approach to the western rim overlook, accessed by way of slickrock playground through which a route is identified with cairns. At ride's end, the view down on and across the Colorado River is sublime; behind, the shocking red fins of Behind the Rocks, jutting in front of the pure white La Sals (provided it is spring or early summer), is an equally inspiring sight. The 12-mile out-and-back is aerobically moderate in difficulty and intermediate to advanced in its technical challenge.

General location: 5 miles southwest of Moab.

Elevation change: You'll gain approximately 1,100 feet on the ride.

Season: March through mid-May and September through November are best. Summers in the Moab area are very hot, so head out at first light if your visit falls during that season.

Services: All services are found in Moab. Stock up on food and water there.

Hazards: Ride with care along the Kane Creek Road, which can carry substantial car traffic, and also when descending to Kane Springs Creek. Walk your bike if prudence suggests it.

Rescue index: Like many rides in southern Utah, the outing visits remote, hard-to-access country. Other mountain bikers will likely be encountered on the ride.

Land status: Bureau of Land Management.

Maps: National Geographic/Trails Illustrated's *Moab Map* (available at local bike shops).

Finding the trail: From the junction of Main Street and Kane Creek Boulevard in Moab (0.75 mile south of the corner of Center and Main), go 0.75 mile west on Kane Creek Boulevard, then veer left onto paved Kane Creek Road. In just under 5 miles you'll cross a cattle guard onto dirt; continue for a little less than 1 mile, then turn right into the obvious parking area.

Source of additional information:

> Moab Multi-Agency Information Center
> Center & Main
> Moab, UT 84532
> (435) 259-8825

Notes on the trail: Pedal southwestward up Kane Creek Road for about 0.5 mile, then turn right onto the signed Amasa Back Trail. After tackling the rough descent to the creek, bushwhack left through brush for approximately 50 yards and you'll probably find stepping stones placed across the creek (subject to change, but Kane Springs Creek should be easy to cross nonetheless). Climb out of the creek bottom over ledges and loose rock. As you gain elevation, ignore side spurs going this way and that—except for the one going right immediately after you cross to the west side of the "back." Less than a mile long, it passes through some sandy areas en route to a dramatic rimrock viewpoint looking over at the bulk of Poison Spider Mesa, standing tall above the Colorado River. Back on the main route, you'll soon cross over an exposed pipeline and under a power line; they, along with the left-hand spur encountered shortly thereafter, drop into the depths of Jackson Hole, an abandoned Colorado River meander. White paint on rocks and/or cairns mark the last 1 mile-plus of the route, which ends at 6 miles at an unforgettable exposed overlook above the Colorado, across the river from the Potash plant.

RIDE 22 · Slickrock Bike Trail

AT A GLANCE

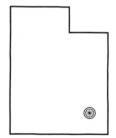

Length/configuration: 12.5-mile combination, consisting of a 5-mile out-and-back (2.5 miles each way) connecting to a 7.5-mile loop.

Aerobic difficulty: Aerobically very tough, with dozens of exceedingly steep climbs

Technical difficulty: Very difficult, with steep climbs and descents over sandstone with a surface like sandpaper. The trail includes tricky ledges, catchy sand traps (often containing cactus), and knee-buckling exposure.

Scenery: Could be another world; worth a moon walk even if you've forgotten your bicycle

RIDE 22 · Slickrock Bike Trail

Map showing the Slickrock Bike Trail area near Moab, including Arches National Park, Colorado River, Negro Bill Canyon Wilderness Study Area, Ice Box Canyon, Natural Selection Viewpoint, Shrimp Rock, Swiss Cheese Ridge, Lion's Back, Abyss Canyon, Practice Loop, Hell's Revenge Jeep Trail, Moab Dump, Sand Flats Rd., and routes to Cisco, Monticello, and Porcupine Rim Trail.

Special comments: The Slickrock Bike Trail is the ultimate for fat-tire enthusiasts

Mountain bikers the world over talk in sometimes reverent (but more often raving) tones about the Slickrock Bike Trail—whether it's about their experience riding it or their hopes of one day doing so. The distance—a measly 12.5 miles—belies the trail's difficulty. Still, 15 years ago, when only a few hardy pioneers were attempting the raucous rock, no one could have guessed how extremely far the envelope of slickrock tricks would be pushed by the turn of the millennium. Today, literally hundreds complete the trail on a normal spring break weekday. You'll see young girls and boys making moves you cannot believe, along with college co-eds, men and women of baby boomer vintage, whole families, and even the occasional dog (usually not on a bike, and typically very thirsty).

The Slickrock Trail was laid out in 1969 by Dick Wilson, who thought he was creating a one-of-a-kind experience for motorcyclists, not bicyclists. That notion changed dramatically after mountain bikes came to be around 1980. Wilson, then a Moab schoolteacher and newspaper man, rode a diminutive 90-cc bike as he explored the sea of slickrock hovering over Moab, progressively piecing together the best trail he could by incorporating certain features and eliminating others. Wilson marked his intended route with chalk, which BLM crews subsequently followed with paint cans in hand.

The trail is manageable by most mountain bikers, so long as they're prepared to walk when necessary and to devote several hours to getting through it. Strong neophytes with good balance and innate nerve will improve vastly over the course of riding the trail just once, as they quickly learn just how unslick slickrock is. (The story goes that the term *slickrock*, a generic name for smooth sandstone like this, derives from the fact that the rock was the bane of shod horses, who did indeed find it slick as ice.) It's highly recommended, prior to committing to the full 12.5-mile trail, that you sample the much easier but still challenging practice loop that's between two and three miles in length.

General location: 4 miles east of Moab.

Elevation change: You may never get more than a couple of hundred feet higher than the trailhead, yet the roller-coaster nature of the trail nets a gain of some 2,000 feet.

Season: March through mid-May and September through November are best. Summers in the Moab area are very hot, so head out at first light if your visit falls during that season.

Services: All services are found in Moab. Stock up on food and water there. Designated campsites are located east of the trail on Sand Flats Road.

Hazards: Most of the Slickrock Bike Trail traverses very hard and abrasive rock. It hurts to fall on it, and opportunities to fall abound. Fact is, you probably will not return home completely unscathed. Wear your helmet. It's also hot and thirsty out there, so pack along plenty of water. The designated trail is marked with white paint, and particularly hazardous places are marked with yellow "fried eggs."

Rescue index: You will meet other mountain bikers (possibly hundreds) on this ride—members of the Moab Bike Patrol perhaps among them. Still, be responsible for yourself and don't count on needing rescued.

Land status: Bureau of Land Management.

Maps: Several maps, some quite detailed and pointing out named features and side spurs along the way, are available at local bike shops and at the Moab Multi-Agency Information Center. You can also obtain a map at the Sand Flats Recreation Area entrance station.

Finding the trail: From the corner of Center and Main in downtown Moab, go south on Main and turn left in 3 blocks onto 300 South. Four blocks later, turn right onto 400 East, then go past Locust and turn left onto Mill Creek Drive. At the stop sign, bear left/straight onto Sand Flats Road, arriving at the entrance station to Sand Flats Recreation Area in another 1.5 miles. After forking over your fee ($5 for a 3-day pass at this writing), continue 0.5 mile to the huge paved parking area, located on the left side of the road.

Source of additional information:

Moab Multi-Agency Information Center
Center & Main
Moab, UT 84532
(435) 259-8825

Notes on the trail: From the parking lot, follow the white-paint dashes across the cattle guard. You'll come to a junction in less than 0.5 mile; a right takes you around the practice loop. Left continues the main trail, on which you'll meet up with the other end of the practice loop in another 0.5 mile. Go left here, climbing a ridge to the point where the main loop starts. You're 2.5 miles cumulative from the parking area. The ensuing 7.5-mile loop can be ridden in either direction, although clockwise is somewhat easier. After closing the loop, return to the parking area by way of the same 2.5-mile spur you set out on.

RIDE 23 · Porcupine Rim

AT A GLANCE

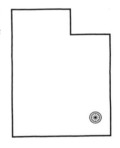

Length/configuration: 21-mile point-to-point (31-mile loop optional)

Aerobic difficulty: Moderate; the ride begins with a testy 800-foot climb

Technical difficulty: One of the area's most challenging trails. Riding surfaces include rough old prospecting road, ledgy double-track, very technical single-track, and pavement.

Scenery: Sock-knocking-off views down on Castle Valley from the rim

Special comments: As far as Moab-area rides are concerned, second in popularity only to the Slickrock Bike Trail. Commercial shuttles run between town and the trailhead.

Porcupine Rim is arguably the most diverse of all local Moab rides and definitely one of the most memorable. Aerobically it is moderately difficult, with an 800-foot elevation gain right off the bat. Technically, it's extremely challenging. An extended climb to the head of Negro Bill Canyon (named for mulatto William Granstaff, a prospector-settler who came to the area in 1877) on a narrow mining track is followed by an unforgettable stretch of double-track leading along the edge of Porcupine Rim, with stomach-churning views straight down on Castle Valley. From a jungle of juniper-piñon, sandstone outcrops, and cacti, you'll begin a long descent down rugged double-track teeming with drop-offs that often come at you when you least expect it. This leads to single-track, sometimes smooth and other times boulder-strewn. The trail deposits you onto UT 128, and the final six miles back to town are paved.

Not long ago, staying on this route could be troublesome. Now, however, it is quite well marked with a combination of Carsonite posts, cairns, paint on rock, lines of stones blocking "wrong-way spurs," and tire tracks left by previous hordes of cyclists.

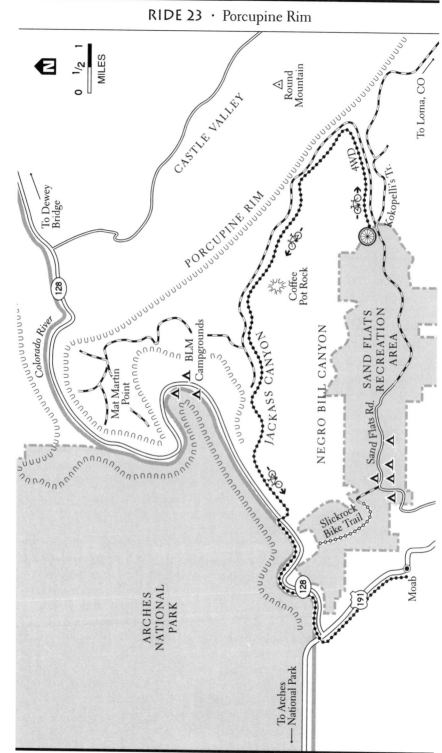

Looking back at
Porcupine Rim from
Castle Valley.

The ride as described, a 21-mile point-to-point, begins at the offical Porcupine Rim trailhead and ends in Moab. (Several commercial operators run shuttles out of Moab to the trailhead; inquire at one of the bike shops for a current listing of names and phone numbers.) If your endurance is outstanding, you may opt to turn the ride into a 31-mile loop beginning and ending in Moab. In this case, simply follow the directions under "Finding the trail" to start the ride. Another strategy—the one commonly used by those allergic to highway riding—is to leave a car at the Negro Bill Canyon parking area, adjacent to where the Porcupine Rim Trail meets UT 128. To find it, drive about six miles upstream along the Colorado River on US 191 and UT 128.

General location: 10 miles east of Moab.

Elevation change: An 800-foot gain in altitude is followed by a 3,000-foot drop.

Season: April through early November. The high elevations of the rim can hold snow well into spring.

Services: All services are available in Moab. Stock up on food and water there.

Hazards: Ledges on the double-track often appear unexpectedly; keep your speed in check, as it's easy to get going too fast. Parts of the single-track are rideable only by ultra-expert bike handlers; overconfidence can send you over the bars. Don't be afraid to walk. The last 6 miles follow busy highways, where you'll want to ride with extreme care—particularly because you'll be hot, tired, and thirsty by the time you get there.

Rescue index: Very remote and hard-to-access terrain. You will, however, encounter other cyclists, and the Moab Bike Patrol maintains a presence on this trail.

Land status: Bureau of Land Management.

Maps: Procure at local bike shops and Moab Multi-Agency Information Center.

Finding the trail: From the corner of Center and Main in downtown Moab, go south on Main and turn left in 3 blocks onto 300 South. Four blocks later, turn right onto 400 East, then go past Locust and turn left onto Mill Creek Drive. At the stop sign, bear left/straight onto Sand Flats Road, arriving at the entrance station to Sand Flats Recreation Area in another 1.5 miles. After paying your fee ($5 for a 3-day pass at this writing), continue up the road, passing the trailhead of the Slickrock Bike Trail in 0.5 mile. About 2 miles past here, the road turns to gravel. In another 4 miles (9.5 miles total from downtown), you'll arrive at the trailhead. If the small parking area is full, park along the north side of the road, pulling off as far as practical.

Source of additional information:

Moab Multi-Agency Information Center
Center & Main
Moab, UT 84532
(435) 259-8825

Notes on the trail: From the trailhead, follow the Porcupine Rim Trail sign leading north off Sand Flats Road (Sand Flats is also signed as Kokopelli's Trail). Begin a sustained climb toward the head of Negro Bill Canyon. The fist few miles present some technical challenges, but for the most part they're just an aerobic/anaerobic grunt. At 1.5 miles you'll see a spur going right, back toward Sand Flats Road. Don't take it. Finally, up top, after a breath-stealing flirtation with the edge of the rim, head back "inland," where you'll progressively encounter a trio of potentially confusing junctions; the wrong way will probably be barricaded with stones. Bear right at all three. After passing the third, where a sign marks the Porcupine Rim Trail, ride onto single-track, much of it stellar with a high cruisability quotient, but just as often ultra-technical, as it desends above Jackass Canyon. You'll run into UT 128 at 15 miles. Cross it very carefully, turn left, and ride 3.5 miles to US 191; then go left and continue for another 2.5 miles to the corner of Center and Main in downtown Moab.

RIDE 24 · Onion Creek–Kokopelli

AT A GLANCE

Length/configuration: 22-mile out-and-back (11 miles each way)

Aerobic difficulty: The 8.5-mile climb to Fisher Valley gains 1,400 feet, with some rather steep pulls out of creek crossings

Technical difficulty: The hard-surfaced two-wheel-drive and sandy four-wheel-drive roads followed are technically easy. The stream crossings, too, are low in technical challenge.

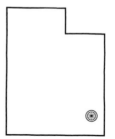

RIDE 24 · Onion Creek–Kokopelli

Scenery: Terrific up-close views of the La Sals as you proceed from redrock desert to the more verdant environs of Fisher Valley

Special comments: The ride involves 22 stream crossings each way (44 altogether). Your bike's moving parts may hate this ride, but you're gonna love it.

This 22-mile out-and-back (11 miles each way) is memorable for its nearly two dozen stream crossings, which may occasionally require first gear to pull out of. The creek crossings are double the fun on the way out. The route serves up a good aerobic workout but is technically easy, with its good gravel- and sand-surfaced roads.

A geologic puzzle of Cutler and Moenkopi sediments.

Down low you'll be surrounded by distinctive towers and rimrocks, a geologic puzzle of purplish and dark red Cutler and Moenkopi sediments. These soon give way—after you cross a high bridge spanning a pinched canyon narrows—to desert slopes that may lead you to believe you've left Utah for Arizona. Still higher up, things turn greener as you enter Fisher Valley, a broad, pleasing basin of ranch lands embraced by mountains and mesas.

Numerous good campsites lie along the first seven miles of the route inside the Colorado Riverway Recreation Area. Also, back out along UT 128 is a string of somewhat more developed BLM campgrounds.

General location: 23 miles northeast of Moab.

Elevation change: You'll gain approximately 1,400 feet on the ride out.

Season: March through mid-May and September through November are best. Summers in the area are very hot, so head out at first light if your visit falls during that season.

Services: All services are available in Moab. Stock up on water there. Onion Creek's water is not potable even when filtered.

Hazards: Avoid during rain, when some road surfaces will muck out and there's flash-flood potential.

Rescue index: You'll probably pass campers throughout the first 7 miles of the ride, which are within the Colorado Riverway Recreation Area.

Land status: Bureau of Land Management.

Maps: National Geographic/Trails Illustrated's *Moab Map* (available at local bike shops).

Finding the trail: From the corner of Center and Main in downtown Moab, go 2.5 miles north on US 191 and turn right onto UT 128 to follow the Colorado River upstream. Just over 20 miles later, turn right up Onion Creek toward the signed "Taylor Livestock/Fisher Valley Ranch." Proceed for 0.75 mile and park in one of many pullouts found on boths sides of the road.

Source of additional information:

Moab Multi-Agency Information Center
Center & Main
Moab, UT 84532
(435) 259-8825

Notes on the trail: Begin riding up-canyon on a well-graded, two-wheel-drive surface, immediately crossing Onion Creek and picking up the first of a great deal of red dirt your wet tires will meet. At just over 5 miles, at stream crossing number 20, that sulfur smell comes from nearby Stinking Springs. Leave the Colorado Riverway Recreation Area at 7 miles to begin climbing in earnest. At the top of the 1.5-mile ascent you'll pass through a green metal gate and enter the high Fisher Valley. One mile beyond here, turn left onto Kokopelli's Trail (signed as such, but only for those coming from the other direction), where the route becomes a sandy four-wheel-drive road. One-half mile later follow the makeshift trail dropping left to avoid a washout. After another mile, with a knob of white gypsum to your right, you'll arrive at the recommended turnaround. Beyond here the trail begins to seriously lose elevation.

RIDE 25 · Dewey–Koko 1

AT A GLANCE

Length/configuration: 17.5-mile combination consisting of an 11-mile out-and-back (5.5 miles each way) connecting with a 6.5-mile loop

Aerobic difficulty: Quite a workout—some 2,000 feet of climbing

Technical difficulty: Four miles are moderately technical, over sandy and/or rocky four-wheel-drive roads. The rest of the ride follows graded gravel roads, often embedded with vision-blurring cobbles.

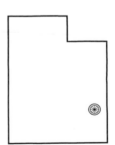

Scenery: The improved Entrada Bluffs Road visits an intriguing mix of dry-country mesas and ridges, while the four-wheel-drive trail dives through a verdant canyon oasis

Special comments: The ride incorporates a stretch of the popular Kokopelli's Trail

The original Dewey Bridge, located not far downstream from where the Dolores River merges with the Colorado River, was important to early settlers in the region as a place of rare opportunity where they could transport supplies from one

RIDE 25 · Dewey–Koko 1
RIDE 26 · Dewey–Koko 2

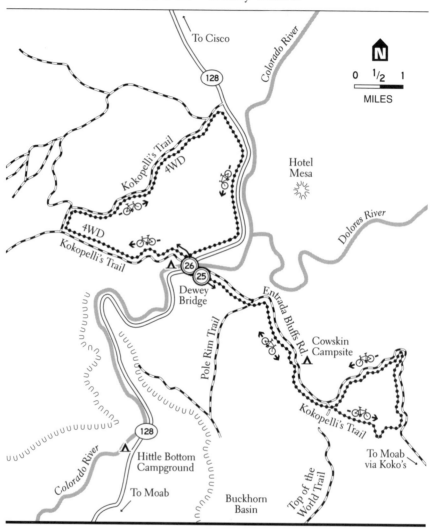

side of the Colorado to the other—supplies coming from Colorado destined for Moab and points beyond. Today the site provides an important river crossing for Kokopelli's Trail riders. Two good rides beginning here (this one and Ride 26, Dewey–Koko 2), each quite distinct in character, incorporate segments of this world-class, long-distance cycling route. If you'd like to explore the area for a couple of days, be aware that there's a designated BLM campground on the other side of the highway from where the rides begin. Also, on this ride you'll pass good campsites at just over 1 mile (in an area of slickrock) and at 3.5 miles.

The outing makes a good morning or evening ride, as it involves a long, potentially very hot uphill. The scenery seems to change at every bend in the road. At about three miles, you'll top a rise and look back far to the north-northwest, across Grand Valley at the imposing Roan Cliffs and Book Cliffs. Farther up the road, sandstone bluffs and mesas preclude long-range vistas. As you approach the end, you'll look down on irrigated-green cow bottoms clashing magnificently with their stark surroundings. The drive to the trailhead from Moab is nothing to sneeze at either, as the road winds below the impossibly red walls of the river's canyon and past features including the phenomenal Fisher Towers.

The 17.5-mile ride involves an out-and-back spur leading to a 6.5-mile loop. It provides a prolonged aerobic workout as it ascends five miles on gravel, as well as a splash of technical riding on a sandy, rock-strewn four-wheel-drive trail. The descent at ride's end can be quite bumpy, over a gravel suface with embedded cobbles.

General location: 34 miles northeast of Moab.

Elevation change: Approximately 2,000 feet are gained in 3 distinct climbing sessions.

Season: March through mid-May and September through November are best. Summers in the area are very hot, so head out at first light if your visit falls during that season.

Services: All services are available in Moab. Stock up on water there. A BLM campground is located on the other side of the highway from where the ride starts.

Hazards: Take special care on the four-wheel-drive sections and during the fast downhill exit.

Rescue index: Part of the ride takes place on good gravel roads, where auto traffic is possible. Otherwise, if help is needed, flagging down a motorist back along UT 128 (or contacting a camper at Dewey Bridge Recreation Site) will be the best bet. You're far enough from Moab that you may not encounter other cyclists on this ride.

Land status: Bureau of Land Management.

Maps: Latitude 40's *Moab East* map (available at local bike shops).

Finding the trail: From the corner of Center and Main in downtown Moab, go 2.5 miles north on US 191, then turn right onto UT 128 to follow the Colorado River upstream. In 31 miles—immediately before crossing the Colorado on a modern bridge—turn right and park at the parking area for the old Dewey Bridge. (Ride 26, Dewey–Koko 2, also begins here.)

Source of additional information:

Moab Multi-Agency Information Center
Center & Main
Moab, UT 84532
(435) 259-8825

Notes on the trail: From the south end of the old Dewey Bridge, ride southeast onto Entrada Bluffs Road, also signed as Kokopelli's Trail. Climb on the main road to 5.5 miles, then turn right off the main road onto a sandy track, a continuation of the signed Kokopelli's Trail. Where Top of the World Trail goes right, keep following the Kokopelli's Trail symbols, prominently displayed on Carsonite posts. Drop deeply into a tight canyon at about 6 miles to cross a creek bed, which may have running water. From there, begin a very steep uphill push of 200 vertical feet over less than 0.5 mile. The trail again becomes rideable after that. Between 7.5 and 8 miles, with Blue Chief Mesa immediately on front, turn left at the T onto a four-wheel-drive road, leaving Kokopelli's Trail. Soon you'll round the head of canyon to begin a bumpy desent over slickrock and loose rubble. At 9 miles bear right, and 0.25 mile later pass through a fence line. Recross the creek bed and ascend to turn left and rejoin the high-grade Entrada Bluffs Road. (Right drops to a dead end at the Entrada Ranch on the Dolores River.) Commence climbing on good gravel at approximately the same angle as that assumed by the strata of sandstone to your right. As you ascend, note the remarkable gash in the plateau made by the creek bed you've crossed twice. Finally, at roughly 11.5 miles the grade breaks, and 0.25 mile later you'll close the loop. Fly down the 5.5 miles you earlier ascended.

RIDE 26 · Dewey–Koko 2

AT A GLANCE

Length/configuration: 15-mile loop

Aerobic difficulty: Moderate, with a steady, sometimes steep climb to the ride's apex

Technical difficulty: Moderately difficult riding through sand and over slickrock. Other surfaces include high-grade dirt and paved roads.

Scenery: Great overlook on the Colorado River early in the ride, and the high point offers a spectacular view looking down Bull Canyon at the lofty La Sals

Special comments: The ride incorporates a stretch of the popular Kokopelli's Trail

Like Ride 25, Dewey–Koko 1, this 15-mile loop begins and ends at the parking area of the historic Dewey Bridge and incorporates a segment of the heralded Kokopelli's Trail. Yet the terrain traversed is surprisingly dissimilar to that of the previous ride. Route finding can be tricky, but Kokopelli's Trail is usually well signed. In the not improbable case that a sign has been removed from a crucial junction, bike tracks can probably be discerned and followed. Nevertheless, keep a close eye on "Notes on the trail."

At the ride's beginning you'll pass through a rural subdivision, under development at this writing, so the situation may be slightly different than what is presented here. Soon you'll come to a canyon of bizarre sandstone formations, resembling whatever your imagination chooses (I saw goalposts, a can opener, and a unicorn horn). Surfaces include a fair amount of sand and slickrock, making the ride moderately technical, along with high-grade dirt road and 4.5 miles of paved UT 128. The highway here is typically low on traffic, and it has a fairly wide shoulder for most of the distance. A good 800 feet of climbing are involved in the first six miles, earning the ride a moderately difficult aerobic rating as well.

General location: 34 miles northeast of Moab.

Elevation change: You'll gain approximately 800 feet over the first 6 miles.

Season: March through mid-May and September through November are best.

Summers in the area are very hot, so head out at first light if your visit falls during that season.

Services: All services are available in Moab. Stock up on water there. A BLM campground is located on the opposite side of the highway from where the ride starts.

Hazards: Sand traps may catch you off guard, and you'll want to ride defensively over the 4.5 miles of UT 128.

Rescue index: Remote and hard-to-access terrain, other than the 4.5 miles along UT 128. Motorists or campers at Dewey Bridge Recreation Site could be summoned in a pinch. You're far enough from Moab that you may not encounter other cyclists on this ride.

Land status: Bureau of Land Management.

Maps: Latitude 40's *Moab East* map (available at local bike shops).

Finding the trail: From the corner of Center and Main in downtown Moab, go 2.5 miles north on US 191, then turn right onto UT 128 to follow the Colorado River upstream. In 31 miles—immediately before crossing the Colorado on a modern bridge—turn right and park at the parking area for the old Dewey Bridge. (Ride 25, Dewey–Koko 1, also begins here.)

Source of additional information:

Moab Multi-Agency Information Center
Center & Main
Moab, UT 84532
(435) 259-8825

Notes on the trail: From the parking area, ride up onto the highway bridge, cross to the north side of the river, and turn left/north onto blacktop at the point where you're flush with the exit ramp of the old bridge. After approximately 0.25 mile, go right onto a wide, packed-sediment road, following the Kokopelli's Trail sign. One-half mile from that point you'll turn right at the T, continuing to follow Kokopelli's Trail as it drops off the main road onto a sandy four-wheel-drive track. In the midst of a tough little uphill, you'll earn a dramatic look over the Colorado River below. At 1.5 miles, after climbing a slickrock ramp through an old pole fence, top a rise and coast down around the head of a wash. After another mile you'll have pumped your way up to a plateau. After dropping through a succession of draws, climb back up and arrive at a major junction at just under 4.5 miles. Here, in front of a sandstone monolith, turn right to continue climbing through sand (left, descending Yellow Jacket Canyon toward Squaw Park, could offer some fun exploring if time permits). At 5 miles, after crossing a wash and ascending through a fence line, curve right to continue on Kokopelli's Trail. (This is an important junction, as the trail going left eventually drops into the wrong canyon.) Follow the Carsonite posts across an expanse of slickrock to pick up a red-dirt track at 5.5 miles. At the top of a nasty little climb, at just under 6 miles, you'll arrive at the ride's high point, with a broad view looking out on where you just came from. Bear left on the more distinct track, then continue left where a slickrock track goes right. At 6.5 miles cross another short patch of slickrock, beyond which the trail climbs drastically for 0.25 mile to surmount a rocky rim. One-quarter mile beyond here you'll arrive at an important junction, where you'll veer left to follow Kokopelli's Trail (right feels like the "natural" way to go). In another mile cross a big, dry, rocky wasteland, following the trail straight through a saddle rather than bearing left along the draw. At 8.5 miles the last climb of note is followed by a descent over dark, evil-looking angular rock. In another mile go straight rather than left, and at just over 10 miles turn right onto UT 128 (Kokopelli's Trail goes left). From here it's 4.5 miles back to the beginning point.

RIDE 27 · Dancing with Cottonwood Creek

AT A GLANCE

Length/configuration: 22-mile combination consisting of a 5.5-mile out-and-back (2.7 miles each way), connected to a 16.5-mile loop

Aerobic difficulty: Moderate, with quite a bit of climbing involved

Technical difficulty: Moderate, with some short, tough hills over loose rock and sand, water, and cobbles in the creek bottoms. Other riding surfaces include graded gravel, double-track of packed sediments and embedded cobbles, faint dirt double-track, and cattle trail.

Scenery: Impressive, as you climb onto the northwest flanks of the Abajo Mountains

Special comments: Route finding can be a real challenge, so an accurately calibrated cyclometer is highly recommended

This ride, along with the next three, is centered out of the Needles District of Canyonlands National Park. The Needles District's Squaw Flat Campground is a long way from anywhere, so you should plan to camp there if you'd like to bag more than one of these rides. Here's how to get to Squaw Flat Campground: From Moab, drive 38 miles south on US 191 and turn west onto UT 211. (If coming from the south, the turn onto UT 211 is 17 miles north of Monticello.) Follow the narrow two-laner as it wends through a relatively lush valley (watch for deer on the highway). Take a break at Newspaper Rock State Park to click the obligatory photo of the beautiful prehistoric rock art decorating a large sandstone panel. On entering Canyonlands National Park 33 miles after leaving US 191, you'll pass the attractive new Visitor Center, which replaced a tacky double-wide trailer that long served as National Park Service offices here. Three miles inside the park you'll come to Squaw Flat Campground. Campsites can be hard to come by, so if possible arrive between 8 and 10 a.m. and join the other vehicular vultures waiting to swoop in on a site evacuation. Just be careful not to run over any rabbits as you circle the grounds. (Site 7-A is my favorite, by the way.)

This 22-mile spur-and-loop combination encompasses a wide array of terrain types and riding surfaces, including steep pitches of loose rock, sand, wet and rocky creek bottom, graded gravel, double-track of packed sediments and embedded cobbles, faint dirt double-track, and cattle trail. It is aerobically and technically moderate in difficulty; the biggest challenge is staying on the route—which explains the lengthy "Notes on the trail" section. Listen for the melodic call of western meadowlarks early on, as you ascend and then traverse a gorgeous, piñon pine–studded

RIDE 27 · Dancing with Cottonwood Creek

bench at the base of a high rimrock ridge; watch for cactus thorns as you follow the cow path in the 7.5-mile range. About 18 miles into the ride, Stevens Canyon Road becomes indisinguishable from the North Cottonwood Creek wash (this may have been a temporary situation, however, and fixed by the time you get there).

General location: 60 miles southwest of Moab.

Elevation change: You'll gain several hundred feet climbing away from the trailhead, then repeatedly lose and gain elevation as you alternately cross ridges and drainages coming down off the Abajos.

Watch closely for prehistoric rock art en route to the trailhead.

Season: April through May and September through October are best. Summers in the area are very hot, so head out at first light if your visit falls during that season. No-see-ums are a nuisance in summer.

Services: Water is available at Squaw Flat Campground and at the Visitor Center. Needles Outpost, a private enterprise located approximately 1 mile east of the Canyonlands National Park entrance station (or 4 miles east of Squaw Flat Campground) sells gas, firewood, limited groceries, and showers (but not beer!). It also has overflow camping available.

Hazards: You'll need to drive through a wide creek (wide in spring, anyway) to get to the trailhead. Inquire at the Canyonlands National Park Visitor Center about current water depth and crossing strategy. If it looks like rain will fall, it's better to avoid this ride altogether, because parts of the route become intimate with canyon washes. Beware of tire-threatening cacti on and around the cow path at mile 7.5.

Rescue index: You're far away from civilization on this ride. Flagging down a motorist on UT 211 or summoning a cowboy at the Dugout Ranch (adjacent to where you turn off UT 211) will probably be your closest available help.

Land status: BLM and Manti–La Sal National Forest.

Maps: *Canyon Country Off-Road Vehicle Map: Canyon Rims Recreation Area* by F. A. Barnes (widely available in the area).

Finding the trail: From the cattle guard marking the eastern boundary of Canyonlands National Park, drive 11.5 miles southeast on UT 211. Turn right/south toward

"Beef Basin–Elk Mountain" onto a good gravel road. In less than a mile you'll arrive at the possibly intimidating creek ford. Just past 4 miles after turning off the highway you'll cross a cattle guard. Park on the left immediately past it.

Source of additional information:

Moab Multi-Agency Information Center
Center & Main
Moab, UT 84532
(435) 259-8825

Notes on the trail: From where you parked, coast down the dirt track to cross Cottonwood Creek below a small dam. (Check out the waterfall roughly 200 feet to the left.) After negotiating the creek you'll skirt a pleasant, cottonwood-embraced campsite. After 0.25 mile, go left onto the main Stevens Canyon Road (County Road 104-A), a relatively high-grade, lane-and-a-half-wide road of packed sediments and cobbles. At just over 2.5 miles, bear left onto the Hop Canyon Road/Trail, as Stevens Canyon Road drops steeply to the right. The route devolves into a double-track, winding through gorgeous piñon-studded benchlands underlying a lofty line of rimrock cliffs. You'll ride amid jumbles of rock as you go up and down through drainages, passing the occasional slop-camp fire ring. At 4 miles pass through a fence line running along a draw. At about 5.5 miles the slopes of the Abajos come into view on the left. At 7 miles descend, then begin climbing a very steep, rocky pitch. One-half mile from the bottom you'll see a cattle pond on the right (it may be dry). Continue through wash sand, pop up on the other side of the wash, then bear left onto a cow path, keeping the wash close to your left. In approximately 250 yards, the trail empties onto a faint double-track; follow it, keeping close to the cliffs. Watch out for cacti! You'll climb to 8.5 miles cumulative and begin descending. At the fork at roughly 9 miles go left downhill, rather than veering right to stay at the same elevation. Soon you'll swing through a small drainage to follow the sandy double-track as it sidehills around a ridge. At 9.5 miles, with a big "castle butte" directly ahead, start dropping quite steeply. In 0.5 mile cross through another drainage, then come to a rim overlook to see your ensuing descent. Note the old rock cabin below. At approximately 11 miles, as you descend along a chiseled ledge, bear right where a double-track forks left up Hop Creek. At 11.5 miles ford Hop Creek in a setting of tall grasses and sagebrush, then ford the larger North Cottonwood Creek. Whoop-de-doos skirting around erosional sloughs take you to a gate in a fence line (leave it as you found it); then, in the 13-mile range, you'll cross the creek a couple of times. At 13.5 miles on the right is an old sandstone-block house and dilapidated log cabin with a sod roof; just beyond those, bear right onto the initially high-grade Stevens Canyon Road. At 16.5 miles you'll see an old cabin (with newer addition) on the right; just under 0.5 mile from there a spur goes left, climbing to the main Cottonwood Canyon Road. That's *not* the route; if you happen to be caught in a rainstorm, however (like the author was), you might want to go that way to avoid potentially hazardous wash riding. At 18 miles the road drops into the creek bottom and stays there for nearly a mile. At approximately 19 miles, at the top of a steep hill, close the loop and continue down on Stevens Canyon Road. Recross the creek and return to the beginning point at 22 miles.

RIDE 28 · Hart's Draw

AT A GLANCE

Length/configuration: 17-mile out-and-back (8.5 miles each way)

Aerobic difficulty: Easy to moderate

Technical difficulty: Easy to moderate, with some tough grunts out of drainages on surfaces of loose sand. Other surfaces include dirt and packed-sand double-track.

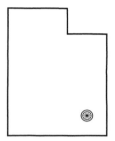

Scenery: Hart's Draw forms the southern rim of Hatch Point, a popular overlook within the Canyon Rims Recreation Area. Most folks look down from Hatch Point; on this ride, you'll look up at the point and deep into its chasm innards.

Special comments: A wide-open view ride that makes for a good bike-packing overnight

This 17-mile out-and-back (8.5 miles each way) is a refreshingly easy ride in terms of both technical and aerobic difficulty. Still, several draw crossings over the second half of the ride do present a bit of a test of technical skills and leg strength. Riding surfaces include sand, both loose and hard-packed, and dirt double-track. It's not a long ride, and the route is mellow enough that one could pull a trailer full of camping gear. Some good dispersed campsites are found at the turnaround, with plenty of juniper and sage firewood nearby. Even if you don't camp, the adventure is not necessarily over at the turnaround: Macomb Canyon and other irresistibly deep, colorful clefts in the plateau beg you to explore on foot. On the way back to the trailhead, you can't miss the unmistakable profile of the Sixshooter Peaks pointing their barrels at the sky.

General location: 65 miles southwest of Moab.

Elevation change: There is a ride in southern Utah that doesn't gain hundreds of feet after all!

Season: March through May and September through November are best. Summers in the area are very hot, so head out at first light if your visit falls during that season. No-see-ums are a nuisance in summer.

Services: Water is available at Squaw Flat Campground and at the Needles District Visitor Center. Needles Outpost, a private enterprise located approximately 1 mile east of the Canyonlands National Park entrance station (or 4 miles east of Squaw Flat Campground), sells gas, firewood, limited groceries, and showers. It also has overflow camping available.

Hazards: Sand in the draw crossings over the second half of the route could grab a tire.

Rescue index: Flagging down a motorist on UT 211 or returning to the Visitor Center at the Needles District will probably be the closest available help.

Land status: Bureau of Land Management.

Maps: *Canyon Country Off-Road Vehicle Map: Canyon Rims Recreation Area* by F. A. Barnes (widely available in the area).

RIDE 28 · Hart's Draw

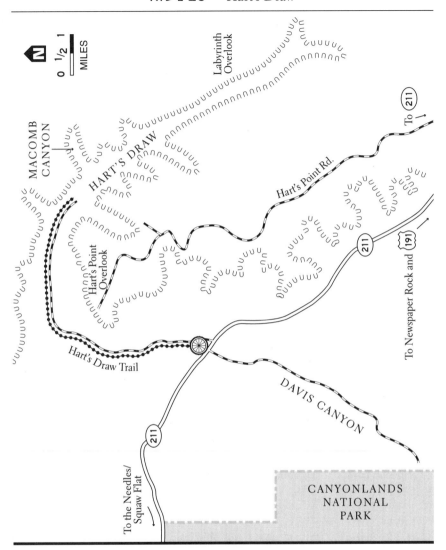

Finding the trail: Six miles east of the cattle guard marking the east boundary of the Needles District of Canyonlands National Park (just past milepost 7), turn north and park to the side of the gate, taking care not to block access. (For details on finding the Needles District, see Ride 27, Dancing with Cottonwood Creek.)

Source of additional information:

Moab Multi-Agency Information Center
Center & Main
Moab, UT 84532
(435) 259-8825

Notes on the trail: Open the metal gate, then pass through and close it. In 0.1 mile, go left on the dirt track rather than continuing straight toward the big canyon. (Continuing straight, however, does offer an intriguing, 3.2-mile round-trip spur—as the author learned when he went the wrong way on his first try.) Begin coasting down on sand and packed sediments. After about 0.75 mile pass through an old fence line. At 2 miles you'll descend through a wash (ignore the double-track forking left as you zip down), then climb onto a juniper-studded knob. At 3 miles skirt around the northwest toe of Hatch Point. Continue veering right where a double-track forks left. At just past 4.5 miles cross a draw, and then, in about 0.5 mile, round a right-hand bend to view a long straightaway. Here you'll begin slamming down and pulling out of numerous sandy washes coming off Hatch Point, each separated from the next by a long straight section. Note the "reclining camel" formation to the right. At 6.5 miles cross a major draw; a little over a mile later curve right through a broad, grassy swale. At 8 miles you'll pass an inviting campsite. At 8.5 miles, immediately after a sandy draw, the route peters out into a web of cattle paths.

RIDE 29 · Colorado River Rim

AT A GLANCE

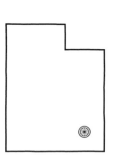

Length/configuration: 15-mile out-and-back (7.5 miles each way)

Aerobic difficulty: Easy

Technical difficulty: Moderately easy over four-wheel-drive road with some sand and slickrock

Scenery: Tremendous perspectives of the Needles, Island in the Sky, and the Salt Creek and Colorado River Canyons

Special comments: Combine this ride with a visit to the excellent Needles District Visitor Center

This 15-mile out-and-back (7.5 miles each way) following a four-wheel-drive road is navigationally straightforward and quite easy both aerobically and technically—although there is some sand, along with a couple of extended stretches of slickrock that offer moderate challenges and immoderate fun. The ride takes place almost entirely within Canyonlands National Park's Needles District and serves up some of the district's most stupendous vistas. You'll see the namesake Needles, Island in the Sky, Dead Horse Point, the La Sals rising above the cliffs of the Canyon Rims Recreation Area, the Abajo Mountains, the gooseneck of the Colorado River known as "The Loop," and the deep notch carved by Salt Creek as it nears its merging with the Colorado. All in all, this is one of the best-views rides in southern Utah. On the way out, just past 2.5 miles, you'll cross Salt Creek, where you can leave your bike and hike about 0.25 mile downstream to the Lower Jump, where the creek tumbles over rimrock in dramatic fashion.

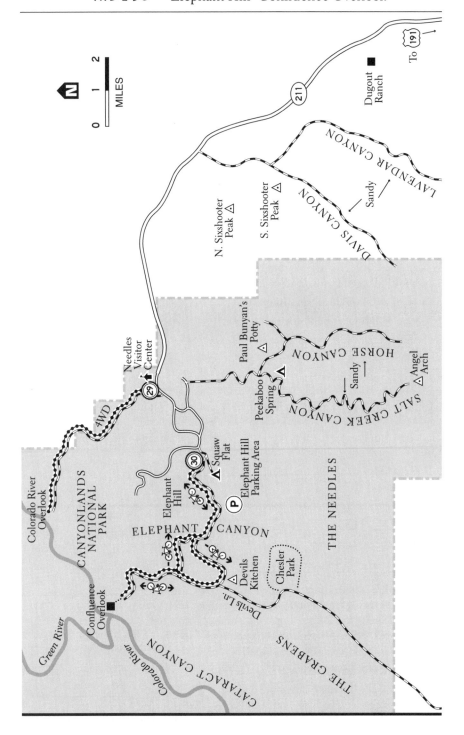

General location: 70 miles southwest of Moab.

Elevation change: Only about 150 feet of elevation differential.

Season: March through May and September through November are best. Summers in the area are very hot, so head out at first light if your visit falls during that season. No-see-ums are a nuisance in summer.

Services: Water is available at Squaw Flat Campground and at the Needles District Visitor Center. Needles Outpost, a private enterprise located approximately 1 mile east of the Canyonlands National Park entrance station (or 4 miles east of Squaw Flat Campground), sells gas, firewood, limited groceries, and showers. It also has overflow camping available.

Hazards: Some patches of sand could grab a tire. Don't get too close to the rim at ride's end, or you'll chance pulling a Wile E. Coyote.

Rescue index: Help can be obtained at the Visitor Center, where the ride begins.

Land status: National Park Service, BLM.

Maps: *Canyonland Official Map and Guide*, available at the Visitor Center.

Finding the trail: Either ride or drive from Squaw Flat Campground to the Needles District Visitor Center (constructed in 1991 to supplant an old double-wide trailer). Park in the Visitor Center parking lot. (For details on finding the Needles District, see Ride 27, Dancing with Cottonwood Creek.)

Source of additional information:

> Moab Multi-Agency Information Center
> Center & Main
> Moab, UT 84532
> (435) 259-8825

Notes on the trail: Begin riding on the road immediately behind the Visitor Center, passing through a fence line and forking left to coast downhill. At just over 2.5 miles you'll cross Salt Creek. At 6 miles begin a mile-long stretch of slickrock that's a total blast. At 7.5 miles arrive at a parking area, where you can continue by foot about 100 yards to the amazing Colorado River overlook.

RIDE 30 · Elephant Hill–Confluence Overlook

AT A GLANCE

Length/configuration: 23-mile combination ride consisting of a 9-mile out-and-back (4.5 miles each way) leading to a 7-mile loop, with another 7-mile out-and-back (3.5 miles each way) beginning 4.5 miles into the loop (have you got all that?)

Aerobic difficulty: Moderate

Technical difficulty: The route begins on gravel, then follows challenging four-wheel-drive roads over the steep pitches of Elephant Hill and through long stretches of deep sand

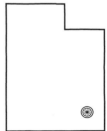

Scenery: A special treat awaits at the end of the second spur: a view 1,000 feet down on the aptly named Green River as it flows into the more often chocolate-colored Colorado

Special comments: Because of sand, the ride will be easier after periods of rain and more difficult after prolonged dry spells

This 23-mile ride consists of a pair of out-and-back spurs shooting off from a 7-mile loop. Early on it crosses Elephant Hill, notorious far and wide among the four-wheel-drive crowd as a challenge to one's driving skills (you'll understand why). The unlikely road was bulldozed in the late 1940s by J. A. Scorup, then an owner of the S&S Cattle Company empire, whose headquarters was at the Dugout Ranch (see Ride 27, Dancing with Cottonwood Creek). The first (and last) three miles of the ride are over good gravel, whereas the rest is over smooth and ledgy slickrock and typically very sandy four-wheel-drive road. You'll pass a couple of backcountry campsites on the loop; to take advantage of them, however, you'd want to pack bivouac-style because hauling a heavy load through the sand would be misery defined. You'll also need to register at the Visitor Center to use the backcountry sites. You can make the ride six miles shorter by driving three miles to the Elephant Hill parking area, but the ride on gravel to that point provides a good warm-up for the rigors of "the hill," atop which you'll gain tremendous views of the Sixshooter Peaks and other distant and nearby features. Elephant Hill is about one mile from base to base, with a quarter mile of slickrock and sand on top, plus very technical ascents and descents both coming and going. To get to the confluence overlook you'll need to leave your bike at the parking area, where a primitive bike rack is located, and hoof it half a mile to the viewpoint. You might want to bring along a lock to secure your bike, although it would be truly amazing to run into a bike thief in this remote spot.

General location: 75 miles southwest of Moab.

Elevation change: Overall not much, but a lot of short ups and downs.

Season: March through May and September through November are best. Summers in the area are very hot, so head out at first light if your visit falls during that season. No-see-ums are a nuisance in summer.

Services: Water is available at Squaw Flat Campground and at the Needles District Visitor Center. Needles Outpost, a private enterprise located approximately 1 mile east of the Canyonlands National Park entrance station (or 4 miles east of Squaw Flat Campground), sells gas, firewood, limited groceries, and showers. It also has overflow camping available.

Hazards: Deep sand and steep, ledgy pitches on Elephant Hill and the Silver Stairs.

Rescue index: Help can be obtained at the Visitor Center or at Squaw Flat Campground.

Land status: National Park Service.

Maps: *Canyonland Official Map and Guide*, available at the Visitor Center.

Finding the trail: The ride begins in the Needles District's Squaw Flat Campground. (For details on finding the Needles District, see Ride 27, Dancing with Cottonwood Creek.)

Spinning through the protected confines behind Elephant Hill.

Source of additional information:

Moab Multi-Agency Information Center
Center & Main
Moab, UT 84532
(435) 259-8825

Notes on the trail: From Campground Loop B, ride onto the gravel Elephant Hill Road. Climb for 1 mile on the wide road, then descend for 0.5 mile to level out along Big Spring Canyon. At just under 3 miles you'll come to a parking area with restrooms (optional starting point). Grunt up Elephant Hill and marvel at why anyone would feel obliged to maneuver their four-wheel-drive up and down it. Note the patches of artificial, erosion-reducing "pavement." Start riding on a sandy four-wheel-drive road at about 4 miles, bearing left at 4.5 miles onto the signed one-way road. Sand flats broken by short ups and downs lead to a tough section over big rocks at 6 miles. Three-quarters of a mile later go right onto Devils Lane (the Devils Kitchen camping area is to the left, with restroom, picnic tables, and cave overhang). At 7.5 miles, with a sign pointing left to "Chesler Park 5 miles," go right toward the signed "Confluence Overlook 4 miles" to ride through an open, sandy park embraced by low rimrock. A little more than 1 mile from there you'll descend the ledge-rock Silver Stairs, looking ahead at the La Sals. At 9 miles, at a junction where right is signed "Elephant Hill 3 miles," leave the loop by riding straight ahead onto a spur leading to the confluence overlook. At 11.5 miles bear right where a double-track goes left toward Cyclone Canyon. One mile past there you'll come to a parking area, where you'll need to park your bike and continue by foot 0.5 mile to the confluence overlook. Back on the bike, backtrack 3 miles, then proceed left on the road toward "Elephant Hill 3 miles." (Just before you get to the turn there's a spur going left to another campsite with a picnic table.) At 18.5 miles total, close the loop. Bear left, retackle Elephant Hill, and return to Squaw Flat Campground at 23 miles.

RIDE 31 · Hovenweep

AT A GLANCE

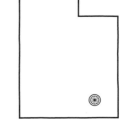

Length/configuration: 21.5-mile combination, consisting of a 10-mile out-and-back (5 miles each way), connecting to an 10.5-mile loop along which you'll take another short spur (0.5 mile each way)

Aerobic difficulty: Easy to moderate, with some abrupt little climbs in the 8- to 11-mile range

Technical difficulty: Technically easy, with riding surfaces of chipseal, gravel, packed sand, and some ledge rock

Scenery: The high plateau known as Sage Plain is dissected by juniper-studded canyons, with the Abajo and more distant La Sal mountains rising to the north

Special comments: A quiet ride through sacred country—most of it in Colorado, but beginning and ending in Utah

Even if no bike ride or prehistoric ruins awaited, the drive to Hovenweep National Momument from points west would be worth doing: flood plains chock-full of Navajo frame houses and hogans, sitting beneath slickrock hills spotted with junipers. Absolutely beautiful.

The ride, quite easy both aerobically and technically, follows remote roads of chipseal, gravel, and sand surfaces, with a bit of ledge rock thrown in for good measure. A loop of 10.5 miles connects two spurs, combining for a total mileage of 21.5. Rather like New Mexico's Chaco Canyon National Historical Park, another park created to preserve Anasazi ruins, Hovenweep National Monument is way out there and consequently relatively rarely visited. When the wind's not blowing, there might not be a quieter place on earth—just the occasional gargling raven, screeching jay, or chortling squirrel. The quiet fits, permitting you not only to see the past but to hear the ghosts of prehistoric times.

The ride visits the outlying Horseshoe and Hackberry group ruins, which, like the other centers of settlement at Hovenweep, were inhabited approximately 1150 to 1300 A.D. by ancestral Puebloan farmers, who built check dams and terraces to conserve and improve the soil. Hovenweep sits on Cajon Mesa, a component of the larger Great Sage Plain, which covers a vast area of the Four Corners. The name Hovenweep—"deserted valley" in the Ute Indian language—was given to the area in 1874 by William Henry Jackson, the legendary explorer-photographer best known for composing the earliest photographs taken of the Yellowstone–Teton region. (Those photos helped lead Congress to authorize the creation of the world's first national

RIDE 31 · Hovenweep

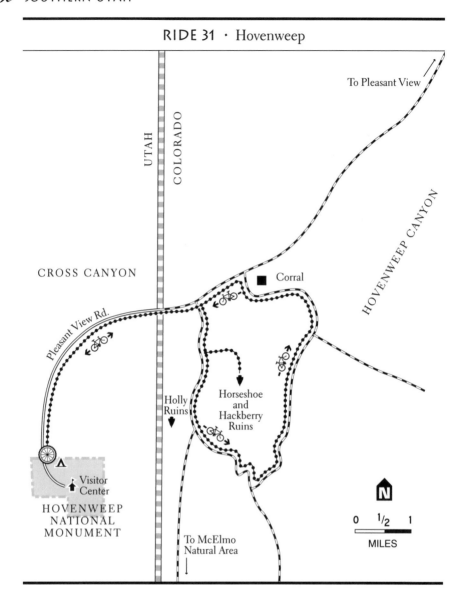

park.) Hovenweep contains six distinct groups of buildings, with several tall towers of particular curiosity to archaeologists: Were they lookout towers, storage bins, or ceremonial temples — or perhaps multifunctional structures?

General location: Straddling the Utah–Colorado border some 45 miles southeast of Blanding.

Elevation change: From the ride's mile-high beginning point you'll gain approximately 700 feet.

Season: March through May and September through October are best. Summers are very hot and winters, though riding is generally possible, can be quite cold.

Services: Hovenweep National Monment has a pleasant 30-site campground with water but no other services (other than a few snacks for sale at the tiny Visitor Center). Blanding or Bluff, Utah, and Cortez, Colorado, are the nearest full-service towns.

Hazards: Cactus thorns and the occasional patch of sand; if the weather is right, watch for rattlesnakes when you're hiking around the ruins.

Rescue index: Four-wheel-drive rigs may be traveling the more remote stretches of the route, but don't count on it. Flagging down a motorist on the Pleasant View Road or returning to the park Visitor Center will be your best bets for emergency help.

Land status: National Park Service and BLM.

Maps: A map of the route ("Tour Two: Holly-Hackberry-Corral Loop") is available at the park Visitor Center.

Finding the trail: Fifteen miles south of Blanding on US 191 (or 11 miles north of Bluff), turn east onto UT 262. In a few miles you'll enter the Navajo Reservation; just follow the signs to Hovenweep whenever you're confronted with a choice of ways to go. The ride begins in the park campground, located about 31 miles from where you turn on to UT 262. The access route is paved except for a stretch of approximately 200 yards in front of the reservation's Full Gospel Church.

Source of additional information:

Hovenweep National Monument
McElmo Route
Cortez, CO 81321
(970) 749-0510

Notes on the trail: Leave the campground, crossing a cattle guard in 0.5 mile and bearing right away from the Visitor Center road. At the stop sign, turn right onto the chipsealed Pleasant View Road. At just under 4.5 miles, cross a cattle guard to enter Colorado and ride onto a dirt surface. At 5 miles, leave the main road by turning right onto the first sand road past a "San Juan Resource Area BLM" sign. The turn is also marked with a Carsonite post sporting a bicycle symbol. Stay on the more distinct road as double-tracks go left then right over the next 0.5 mile, then turn left onto the spur road marked "Dead End" (despite another sign that points straight ahead to Hackberry and Horseshoe). Cross a wash, then encounter a couple of minor slick-rock ledges. Half a mile after turning, come to a green gate, which you'll have to walk around. In another 0.25 mile, at a T, stash your bike and explore the ruins by foot. (Horseshoe Unit is to the right, Hackberry Unit to the left.) After backtracking to the main road, turn left. In a little less than 1 mile, at 8 miles cumulative, turn right toward the Holly Unit. In 0.5 mile, turn right back on the better road, as it drops into a canyon. In a little over 0.25 mile you'll turn left onto a lesser traveled track, as the main road curves right toward McElmo Natural Area. Twist down into a rocky labyrinth, then climb rather steeply to a little past 10.5 miles cumulative. Immediately before topping the hill marked by a large lone juniper, take the first left onto a sandy road, riding north past some ponds (they may be dry). At 13 miles cumulative, continue straight where a track drops left. In 0.25 mile, pass through an opening in a fence line and continue straight where a track drops steeply to the right into Hoven-weep Canyon. A couple of miles farther along you'll pass some picturesque old corrals, then turn left onto Pleasant View Road. A mile from that point you'll close the loop, returning to the campground at 21.5 miles.

RIDE 32 · Valley of the Gods

AT A GLANCE

Length/configuration: 27-mile loop

Aerobic difficulty: Dishes out a good workout, with some 1,500 feet of elevation gain

Technical difficulty: Easy, over pavement, graded native dirt, sporadic drift sand, and some rocky segments

Scenery: You've gotta see it to believe it

Special comments: Like a miniature, abandoned version of Monument Valley, which can be seen to the southwest during this ride

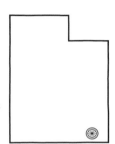

This 27-mile loop following paved and dirt/sand roads is aerobically moderate in difficulty and technically easy, yet even the most expert of riders will rave over its colorful brand of desolate beauty. Buttes, spires, and sandstone idols with evocative names like Castle Butte, Seven Sailors, Southern Lady, and Rooster Butte will keep you company as you spin through this empty expanse of San Juan County. Valley of the Gods Road is 16.5 miles long, with the remaining 10.5 miles of the route following paved highways.

General location: 20 miles west of Bluff, or 5 miles northwest of Mexican Hat.

Elevation change: The high point is 900 feet loftier than the low, and cumulative gain is around 1,500 feet.

Season: March through May and September through November are best.

Services: All services are available in Bluff, with somewhat more limited services found in Mexican Hat. Fill up on water in one of those towns. Camping is available at Goosenecks State Park, 3 miles southwest of the trailhead. The park is renowned for its overlook on a spectacular entrenched meander of the San Juan River. Dispersed camping is permitted on the BLM lands of this ride, too. You'll also pass the Valley of the Gods Bed-and-Breakfast one-half mile after turning onto Valley of the Gods Road (6 miles into the ride).

Hazards: Don't try it during a rainstorm. The highway can occasionally carry a fair bit of traffic, but sight distances are good. Still, ride defensively.

Rescue index: Motorists might be met on the unpaved portions of the route, and they will be encountered on the paved parts.

Land status: Bureau of Land Management.

Maps: DeLorme *Utah Atlas & Gazetteer*, page 22.

Finding the trail: Go 20 miles southwest of Bluff on US 163 (Mexican Hat is 4 miles south from here), then 1 mile northwest on UT 261. The point is also the turnoff to Goosenecks State Park. Park in a wide spot well off the road.

RIDE 32 · Valley of the Gods

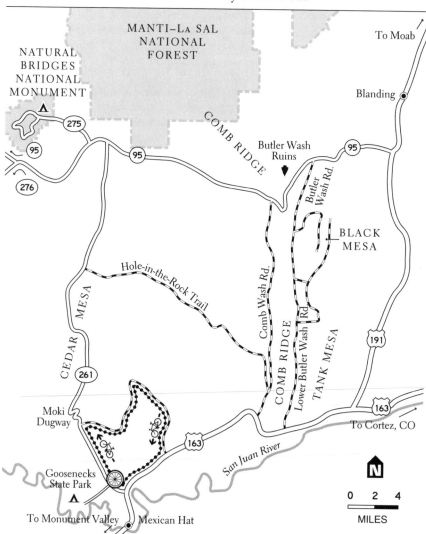

Source of additional information:

San Juan County Multi-Agency Visitor Center
P.O. Box 490
117 South Main
Monticello, UT 84535
(435) 587-3235

Notes on the trail: Ride northwest on UT 261, taking aim at Cedar Mesa. At 5.5 miles, immediately before the highway begins crawling up the impossible Moki Dugway, turn right onto dirt County Road 242/Valley of the Gods Road and pass a ranch/B&B. Begin climbing up and down through draws, soon to flirt with the drastically eroded flank of Cedar Mesa. You'll enter a scattered forest of juniper, and at just over 14 miles top out in a saddle connecting Castle Butte (on the right) with Cedar Mesa. Beyond here, your surroundings change drastically. At 19 miles swing right to see an endless vista incorporating Valley of the Gods and Monument Valley, rising on the distant side of the San Juan River. At just under 22 miles, after crossing the bed of Lime Creek, turn right onto US 163 and ride 4 miles to the Mexican Hat Junction, where you'll turn right onto UT 261 to ride the remaining mile back to the beginning.

RIDE 33 · Monument Valley

AT A GLANCE

Length/configuration: 11.5-mile combination, consisting of a 6.5-mile out-and-back (3.2 miles each way) connecting to a 5-mile loop

Aerobic difficulty: Easy, except the climb back out to the Visitor Center

Technical difficulty: Easy, over good dirt roads that may include sand traps or, if it's been raining, mud pits

Scenery: Spectacular and, if you're a fan of classic westerns—or four-wheel-drive vehicle ads—vividly familiar

Special comments: Okay, maybe the ride *is* in Arizona, but you're so close that you've just got to do it! Anyway, Monument Valley has a Utah mailing address and phone number

This 11.5-mile ride comprises a 6.5-mile out-and-back (3.2 miles each way), along with a 5-mile loop. It is aerobically and technically quite easy, over a graded native surface that in dry weather can dish out quite a bit of sand and, in wet weather, mud holes and erosional sloughs and troughs. The climb at the very end is the only tough hill. By no means is this a solitude ride, yet you're constantly looking out over some of the emptiest country on earth. Here you may encounter a greater number of foreign visitors than anywhere in the Southwest outside the Grand Canyon. You'll also come across a lot of flatlanders driving rental cars where they probably shouldn't be. The loop is open during daylight hours only, and travel off the main route is considered trespassing, as roughly a hundred Navajo families live in the 30,000-acre valley. In addition to 1,000-foot-high erosional-remnant figures—most of them named by pioneer trader Harry Goulding; the Navajos simply called it Valley of Standing Rocks—like the Mitten Buttes and Rain God Mesa, you'll encounter gorgeous sand dunes and long-range vistas over the land of the Dineh. John Ford and other moving- and still-picture legends have exposed lot of film in Monument Valley, and so can you—but remember: If you want to take home pictures of the Native Americans or their compounds, ask permission first and expect to pay a courtesy fee. (By the way,

RIDE 33 · Monument Valley

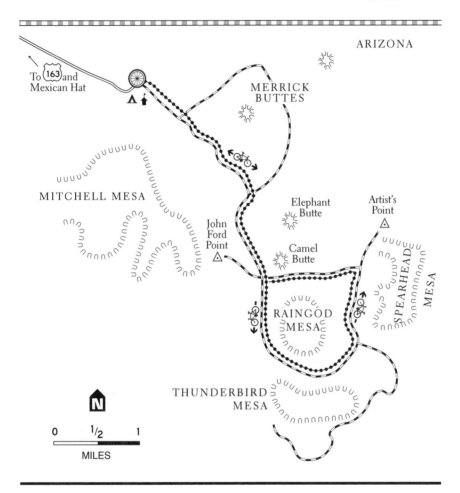

UTAH

ARIZONA

To (163) and
Mexican Hat

MERRICK
BUTTES

MITCHELL MESA

Elephant
Butte

Artist's
Point

John
Ford
Point

Camel
Butte

SPEARHEAD MESA

RAINGOD
MESA

THUNDERBIRD
MESA

N

0   1/2   1

MILES

Arizona does not abide by Daylight Savings Time, but the Navajo Reservation does;
leave your watch on Utah time and you'll be set.)

General location: 28 miles southwest of Mexican Hat (which is 50 miles southwest
of Blanding).

Elevation change: After losing 400 feet right off the bat, you'll ride relatively level terrain for the majority of the route at a mile-high elevation. In all, you'll gain around
750 feet.

Season: March through May and September through November are best. Summers
can be very hot and winters quite cold.

Services: All services are available in Bluff, with somewhat more limited services found in Mexican Hat. Closer by, Goulding's Lodge has accommodations, tent and RV sites, dining, and limited groceries. The Monument Valley Tribal Park Visitor Center also has water and some food available, along with a commercial campground.

Hazards: There will probably be a fair amount of traffic on the route, both private vehicles and tour buses. Posted speed limits and the nature of the road demand that vehicles move slowly, but ride defensively all the same. You may encounter Navajos' dogs, but they're generally quite meek.

Rescue index: A lot of motorized vehicles travel the route.

Land status: Navajo Nation.

Maps: A map of the loop, with scenic and historic turnouts numbered to relate to signs on the ground, is available at the Visitor Center. (It does, however, exaggerate the distance.)

Finding the trail: From Mexican Hat, drive south on US 163, crossing the San Juan River and entering the Navajo Indian Reservation. In about 21 miles, turn left/southeast off the main road to pass through a row of Indian-goods sales shacks (a right turn at that point leads to Goulding's Lodge, with its historic trading post, John Wayne cabin, and modern resort). In 1.5 miles enter Arizona, and in another 2.5 miles arrive at the entrance to Monument Valley Tribal Park ($2.50 entrance fee at this writing). Park in the Visitor Center parking lot.

Source of additional information:

Monument Valley Tribal Park
P.O. Box 360289
Monument Valley, UT 84536
(435) 727-3287

Notes on the trail: From the parking lot, ride onto the well-signed scenic drive and immediately dive into the flats of the valley. At just under 3 miles you'll pass the spur going right to Three Sisters and John Ford's Point. One-half mile beyond there go straight, following the "One Way" arrow. At 4.5 miles bear left to stay on the main route, and then, in another mile, turn right after a wash at the T to stay on the main route. At about 6.5 miles, bear left (straight ahead goes 0.25 mile to Artist's Point, an overlook that should not be missed). At 8 miles-plus you'll turn right downhill, closing the loop. Climb out of the one of the world's most beautiful holes, returning to the parking lot at 11.5 miles.

RIDE 34 · Comb Ridge

AT A GLANCE

Length/configuration: 47-mile loop

Aerobic difficulty: Difficult if attempted as a 1-day ride; moderate as a 2-day trip

Technical difficulty: Moderately easy, over packed sediment roads with some loose sand, as well as 8 miles of pavement

Scenery: Comb Ridge is an immense hunk of sandstone; an 80-mile-long, north–south-running anticlinal uplift. On the east side the rock is lightly hued and gently sloping, but on the west the ridge looks like a sheared-off birthday cake containing red dye number 11.

Special comments: It's recommended that you do this as a 2-day bike-packing trip, or meet up with a support vehicle on the pavement at the end of the first day

This 47-mile loop following roads of packed sedimient and loose sand (along with 8 miles of pavement) is technically rather easy and aerobically moderate—*if* you take the recommended two days to do it. Only the fittest of riders should attempt the ride in one day and with *lots* of water aboard. (For a shorter day outing, consider an out-and-back from the trailhead up CR 262, into the Butler Wash area. Stunning side canyons cut into Comb Ridge will invite you to spend hours exploring by foot.) Although the "Notes on the trail" section is rather extensive, route finding is actually quite easy: Just stay close to Comb Ridge whenever faced with a choice of ways to go. To begin, after turning off the highway, you'll head north along the abrupt west wall of the ridge, generally gaining elevation as you zip up and down through a repetition of dry washes. Off-road travel is prohibited between the two highways because of the wilderness-study status of much of these lands.

As you traverse this impossibly dry, remote country, imagine doing it in a horse-drawn wagon in 1880, like a large group of Mormon pioneers did. Summoned by their leader to set up a colony along the San Juan River (he wanted to beat non-Mormon Anglos to the punch in establishing relations with the local Native American populations), the intrepid Latter-day Saints made their arduous Hole-in-the-Rock trek from Escalante, through the Hole-in-the-Rock, across the Colorado River, and over an infinity of slickrock country. San Juan Hill, where they crossed the nearly sheer face of Comb Ridge, was one of the toughest challenges of all. Their ultimate goal: a settlement at the mouth of Cottonwood Creek that they called Montezuma. Today the town is known as Bluff.

General location: Five miles west of Bluff.

Elevation change: The high point is 1,100 feet above the low point.

Season: March through May and September through November are best. Summers can be very hot and winters quite cold.

RIDE 34 · Comb Ridge

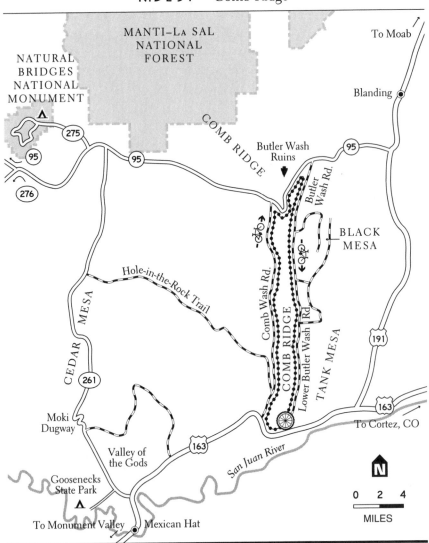

Services: All services are available in Bluff. Fill up on water there.

Hazards: The route can be quite sandy after prolonged dry spells. Conversely, after rains, parts of it may be impassable. Use special care when riding the highway segments.

Rescue index: Other than the highway stretches, the ride is remote. You may meet off-road vehicles, but don't count on it.

Land status: Bureau of Land Management.

Maps: DeLorme *Utah Atlas & Gazetteer*, page 22.

Finding the trail: From Bluff, go 5 miles west on US 163. Park in a wide spot at the right-hand turn to Lower Butler Wash Road/CR 262.

Source of additional information:

BLM San Juan Resource Area
P.O. Box 7
435 North Main
Monticello, UT 84535
(435) 587-2141

Notes on the trail: From the parking area, ride west on US 163, coasting down to Butler Wash and then ascending Comb Ridge. After coasting to Comb Wash, climb to 3 miles cumulative and turn right onto Butler Wash Road/CR 235. At just over 5 miles total, bear right where a similar-surfaced track goes left (it's part of the Hole-in-the-Rock Trail, an intriguing adventure in its own right). Cross through Comb Wash, then hit cattle guards at 8 and 11.5 miles. At 15 miles enter an area of subdued, stratified sandstone bluffs on the left—they contrast markedly with the shocking red walls of Comb Ridge to the right—and pass a grove of cottonwoods. At about 20 miles you'll recross Comb Wash, then do so again before turning right onto UT 95, the Bicentennial Highway (paving was completed in 1976), at 21 miles to climb again through the bowels of Comb Ridge. At 23.5 miles on the left is the parking area and trailhead for Butler Wash Ruins, where a mile-long hiking trail leads to a viewpoint overlooking Anasazi ruins. Continue up to 26 miles, then turn right onto Butler Wash Road/CR 230. After edging up rimrock and twisting in and out of a succession of drainages, the road straightens out at 30 miles, although still crossing drainages coming off the west slope of Black Mesa. Continue straight at 31 miles where another fork goes left. After crossing a cattle guard, and then, 0.5 mile later, passing through a draw at 37 miles total, go right to continue skirting Butler Wash and paralleling Comb Ridge, rather than going left onto the other good road. At 39 miles another road comes in from behind left. At about 44 miles you'll climb onto the flanks of Tank Mesa. Soon after crossing a cattle guard, bear left onto gravel and close the loop at 47 miles.

RIDE 35 · Natural Bridges National Monument

AT A GLANCE

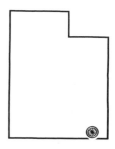

Length/configuration: 9-mile combination consisting of a 0.5-mile out and back (0.25 mile each way) leading to an 8.5-mile loop

Aerobic difficulty: Easy

Technical difficulty: Easy; the route is entirely on blacktop

Scenery: Some of the most beautiful canyons in all of canyon country

Special comments: Who says a good mountain bike ride can't be paved?

What's a road ride doing in a mountain bike guide, you ask? Well, once laying eyes on it, no cyclist in his or her right mind could resist this smooth, narrow ribbon of blacktop weaving above some of the most amazing canyons you'll ever see.

RIDE 35 · Natural Bridges National Monument

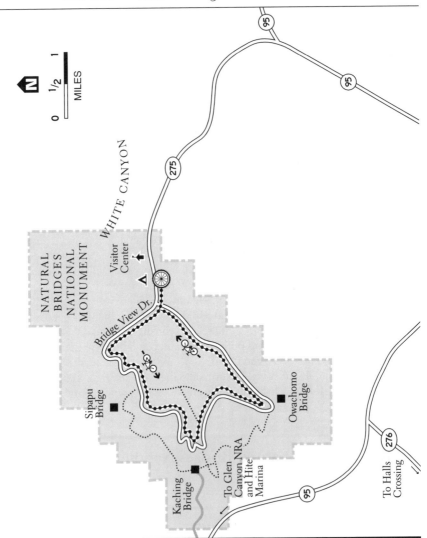

The scene is particularly stunning in late October, when the deep clefts of vividly hued rock brim with the brilliance of fall brush, all of it framed by the surrounding mesa's subdued juniper green and darker stone. If the ride wasn't in this book you might neglect visiting Natural Bridges National Monument altogether, which would be a shame when you're so close. Traveling to Natural Bridges from the Mexican Hat area—where you are/were if you've just done one or more of the previous several rides—in itself offers an unending visual spectacle, along with this very special treat: the drive up the improbable Moki Dugway, which you can't believe is there until you are there, and even then you're not sure where it could possibly go next. Blasted and bulldozed from the cliff face during the 1950s uranium boom, the dugway ascends

This ribbon of blacktop reveals some of southern Utah's most incredible canyon views.

1,100 vertical feet in just three miles, as it climbs a series of gravel switchbacks from the floor of Valley of the Gods to the top of Cedar Mesa, elevation 6,000 feet.

The 9-mile ride, consisting of a short spur and an 8.5-mile loop, is entirely on pavement, earning it an easy rating both aerobically and technically. Do it early in the morning or late in the day to avoid the mid-day traffic, which can be substantial. The outing is nothing for the keen mountain biker if not an exercise in restraint: You skirt slickrock expanses that'll make your body buzz with anticipation, yet pedaling off the paved road is a no-no in the national monument. Ride here before visiting Moab and you'll be primed for the Slickrock Bike Trail. Consider bringing a cable lock so you can secure your bike to a railing and partake of the monument's outstanding hikes, working off some of that spare energy by slickrocking on foot.

General location: 50 miles west of Blanding, or 45 miles north of Mexican Hat.

Elevation change: The ribbon of blacktop starys fairly level as it curves above the canyons below. If you hop off your bike to visit any of the 3 major natural bridges—Sipapu, Kachina, and Owachomo—the elevation loss (and gain in reverse) is substantial and steep.

Season: April through October are best, although the monument is open year-round.

Services: The nearest full-service town is Blanding, 50 miles east. Mexican Hat, 45 miles south, has somewhat more limited services. No services other than water are available within the national monument, and the campground water is turned off in winter.

Hazards: Watch for car traffic on the loop, and keep your eyes on the road—tough as it may be in such surroundings.

Rescue index: Help is available at the park Visitor Center.

Land status: National Park Service.

Maps: *Natural Bridges Official Map and Guide*, available at the Visitor Center, or DeLorme *Utah Atlas & Gazetteer*, page 22.

Finding the trail: From the junction of UT 95 and UT 261 (42 miles west of Blanding or 37 miles north of Mexican Hat) go west onto UT 95 and then, in about 2 miles, turn right onto UT 275. In another 5 miles, you'll reach the campground, where the ride begins.

Source of additional information:

> Natural Bridges National Monument
> P.O. Box 1
> Lake Powell, UT 84533
> (435) 692-1234

Notes on the trail: Leave the campground, turning right. In 0.25 mile you'll continue onto a one-way swatch of blacktop. At 1.5 miles cumulative is the Sipapu Bridge overlook; then, in another 0.5 mile, the Sipapu Bridge trailhead. (*Sipapu* is a Hopi term referring, roughly, to "the gateway through which the souls of men come from and return to the underworld.") At 2.5 miles cumulative pass the Horsecollar Ruin trailhead. A couple of miles from there you'll pass the Kachina Bridge overlook, and, at 6.5 miles, the trailhead for the delicate Owachomo Bridge. A mile farther you'll encounter a great view looking up at the Bear's Ears/Elk Ridge. At just over 8.5 miles close the loop, riding back onto a two-way road and regaining the campground at a little under 9 miles.

RIDE 36 · Horsetanks/Glen Canyon

AT A GLANCE

Length/configuration: 12.5-mile loop

Aerobic difficulty: Moderate, with about 1,000 feet of climbing

Technical difficulty: Moderately easy, over packed sand, wash sand, a bit of slickrock, and 3.5 miles of pavement

Scenery: Surroundings of maroon bluffs and an earth grinning with big white teeth, where it's been ripped open by erosional forces

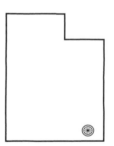

Special comments: The ride begins about a mile from the Colorado River's Narrow Canyon Bridge, within the Glen Canyon National Recreation Area not far from Hite Crossing

This is one of those serendipitous finds I unearthed simply by eyeballing some lines on a map and then investigating where they led. It makes one wonder how many good and great rides in southern Utah have yet to be blazed by fat tires. The 12.5-mile loop, rated aerobically moderate and technically easy, for the most part fol-

RIDE 36 · Horsetanks/Glen Canyon

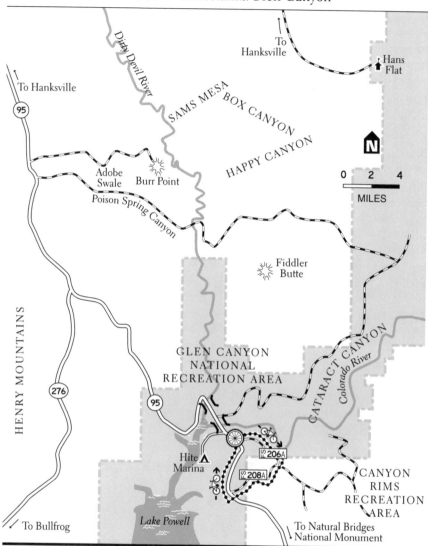

To Hanksville

Dirty Devil River

To Hanksville

95

SAMS MESA BOX CANYON

HAPPY CANYON

To Hanksville

Hans Flat

N

Adobe Swale   Burr Point

Poison Spring Canyon

0   2   4

MILES

Fiddler Butte

HENRY MOUNTAINS

GLEN CANYON NATIONAL RECREATION AREA

CATARACT CANYON

Colorado River

276

95

Hite Marina

206A

208A

CANYON RIMS RECREATION AREA

To Bullfrog

Lake Powell

To Natural Bridges National Monument

lows a road of packed sand that occasionally sees benefit of the blade. There's also a little slickrock and wash sand thrown in, as well as 3.5 miles of paved UT 95.

Another route that looks equally intriguing (but which I haven't explored) is the sand track taking off to the south across the high mesa country from near Fry Canyon Lodge. Fry Canyon is about 23 miles southeast of the trailhead for Horsetanks/Glen Canyon, and you'll pass it if coming in from the Blanding/Natural Bridges area. For most of the distance between Natural Bridges and the trailhead you'll motor alongside and above White Canyon, an amazingly beautiful and beckoning cleft in the plateau. It was by way of old Indian trails following White Canyon that prospector Cass Hite found his way to the Colorado River in September 1883.

There he discoverd a ford, which he dubbed Dandy Crossing. It was one of the very few places between Moab and Lee's Ferry, a span of more than 200 miles, where one could move wagons and livestock from one side of the river to the other in relative safety. The ford soon was known as Hite Crossing, named in honor of the only person living in the area. The original Hite, situated on the opposite side of the river from the present Hite Crossing Marina, was buried by the waters of Lake Powell when Glen Canyon was flooded in 1964.

General location: On UT 95, the Bicentennial Highway, roughly 80 miles northwest of Blanding and 50 miles southeast of Hanksville.

Elevation change: The high point is roughly 800 feet above the low point.

Season: March through May and September through November are best. The elevation is a little over 4,000 feet, or about the same as Moab's, so summers can be extremely hot.

Services: The only services between the 2 full-service towns of Blanding and Hanksville, separated by 130 miles of gorgeous emptiness, are those found at Fry Canyon (lodging, general store, cafe, gas, and camping) and at Hite Crossing Marina, located on Lake Powell approximately 3 miles west of this ride's beginning. Hite has a small store and a public campground. Be forewarned, however: *Do not* put yourself in the position of depending on the services at Fry Canyon or Hite Crossing. The rule out here is to carry several days' worth of both food and water in your vehicle at all times.

Hazards: Probably the biggest hazard is the ride's remoteness. You're *way* out there on this one. Depending on the time of year, you may be lucky to see any car traffic even on UT 95.

Rescue index: You may be able to flag down a motorist on UT 95; alternatively, help can be procured at Hite Crossing Marina.

Land status: National Park Service, BLM.

Maps: DeLorme *Utah Atlas & Gazetteer*, page 29, or the Utah Travel Council's *Southeastern Utah* map.

Finding the trail: From the Colorado River's Narrow Canyon Bridge, drive southeast uphill on UT 95 for just over 1 mile. Park on the east side of the road, off of CR 206a.

Source of additional information:

Glen Canyon National Recreation Area
P.O. Box 1507
Page, AZ 86040
(520) 608-6404

Notes on the trail: Ride up CR 206a/Horsetanks Road amid a landscape of eerily eroded white sandstone on the left and low maroon bluffs on the right, directly toward a miniature "Mexican Hat." At just over 0.25 mile another road comes in on the right, which connects to the highway a bit higher than where you started. As you gain elevation, note the red rock rising above the waters of upper Lake Powell, backdropped by the dark and wild Henrys Mountains. At 3 miles, continue straight where tracks go left (to a grove of trees near a patch of slickrock) and right (up into a canyon). At just under 4 miles a sign marks the end of the "motor travel restricted area," meaning you're leaving Glen Canyon National Recreation Area and riding onto BLM lands; then, at 4 miles, bear right where the road splits into 2 roads of nearly equal quality. In about 0.25 mile, go straight onto CR 208a. Soon you'll ride into a wash bottom; stay in it for about 0.25 mile. At a little over 7.5 miles reenter the signed "motor travel restricted area" (reenter Glen Canyon National Recreation Area, that is). At 9 miles cross a cattle guard, then turn right onto UT 95. In another 3.5 miles you'll return to the beginning point.

RIDE 37 · White Rim Road

AT A GLANCE

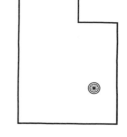

Length/configuration: 100-mile loop

Aerobic difficulty: Moderate. The majority of the route is quite level—but not all of it!

Technical difficulty: Moderate, mostly over packed sediments, as well as some slickrock, loose sand and rubble, gravel, and pavement

Scenery: One of the most scenic rides in Utah, and therefore in the world

Special comments: This legendary multiday, above-the-Canyon-Country adventure should be done with four-wheel-drive vehicle support. If you have trouble organizing your own group, several outfitters in the Moab area and elsewhere offer guided tours on White Rim Road.

Beginning high on Island in the Sky, this loop of 100 miles can be ridden in either direction. Here it is described in a clockwise direction of travel. The ride is technically and aerobically moderate (unless you choose, as some gonzo fitness freaks have, to ride the whole thing in a day), yet its distance and remoteness make it a true adventure that should not be set out on as a lark. The sheer scale of size and distance are an agoraphobic's nightmare and a big-country lover's sweetest dream.

Right off the bat the route plunges down the switchbacking Schafer Trail and onto the White Rim, a sandstone bench nestled between the Island in the Sky and the Green and Colorado River canyon bottoms. Toward the ride's end you'll regain the higher plateau by way of the switchbacks of the Horsethief Trail. The National Park Service rates the White Rim Road moderately difficult for high-clearance, four-wheel-drive vehicles in favorable weather conditions, so your shuttle driver should have good off-road driving skills, and the vehicle should have tire chains and excellent tread. (In wet weather some sections range from harrowing to extremely dangerous to absolutely impassable for bikes and motorized rigs alike.) All mountain bike/vehicle groups must obtain a backcountry camping permit from the National Park Service and stay only at designated campsites. Each site has vault toilets and will hold as many as 15 people and three vehicles. Following is a list of the campsites, their distance from the Visitor Center and the number of individual sites each has: Shafer, 7 miles, 1 site; Airport, 19 miles, 4 sites; Gooseberry, 30 miles, 2 sites; White Crack, 39 miles, 1 site; Murphy Hogback, 45 miles, 3 sites; Candlestick, 55 miles, 1 site; Potato Bottom, 66 miles, 3 sites; Hardscrabble Bottom, 68 miles, 2 sites; Taylor, 75 miles, 1 site; Labyrinth, 77 miles, 2 sites.

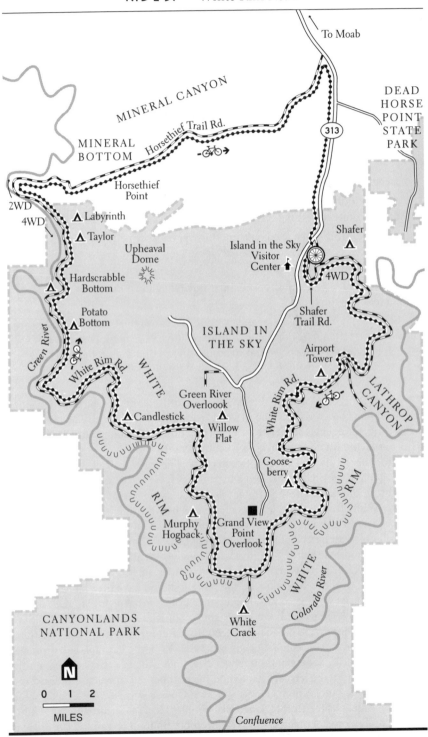

To Moab

MINERAL CANYON

DEAD
HORSE
POINT
STATE
PARK

MINERAL
BOTTOM

Horsethief Trail Rd.

313

Horsethief
Point

2WD
4WD

Labyrinth

Taylor

Shafer

Upheaval
Dome

Island in the Sky
Visitor
Center

Hardscrabble
Bottom

4WD

Potato
Bottom

Shafer
Trail Rd.

Green River

White Rim Rd.

ISLAND IN
THE SKY

Airport
Tower

WHITE

White Rim Rd.

LATHROP
CANYON

Green River
Overloook

Candlestick

Willow
Flat

Gooseberry

RIM

RIM

Murphy
Hogback

Grand View
Point
Overlook

WHITE

Colorado River

CANYONLANDS
NATIONAL PARK

White
Crack

N

0   1   2

MILES

Confluence

Shafer Trail zippers its way down into a fat-tire wonderland.

Although not required, reservations for the campsites are highly recommended, as competition is typically fierce on this popular route, particularly in spring. Most riders take three to five days to complete the ride, so plan your campsites accordingly. Whether or not you make campsite reservations, a backcountry camping permit *is* required.

Current policy for mountain bike/four-wheel-drive trips is as follows: Reservation requests are accepted for the following calendar year by mail or fax only, postmarked or faxed on or after the second Monday of the preceding July. To make a reservation, send your letter and payment to the reservation office no less than two weeks in advance of your trip (and long before that if you want to ensure getting your first choice of dates/campgrounds). Include this information: (1) name and address of trip leader, with day and evening phone numbers, (2) dates and campsites desired, and alternative choices for both, (3) the number of people in your group, (4) the number of vehicles in your group, (5) nonrefundable reservation fee of $25 (maximum of 15 people/three vehicles). If mailed, you can make your check out to National Park Service; if faxing the information, include a Visa or MasterCard number and expiration date. You can also pay by credit card if mailing your reservation. Mail or fax to:

Canyonlands National Park
Reservation Office
2282 S. West Resource Blvd.
Moab, UT 84532-3298
(435) 259-4351
(435) 259-4285 (fax)

You can also call the phone number for information on obtaining the required backcountry camping permit.

General location: 35 miles southwest of Moab.

Elevation change: The high point is approximately 6,300 feet; the low, where you skirt the Green River, is around 4,000 feet.

Season: March through May and September through November are best, with summers getting extremely hot in the bare, wide open.

Services: The nearest full-service town is Moab, where you'll want to stock up on food and water for several days. Take along at least a couple of extra days' worth of both, in case you get stuck or otherwise stalled.

Hazards: Dehydration and mechanical breakdown. Bring lots of water, spare tubes, and other bike parts. Plan on between 1 and 2 gallons of water per person per day.

Rescue index: Plan not to fall down or get sick on this ride, although if you're doing it in spring or fall there'll probably be another party not far ahead and/or behind. Help is also available at the Island in the Sky Visitor Center (the center has a cellular pay phone; credit card required).

Land status: National Park Service, BLM.

Maps: *Canyonland Official Map and Guide.* This and other, more detailed maps are available at the Moab Multi-Agency Information Center or at the Island in the Sky Visitor Center.

Finding the trail: From the corner of Center and Main in Moab go north on US 191 for 11 miles, then turn left onto UT 313 toward Dead Horse Point State Park/Canyonlands National Park. Twelve miles after turning onto UT 313, note the right-hand turn to Mineral Bottom—that's the road on which you'll emerge from the wilds at ride's end. In approximately 9 miles more, a few hundred yards past the national park entrance station, you'll come to a left-hand turn toward the Shafer Trail. Turn left and drop down to the parking area. This is where you'll begin riding (although you'll want to head up the main road a bit farther to take in the Island in the Sky Visitor Center and the nearby vista down on the switchbacks of the Shafer Trail).

Source of additional information:

> Moab Multi-Agency Information Center
> Center & Main
> Moab, UT 84532
> (435) 259-8825

Notes on the trail: This ride is well signed, and it has been described in many places and by many people, in almost microscopic detail in some instances. The best blow-by-blow description I've seen written specifically for mountain bikers is in Todd Campbell's *Above and Beyond Slickrock,* widely available in the Moab area (in that book it's described for counterclockwise travel, however). From the trailhead, you'll immediately drop down the Shafer Trail switchbacks and onto the White Rim Road. Some 70 miles later you'll climb back out via the Horsethief Trail switchbacks. Once back on top, it's about 15 miles through relatively ho-hum surroundings back to UT 313, onto which you'll turn right, returning to the beginning point in another 9 miles. (Note: Several out-and-backs spurring off the White Rim Road offer additional good riding and can add substantially to the total distance.)

RIDE 38 · Kokopelli's Trail

AT A GLANCE

Length/configuration: 145-mile point-to-point

Aerobic difficulty: Difficult, with a cumulative ton of climbing

Technical difficulty: Difficult, with a broad ranges of riding surfaces, including technical single-track, four-wheel-drive road, sand, slickrock, ledge rock, graded gravel and dirt, and pavement

Scenery: An ever changing panorama of desert, sandstone canyons, and high, mountain-flanking mesas

Special comments: Can be ridden self-supported, making it a real test, or by meeting up with a support vehicle nightly at designated points

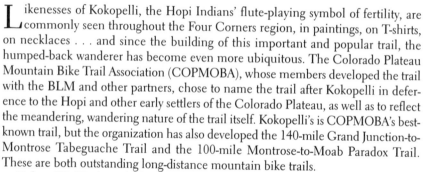

Likenesses of Kokopelli, the Hopi Indians' flute-playing symbol of fertility, are commonly seen throughout the Four Corners region, in paintings, on T-shirts, on necklaces . . . and since the building of this important and popular trail, the humped-back wanderer has become even more ubiquitous. The Colorado Plateau Mountain Bike Trail Association (COPMOBA), whose members developed the trail with the BLM and other partners, chose to name the trail after Kokopelli in deference to the Hopi and other early settlers of the Colorado Plateau, as well as to reflect the meandering, wandering nature of the trail itself. Kokopelli's is COPMOBA's best-known trail, but the organization has also developed the 140-mile Grand Junction-to-Montrose Tabeguache Trail and the 100-mile Montrose-to-Moab Paradox Trail. These are both outstanding long-distance mountain bike trails.

Kokopelli's Trail can be likened to a multiday counterpart to the Slickrock Bike Trail, and it is fitting that riders come from throughout the world to experience it. The 145-mile point-to-point route is remote and rugged. It is a linear jigsaw puzzle, linking all sorts of riding surfaces, including pavement, graded gravel and dirt, ledge rock, slickrock, sandy and/or rocky four-wheel-drive road, existing and newly constructed single-track, and even some historic stagecoach road thrown in for good measure.

Did I mention scenery? From the Mars-scape of the Slickrock Bike Trail the route climbs toward Porcupine and Fisher Mesas. Early views into Castle Valley and of the Fisher Towers' redrock sentinels are followed by a pair of rocky canyons both called Cottonwood, the colorful sandstones of the Entrada Bluffs, and a scenic descent to Dewey Bridge overlooking the broad Grand Valley and distant Roan Cliffs and Book Cliffs. And that's just the first half of the ride!

In case you don't have the time or inclination to ride the entire main route, five loop routes in Colorado—Mary's Loop, Lion's Loop, Troy Built Loop, Steve's Loop, and Horsethief Bench Loop—are all easily accessible from Grand Junction. Moreover, Rides 24 through 26 in this book all utilize portions of Kokopelli's Trail in Utah. If you *are* going to ride the entire trail, with or without a support vehicle, then careful, tedious advance planning with the route maps is a must.

RIDE 38 · Kokopelli's Trail

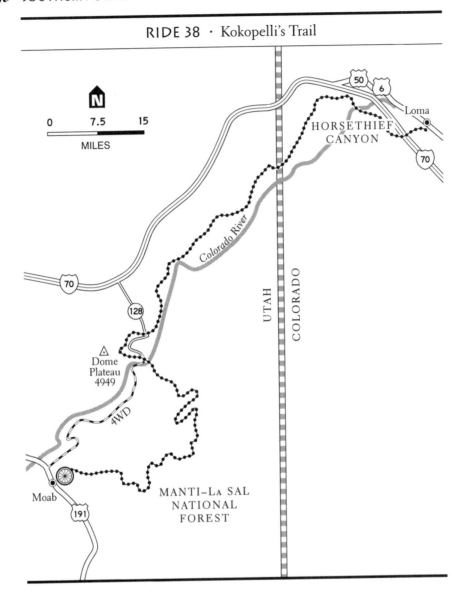

General location: The trail traverses a big piece of real estate separating Moab, Utah, and Loma, Colorado.

Elevation change: The elevation difference between the low point (Loma) and the high point, on the northern flanks of the La Sal Range, is about 4,000 feet. Cumulative gains and losses, however, are much more than this.

Season: April through May and September through October are best. Summers are very hot, yet at the higher elevations you'll chance running into snow and/or cold rain if you try it too early or too late in the year.

The meandering Kokopelli's Trail is well signed for its entire length.

Services: No services are found on the route. Moab, near the western terminus, has all services. Stock up there. If you choose to ride east to west, Grand Junction, Colorado, a major city, is located about 15 miles east of the trailhead.

Hazards: Avoiding dehydration is a major concern. The remote nature of the trail, much of which is quite technical, demands that you go well prepared with tools, spare parts, and first-aid gear, along with the knowledge of how to use it all.

Rescue index: Most of the trail is very remote and difficult to access.

Land status: Bureau of Land Management.

Maps: *Kokopelli's Trail Tips and Loops*, available from COBMOBA.

Finding the trail: From the corner of Center and Main in downtown Moab, go south on Main and turn left in 3 blocks onto 300 South. Four blocks later, turn right onto 400 East, then go past Locust and turn left onto Mill Creek Drive. At the stop sign, bear left/straight onto Sand Flats Road, arriving at the entrance station to Sand Flats Recreation Area in another 1.5 miles. After paying your fee ($5 for a 3-day pass at this writing), continue 0.5 mile to the huge paved parking area, located on the left side of the road. The trail starts here.

Source of additional information:

COPMOBA
P.O. Box 4602
Grand Junction, CO 81502-4602
(970) 243-5602

Notes on the trail: Kokopelli's Trail is well marked with brown-post navigational and reassurance markers set at intersections and at roughly 0.5-mile intervals along the length. A detailed map/route log is available from COPMOBA, and it should be obtained prior to setting out. The following notes are intended only to give you a general idea of what to expect. Beginning at the Slickrock Bike Trail parking area, ride east on the Sand Flats Road for about 17 miles, passing the trailhead for the Porcupine Rim Trail along the way. After a couple of miles on the rugged Porcupine Rim Road, you'll follow the La Sal Loop Road and county roads to, then through, the high, scenic Fisher Valley above Onion Creek. Onward you will continue, through a pair of Cottonwood Canyons, before dropping down to Dewey Bridge (roughly the halfway point), crossing the Colorado River and climbing into the sand and slickrock of Bull and Yellow Jacket Canyons (see Rides 24 through 26). After a very brief paved interlude on UT 128, the trail follows four-wheel-drive roads and single-track trails toward the no-services settlement of Cisco. A series of graded-dirt roads and primitive tracks subsequently leads the 13 miles from near the Cisco Boat Landing toward the Westwater Ranger Station (you'll come within a couple of miles of it). The ensuing 23 miles to Rabbit Valley is largely over old stagecoach road and four-wheel-drive tracks. From there, 9 miles of two-wheel-drive road precede 10 miles of tough single-track and moderately easy four-wheel-drive roads. This stretch includes a long, very steep descent to a bridge crossing of Salt Creek, located about 12 miles from trail's end. The final 4 or 5 miles traverse the maroon shales of the Morrison Formation, while approximating the route of I-70. The eastern terminus is the Loma Boat Launch, off I-70 some 15 miles west of Grand Junction.

PANORAMALAND

Your tubular meanderings through Panoramaland begin at the Colorado River near Hite Crossing Marina. As you enter Panoramaland from Canyonlands— and when you leave it for Color Country—you may wonder just how Utah's official name givers chose to call which region what. Canyonlands could just as accurately be described as Color Country or Panoramaland, and the same is true for the other two—all three names would fit any one of the regions just fine.

Panoramaland has plenty to keep any devoted follower of the fat-tire way busy for weeks, months, even years. *Diversity* is the key word here, from the bleak Burr Desert and Dirty Devil River to the stunning, rock-hard beauty of Capitol Reef National Park to the high, aspen-covered Fish Lake and Sevier Plateaus. Moreover, if you're interested in venturing out that way, the western half of the region is within the Great Basin province: big, dry, basin-and-range country with places wearing descriptive names like Whirlwind Valley, Black Rock Desert, and the Confusion Range. Farther east, although there's still plenty of rock (much of it red), the featured riding is more typically characterized by high mountains and lofty plateaus. On how many rides have you gained a full mile of elevation, for instance? You can in Panoramaland—if you're crazy and you want to—on the aptly named Sevier Grunt and probably on other, undiscovered/unfeatured outings.

Or, take the rugged Fish Lake Plateau, an upland of volcanic origin roughly 750 square miles (a half-million acres) in size. During wet spells, a large share of the roads and trails in the surrounding, lower-lying deserts will be mired in mud, gumbo, and goo. The volcanic soils of the Fish Lake Plateau, however, drain well and quickly, making it a good place to visit if you're unlucky and hit southern Utah during the summer/fall monsoons. Add to the formula great trails and several excellent resorts and Forest Service campgrounds (some with showers!) lining Fish Lake, and it's no wonder the area has become a real summer and autumn haven for mountain bikers. The popular Fish Lake in the Fall Mountain Bike Festival hasn't detracted any from the area's reputation among cyclists, either. For the comfort and convenience of "indoor camping," meanwhile, Richfield, Torrey, and several other full-service towns make excellent centers of operations.

Those intrigued by history will enjoy learning that Panoramaland is home to some of the earliest and best-preserved Mormon settlements in Utah. Drive or ride around the Sanpete Valley towns of Moroni and Spring City, for instance. Both were settled in the middle of the 19th century, and the entire *town* of Spring City is listed on the National Historic Register. Going back even farther in time, prehistory buffs will go bonkers at places like Fremont Indian State Park, out of whose campground two of the featured rides begin and end.

You leave Panoramaland by wending your way through an area you may have already visited, only this time you're coming at it from another direction: Burrville, Loa, and Torrey, by way of State Highways 62 and 24. From Torrey you'll commence the unforgettable climb up Boulder Mountain, on whose northeast flank you drive into Color Country.

RIDE 39 · Burr Point

AT A GLANCE

Length/configuration: 21-mile out-and-back (10.5 miles each way)

Aerobic difficulty: Easy, with a gradual climb to the turnaround

Technical difficulty: Easy, over graded gravel with some sand

Scenery: 10 miles of spinning through the rather bleak Burr Desert reaps an inspiring look down on the Dirty Devil River canyon; heading back, the impressive Henry Mountains erupt from subdued surroundings

Special comments: This curving, moderately hilly road provides a fun desert zip; not a good choice, however, for shade-only tolerant individuals

This ride, rated aerobically and technically easy, dishes up a swath of Burr Desert, a rolling, blackbrush-blanketed expanse of landscape squeezed between UT 95 and the Dirty Devil River. The curiously named river allegedly earned its moniker in 1869 when explorer John Wesley Powell and party passed the mouth of the Dirty Devil (which forms upstream where the Fremont River and Muddy Creek join forces), whose waters they found "exeedingly muddy and (with) an unpleasant odor." One of the men remarked that the river was a dirty devil, and the name remains 130 years later. Where you're headed on this ride, by the way, is not called Burr Point because you're bound to be cold and shivery by the time you get there; rather, it received its name— like other things "Burr" in the region—in honor of John Atlantic Burr (whose middle name resulted from the fact that he was born while his Utah-bound parents were cross-ing the Atlantic). The legendary Burr Trail, located southwest of here and running through the Waterpocket Fold, was blazed by Burr as a cattle trail.

Enough about names. Another of those intriguing but unexplored rides (by the author, anyway) begins just two miles south of this one. From studying the maps, it looks as though one could ride easterly down Poison Spring Canyon, ford the Dirty Devil, then ride up North Hatch Canyon to the juncture inside Glen Canyon National Recreation Area with National Park Service Road 633. A right turn onto this road leads southwesterly above the Colorado River's Cataract Canyon to reconnect with UT 95, near where the Dirty Devil converges with the Colorado just north of Hite Crossing Marina. (A left turn onto NPS 633 leads north to Hans Flat; see Ride 40.) This could make for an outstanding adventure, but before attempting it you'll

RIDE 39 · Burr Point

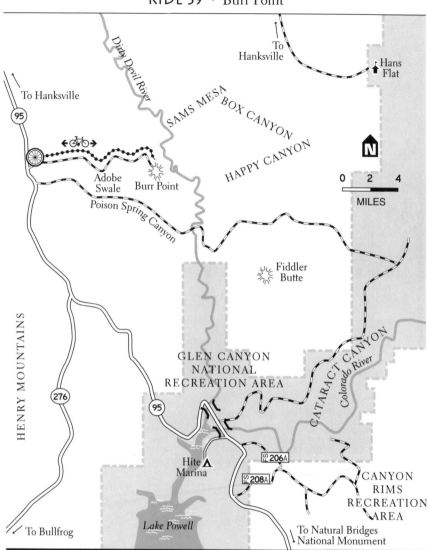

definitely want to check in with the Bureau of Land Management and/or the National Park Service to obtain more information. It appears to be at least 70 miles from one trailhead to the other.

General location: 15 miles south of Hanksville.

Elevation change: 5,000 to 5,500 feet.

Season: March through May and September through November.

Services: The closest services are in Hanksville, 15 miles north. Stock up on water there.

There's little to stop the views out here, other than the Henry Mountains.

Hazards: Auto traffic is a possibility on the route, especially on weekends.

Rescue index: You're in yet another empty corner of southern Utah; flagging down a motorist on UT 95 will likely be your best source of assistance.

Land status: Bureau of Land Management.

Maps: Hanksville 1:100,000 metric map (BLM) or DeLorme *Utah Atlas & Gazetteer*, page 29.

Finding the trail: From Hanksville, go 15 miles south on UT 95 and turn left/east onto the road signed "Dell Seep 5, Adobe Swell 8, Burr Point 11." Pull off the road and park.

Source of additional information:

BLM Henry Mountains Field Station
406 South 100 West
P.O. Box 99
Hanksville, UT 84734
(435) 542-3461

Notes on the trail: Ride east up the gravel road, gradually gaining elevation, through broad-shouldered country backed to the west by the Henry Mountains. Simply stay on the main road wherever primitive forks go left or right. Between 4.5 and 5 miles you'll roller-coaster through some fun draw crossings, and at 8 miles you'll pass the intriguing slickrock expanses of Adobe Swale on your right. At 10.5 miles you'll reach Burr Point, where you can look down on the canyon of the Dirty Devil, as well as across and into Sams Mesa Box Canyon, which feeds the Dirty Devil from the east. Return by the same route.

RIDE 40 · Panorama Point

AT A GLANCE

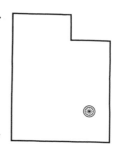

Length/configuration: 17-mile out-and-back (8.5 miles each way)

Aerobic difficulty: Moderate, with the lion's share of the climbing coming at you on the way back

Technical difficulty: Moderate, over four-wheel-drive road with some sand and slickrock

Scenery: They don't call it Panorama Point for nothin'

Special comments: The drive to the trailhead from UT 24 takes almost as long as the ride itself

This ride takes place within Glen Canyon National Recreation Area, in an area immediately west of the Maze District of Canyonlands National Park. It's a long drive in, but any southern Utah explorer worth his saltbrush must be able to say he's seen this incredible spot. Primitive backcountry campsites are found both at Panorama Point and at Cleopatra's Chair (see "Notes on the trail"). Panorama Point makes a fabulous place to camp—if for no other reason than to watch the sun rise over the canyonlands—in a view-abundant setting with some wind protection afforded by bursts of piñon and juniper. To camp, you'll need to procure a backcountry camping permit at Hans Flat Ranger Station.

The 17-mile out-and-back is rated aerobically and technically moderate in difficulty. After negotiating 8.5 miles of rolling, timbered rim country over a four-wheel-drive road containing some respectable stretches of sand and slickrock, you'll reach Panorama Point. Here you gaze out, an infinity encompassing features you viewed from different perspectives if you've accomplished certain other rides in this guide. Spreading out below is the evocative Land of Standing Rocks and the aptly named Maze, decidedly one of the most isolated, inaccessible, and fantastic places in North America; it's a colorful puzzle of narrow, multifingered, randomly eroded box canyons, far too confusing to be contemplated for too long. Farther out you can see the Needles District, Island in the Sky, the distant Abajos and La Sals, and, on a clear day, the high tips of the even more distant San Juan peaks of Colorado. It really is something to behold.

General location: Sixty miles east of Hanksville. As the raven flies, you're about the same distance from Moab; you don't have wings, though, so it's about twice that far by car.

Elevation change: 6,150 to 6,650 feet.

Season: March through October (be aware that even at this elevation summers can be very hot).

Services: Hanksville is the closest full-service town. Stock up there or in Moab.

Hazards: Sand and the remote nature of the trail are your biggest concerns. Also, be sure to bring plenty of water.

RIDE 40 · Panorama Point

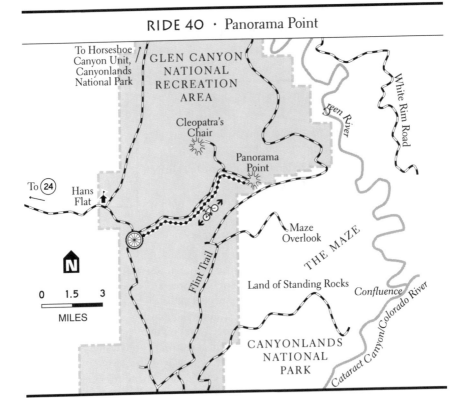

Rescue index: Rescue? Ha! Seriously, emergency assistance can be arranged for at Hans Flat Ranger Station.

Land status: National Park Service.

Maps: DeLorme *Utah Atlas & Gazetteer*, pages 29 and 30, or *Glen Canyon National Recreation Area Official Map and Guide.*

Finding the trail: From Hanksville, drive 14 miles north on UT 24 and turn right/east toward Hans Flat. Proceed through 45 miles of deserted San Rafael Desert to the Hans Flat Ranger Station. From there, continue 2.5 miles toward the Flint Trail, parking off the road at the turn to Panorama Point.

Source of additional information:

Glen Canyon National Recreation Area
P.O. Box 1507
Page, AZ 86040
(520) 608-6404

Notes on the trail: Ride northeasterly on the four-wheel-drive track leading toward Panorama Point. Initially you'll encounter a series of short to moderately long ups and downs, weaving through occasional patches of sand. Continue straight downhill at 4 miles, where a spur goes right (it dead ends in 0.5 mile at an excellent viewpoint). At just past 5.5 miles you'll come precariously close to the canyon rim. In another mile, bear right toward Panorama Point where a left goes 2 miles to Cleopatra's Chair (this spur is worth tacking on if time and energy permit). The last 1.5 miles encompass some moderately technical slickrock and sandy expanses. Don't worry: You'll know when you get to the end, at 8.5 miles, even if you're not equipped with a cyclometer.

RIDE 41 · Capitol Reef Scenic Drive

AT A GLANCE

Length/configuration: 19-mile out-and-back (9.5 miles each way)

Aerobic difficulty: Easy, gaining about 500 feet of elevation on good surfaces

Technical difficulty: Easy, following pavement and well-graded dirt roads

Scenery: Awesome close-ups of the buckled earth and weather-battered rock of the Waterpocket Fold and its universe of slot canyons, sandstone domes, crumbling cliffs, and castlelike turrets

Special comments: A great spin to take out of the Capitol Reef National Park campground early in the morning or after supper, when car traffic will be lighter

This 19-mile out-and-back (9.5 miles each way), rated aerobically and technically easy, begins with with 6.5 miles of paved road, which occasionally crosses through the wash on concrete pads. That is followed by three miles of graded, hard-packed dirt road. Through a world of rock you will go—rocks ranging from the reddish-brown shales of the Moenkopi Formation and the grayer band of Chinle shale (originally deposited as volcanic ash), to the distinctive colors and various shapes assumed by the sandstones of the Wingate, Navajo, and Kayenta formations. Head out at first light and pack a picnic, because the turnaround at Pleasant Creek is an ideal place to spread a feast. You'll find ample shade, along with close-ups of some of the Waterpocket Fold's most spectacular domes; distant views of the juniper-clad, red slopes of lower Boulder Mountain; and the soothing gurgle of mountain water feeding the thirsty desert. En route to the turnaround, short spurs can be ridden up Grand Wash and Capitol Gorge.

Interestingly, until 1962 the main road came into Capitol Reef by way of Capitol Gorge, but the costs of maintenance and clean-up following floods were too great; poke into it and have a look (but not if it looks like rain!) and you'll understand why. Today the Capitol Gorge spur ends about two miles from the Scenic Drive. Good hikes are available along the way, too, including a couple that branch out at the ride's beginning near the campground. One of them goes up Cohab Canyon—short for "cohabitation," an allusion to polygamous Mormons of the 19th century said to have hidden out here to avoid prosecution by the feds.

It'd be tough to do it without getting your feet wet, but if you choose at the turn-around you can continue across Pleasant Creek and explore upstream from the ford,

RIDE 41 · Capitol Reef Scenic Drive
RIDE 42 · Cathedral Valley

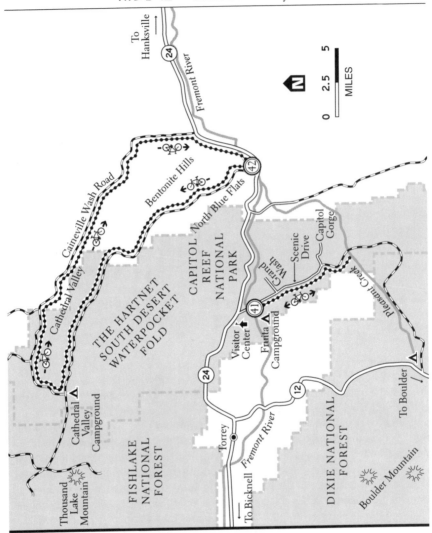

beyond which the road is barely maintained if at all. Alternatively, if you can persuade a companion to provide a shuttle, you can start high up along the Grover-Boulder Highway near Pleasant Creek Campground and coast almost the entire way to Capitol Reef's Scenic Drive by way of Lower Bown's Reservoir. See Ride 54, Rosebud Trail, in Color Country for a description of what would constitute the first few miles of that ride. At this writing, there are also a couple of outfitters in Torrey through which you might be able to arrange a shuttle.

General location: The ride begins at Fruita Campground in Capitol Reef National Park.

A universe of slot canyons, sandstone domes, and crumbling cliffs.

Elevation change: 5,600 to 6,100 feet.

Season: March through November.

Services: Fruita Campground has water. Other services are available in Torrey, 11 miles west of the Visitor Center on UT 24.

Hazards: The paved road is narrow enough that if 2 cars were passing it might not leave enough room for a bicycle. However, the speed limit is 25 m.p.h. Ride defensively all the same, pulling off the road if and when it seems wise.

Rescue index: You'll meet car traffic along this ride. Rangers patrol the area, too.

Land status: National Park Service.

Maps: Canyonlands National Park *Official Map and Guide* or DeLorme *Utah Atlas & Gazetteer,* page 28.

Finding the trail: Fruita Campgound is located 1.5 miles south of the Capitol Reef National Park Visitor Center.

Source of additional information:

Capitol Reef National Park
Torrey, UT 84775-9602
(435) 425-3791

Notes on the trail: Leave the campground, heading south on the paved Scenic Drive. At about 2 miles pass Grand Wash, which, if the road is open, you can pedal into for about a mile. At 4.5 miles you'll cross the Slickrock Divide: Water falling north of here drains into Grand Wash; that falling to the south flows into Capitol Gorge. At 6.5 miles, with Capitol Gorge on the left, continue onto the unpaved

Pleasant Creek Road. You'll immediately begin climbing on a surface of hard-packed, rock-embedded dirt, winding through a scattered forest of juniper and piñon. At just over 9 miles, on a road surface that's now sandier, you'll pass some beautiful old corrals settled beneath a spreading cottonwood canopy, and then, in another 0.25 mile, arrive at the Pleasant Creek crossing. When you're good and ready, retrace your tire tracks to the campground, reached at 19 miles cumulative.

RIDE 42 · Cathedral Valley

AT A GLANCE

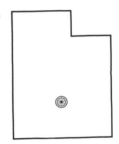

Length/configuration: 65-mile loop

Aerobic difficulty: Moderate, with numerous steep climbs adding up to more than 2,500 feet of elevation gain

Technical difficulty: Easy, over high-clearance two-wheel-drive roads (some sections passable only in dry conditions) of dirt, sand, and bentonite, along with 7 miles of pavement

Scenery: The colorful spires, cathedrals, and igneous dikes and sills of the spectacular and little-visited northern reaches of Capitol Reef National Park are backed by the hovering darkness of basalt-capped Thousand Lake Mountain

Special comments: Best done as a 2- or 3-day bike-packing or vehicle-supported trip

This 65-mile loop is a grand outing, but one that only the fittest riders should attempt in one day, and even then only in the best of weather conditions. Aerobically, the ride is moderate in difficulty, assuming you don't try it in one day (which would jack it up to most difficult); technically, it's easy, over generally smooth roads of sand, bentonite, and compacted sediments. Early in the ride, as you twist your way north/northwestward, going generally uphill, you'll earn great views of the upper end of the Waterpocket Fold, where it collides with Thousand Lake Mountain. After that, the stunning scenery just keeps coming and keeps changing. To close the loop, you'll ride seven miles along paved UT 24.

To begin, you—and your support vehicle, if you have one—must ford the Fremont River, which must not be attempted during high runoff. Nor do you want to set out on this adventure if rain is in the forecast, for much of the route transforms into impassable, ice-slick gumbo in a downpour. Before heading out, check in at the Capitol Reef National Park Visitor Center (1) to inquire about the water depth and safety of the Fremont River ford, (2) to pick up a copy of the self-guiding publication containing interpretive information keyed to tour stops along the route, and (3) to obtain a backcountry camping permit, if you plan to camp at Cathedral Valley Campground. Located about 27.5 miles into the ride, Cathedral Valley is the recommend overnight if you're doing the ride in two days. (Once past 37 miles you can camp just about anywhere, as the route leaves national park lands for BLM lands, where dispersed camping is permitted.) Also, in the 14- to 15-mile range, before entering the national park, you'll pass some good areas for camping where you should plan to stay if you'll be taking three days to complete the ride. In that case, a good spot for overnight number two is just past 50 miles, in a beautiful, protected area of sandstone rims and washes.

General location: The ride begins just east of Capitol Reef National Park along UT 24.

Elevation change: 4,600 to 7,000 feet.

Season: April through May and September through October.

Services: No services are available on the unpaved portions of the route. Drinking water is available at the Visitor Center in Capitol Reef National Park, and 3 miles east of the trailhead on UT 24 there's a modern, commercial campground with a minimally stocked store. All other services can be found in Torrey, 23 miles west of the trailhead. Torrey is the best place nearby to stock up for a 2- or 3-day adventure.

Hazards: Dehydration is the biggest concern; bring a minimum of 1 gallon of water per person per day. Bring bicycle tools and parts, too, as well as first-aid supplies.

Rescue index: The route is very remote. You might meet touring motorists and/or a ranger on patrol; or, you might not. Go prepared for emergencies.

Land status: National Park Service, BLM.

Maps: Capitol Reef National Park *Official Map and Guide* or DeLorme *Utah Atlas & Gazetteer*, page 28.

Finding the trail: From the Capitol Reef National Park Visitor Center, drive 12 miles east on UT 24. Turn north onto the road signed "River Ford/Cathedral Valley" and drop down to park in the shade of the cottonwood grove located about 0.5 mile from the highway.

Source of additional information:

Capitol Reef National Park
Torrey, UT 84775-9602
(435) 425-3791

Notes on the trail: Go north toward Cathedral Valley/Hartnet Road, walking your bike and gear across the Fremont River. At 4 miles you'll ride into North Blue Flats. At about 7.5 miles begin climbing steeply into the Bentonite Hills; then, at just under 11 miles, you'll climb ever higher into the Hartnet, an expanse of cliffs, ledges, and arroyos carved into and out of Salt Wash sandstone. Wash crossings are common. At 13.5 miles pass a spur going left (1.25 miles each way) to the Lower South Desert Overlook. At just under 16 miles you'll enter Capitol Reef National Park, continuing amid sandstone bluffs and dipping in and out of draw crossings. At about 25 miles, now in close proximity to the flanks of Thousand Lake Mountain, the view over the South Desert is remarkable. At 27.5 miles, just after turning right toward "U-24 26 Miles" (and away from the road ascending Thousand Lake Mountain), arrive at Cathedral Valley Campground. From there, a mile-long series of switchbacks drops you into the world of creatures and monoliths of Entrada sandstone inhabiting Upper Cathedral Valley. At 31 miles, to the right are the features known as the Walls of Jericho, the Basilica, and Wall Street. At the junction at 32.5 miles go straight toward "U-24 20 Miles," where a left heads toward Baker Ranch and I-70. Continue crossing draws before ascending a mesa to 37 miles, where you'll bear right toward Lower Cathedral Valley and leave Capitol Reef National Park, riding onto BLM lands. At 44 miles, a couple of miles past the right-hand spur to the temples of the Sun, Moon, and Stars, you'll begin encountering some potentially annoying stretches of loose sand. At 46 miles coast into the sandstone environs of Caineville Wash; then, at 50 miles, commence a 4-mile jitterbug with a jumble of sandstone ledges and rimrock draws. At 57.5 miles, after another interlude of sand and bentonite, turn right onto UT 24 and ride 7 miles to get up and over a series of three ridges before turning back toward the river ford and returning to the trailhead at 65 miles.

RIDE 43 · Torrey/Velvet Ridge

AT A GLANCE

Length/configuration: 14.5-mile loop

Aerobic difficulty: Easy to moderate, with approximately 600 feet of climbing

Technical difficulty: Moderate, over sandy, rock-embedded double-track; smooth to rutted ATV trail; and pavement

Scenery: At ride's beginning you look ahead at the bright-red sandstone breaks of Thousand Lake Mountain; coming back out of the hills you gaze across the fertile Fremont River Valley at the lofty Aquarius Plateau/Boulder Mountain

Special comments: If you arrive during a prolonged dry spell, you may want to do the ride in reverse, so that the sandiest portions will be downhill

This 14.5-mile loop begins at the edge of Torrey, a liberally shaded little town containing some wonderful old stone-block houses and certain newer businesses suggesting that the quaint settlement has been discovered. Following sandy and sometimes rocky four-wheel-drive road, ATV trails through hills of clay, and 4.5 miles of pavement, the ride is rated moderate in both aerobic and technical difficulty. The sandy sections will be in best shape shortly after a rainfall; unfortunately, that's also when the prospect of negotiating the tire-gooping bentonite soils of Velvet Ridge will range from improbable to impossible. Where the road hugs the base of the clay hills to wrap around the heads of several arroyos, look up and notice the clay "fans" coming off the rimrock above; they resemble the statifications of sand in a sand jar in their perfect layers of various shades. Out below, the wetlands and irrigated green hayfields of the Fremont River flood plain provide luscious contrast to the desiccated hills you're traversing. Most of the ride follows a segment of the popular Great Western Trail, a long-distance route that is still under development in Idaho and Montana, but which is complete in Utah. The multiuse trail in some instance splits in two, encompassing one branch for ATVers and a separate route, sometimes miles away, dedicated to nonmotorized uses.

RIDE 43 · Torrey/Velvet Ridge

General location: The ride begins on the west edge of Torrey, located just west of Capitol Reef National Park.

Elevation change: 6,850 to 7,350 feet.

Season: April through October.

Services: Torrey has all services.

Hazards: Some of the sandier stretches could snag a tire. Ride defensively along the 4.5 miles of UT 24, which has a paved shoulder between 1 and 2 feet wide.

Rescue index: There's a chance of encountering ATVers on the unpaved stretches because you're following a section of the Great Western Trail. Otherwise, Torrey, or motorists along the highway, will be the closest available help.

Land status: Private, Fishlake National Forest, BLM.

Maps: Fishlake National Forest visitor map.

Finding the trail: At the west edge of Torrey, turn north onto Sand Creek Road and go 0.75 mile on hard-surfaced gravel. Park at the Great Western Trail (GWT) Torrey trailhead.

Sources of additional information:

Loa Ranger District
Fishlake National Forest
138 South Main
Loa, UT 84747
(435) 836-2811

Teasdale Ranger District
Dixie National Forest
138 East Main
Teasdale, UT 84773
(435) 425-3702

Notes on the trail: From the trailhead, ride toward the big water tank on a sandy, rock-embedded track. In 0.5 mile, beside the tank, you'll see a sign reading "Velvet Ridge—4.5; Hwy. U24 via Velvet Ridge—8.7." Just beyond here, splash through Sand Creek and turn left at the Y on FS 207/GWT (the road you're turning from naturally goes straight toward Holt Draw). At between 1 and 1.5 miles cross the stream again, then, 0.5 mile later, stay to the main track. At 2 miles cumulative bear right on the higher-grade track and continue straight along the signed GWT. A short way from there, where the main track continues straight, go left toward "Velvet Ridge." At just under 3 miles continue straight on the GWT where another track goes right. You'll soon pass a couple of spurs leading to great viewpoints looking down on the Fremont River Valley; whenever presented with a choice, to remain on the main route, just continue following signs for UT 24 and/or the GWT. Eventually, the track skirts the base of the clay hills to get up and around the heads of some otherworldly, void-of-vegetation arroyos before descending a steep, rutted, ugly, hot, barren downhill about 0.5 mile in length. At the bottom, at approximately 9 miles, turn left onto UT 24 and ride for 4.5 miles. At the west edge of Torrey, turn north onto Sand Creek Road, closing the loop in another 0.75 mile.

RIDE 44 · Sevenmile Cruise

AT A GLANCE

Length/configuration: 16-mile out-and-back (8 miles each way)

Aerobic difficulty: Easy to moderate, gaining approximately 1,100 feet of elevation

Technical difficulty: Easy, over well-graded two-wheel-drive road and a short stretch of pavement

Scenery: A medley of rushing streams, silvery sage flats, cattle-filled meadows, volcanic-rubble slopes, stands of aspen, and towering Mts. Marvine and Terrill

Special comments: A great ride to do if you get stuck in a steady rain, not an uncommon phenomenon in the verdant Fish Lake Basin

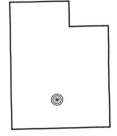

RIDE 44 · Sevenmile Cruise

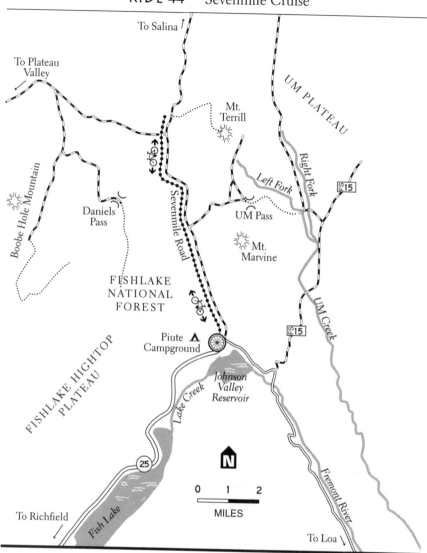

Despite its name, this mellow out-and-back is 16 miles in length (8 miles each way); in reality, though, you can make it as long or as short as you'd like. It is easy to moderate in aerobic difficulty and technically easy, combining well-graded two-wheel-drive road and a short patch of pavement at the beginning/end. The first four miles are coincidental with Ride 47, UM Pass, while beyond the suggested turn-around the road perseveres northward, eventually meeting I-70 a few miles east of Salina. One-half mile before the turnaround, there's also the option of turning west and finding your way on four-wheel-drive tracks to the Plateau Valley, a beautiful mid-elevation basin of birds, streams, and cabins (you drove through it if you came to

Slopes of volcanic rubble are scattered amid a landscape of meadows and silvery sage flats.

Fish Lake by way of Richfield). From there you would return to the Fish Lake Basin via UT 24 and UT 25.

Unlike the more restrictive situation along the paved road between Fish Lake and Johnson Valley Reservoir, where outstanding campgrounds abound—some with showers!—dispersed camping is allowed in the areas traversed on this ride. The turnaround is at the trailhead for the hiking/jeeping track leading up 11,531-foot Mt. Terrill.

General location: 50 miles southeast of Richfield.

Elevation change: 8,800 to 9,900 feet.

Season: June through October.

Services: Meals, accommodations, and some groceries are available at Fish Lake Lodge (7.5 miles southwest of the trailhead) and Bowery Haven Resort (6 miles southwest); drinking water is available at the resorts and at the campgrounds lining Fish Lake. Still, if coming in from the northwest, you'll probably want to stock up on supplies in Richfield; if approaching from the southeast, procure food and camping supplies in Torrey or Loa.

Hazards: You will likely meet a bit of tourist, stock grower, and/or logging traffic on the road in summer, and hunters in October.

Rescue index: Your best strategy in an emergency will be to flag down a passing motorist or to return to Fish Lake Lodge or Bowery Haven Resort. Pay phones are found at the resorts and at some of the Forest Service campgrounds in the area, including Mackinaw. There's also a Forest Service guard station located near Fish Lake Resort.

Land status: Fishlake National Forest.

Maps: Fishlake National Forest visitor map.

Finding the trail: From Fish Lake Lodge, drive a little over 7 miles northeast on pavement and turn left toward Piute Campground, located opposite Johnson Valley Reservoir. Park in the large lower parking area.

Source of additional information:

> Fishlake National Forest
> 115 East 900 North
> Richfield, UT 84701
> (435) 896-9233

Notes on the trail: From the parking lot, ride northeasterly on pavement, turning left at just under 0.5 mile onto the gravel Sevenmile Road toward Gooseberry and Salina. Commence climbing at a fairly gradual, but steady grade. At about 1 mile cumulative you'll pass a trail going left to the Fish Lake Hightop Plateau via Tasha Creek; then, 0.5 mile later, cross a cattle guard into a broad, grassy basin and riparian management area. (Dispersed camping is permitted beyond this point.) Just past 4 miles, note the dirt track on your right; that is the continuation of the UM Pass route (Ride 47). At 7 miles cross a cattle guard, going from the Loa to the Richfield ranger district. The Mt. Terrill Guard Station is tucked in a grove below to the left. At 7.5 miles pass a road going left toward Daniels Pass/Boobe Hole Mountain. This four-wheel-drive road feeds into all sorts of rugged pedaling possibilities, including that of riding to Plateau Valley, as mentioned above. The 8-mile mark, at the pullout for the Mt. Terrill trailhead on the right, is the recommended turnaround.

RIDE 45 · Lakeshore Trail West

AT A GLANCE

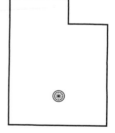

Length/configuration: 10-mile combination ride consisting of a 1-mile spur connected to an 8-mile loop

Aerobic difficulty: Easy to moderate, with a fair bit of climbing involved

Technical difficulty: Easy to moderate, with surfaces ranging from cinder-surfaced trail and pavement to smooth single-track

Scenery: Pelican Overlook provides a wonderful perspective of the surrounding countryside, and the trail also passes through some gorgeous stretches of forest

Special comments: Most of the single-track is buffed, providing a fun ride for anyone, but it is particularly well suited for dampening the cleats of the single-track neophyte

S ample this fun spin prior to tackling the much longer and harder Mytoge Mountain Loop. The 10-mile ride, consisting of a mile-long spur connected to an 8-mile loop, is rated both aerobically and technically somewhere between easy and moderate in difficulty. It makes a perfect introduction to single-track riding because it's neither too long nor too remote. Route finding is a bit of a challenge, but even if you get off track you can hardly go wrong; so long as you head downhill you'll wind up back at the highway. Riding surfaces include cinder-surfaced lakeshore trail, pavement, and smooth single-track.

Fish Lake empties by way of Lake Creek into Johnson Valley Reservoir, out of which flows the Fremont River. The lake occupies a downfaulted valley, or *graben* (German for "gutter" or "trough"), which descended between the fault running along the base of Mytoge Mountain and a second, higher fault at the base of the Fish Lake Hightop Plateau to the northwest. Check out the Forest Service map, and you can see that the mountain, the plateau, and Fish Lake all run parallel to one another. One of the things that makes the Fish Lake Basin so appealing to self-propelled hikers, bikers, and horseback riders is that much of the surrounding forest lands are either off-limits to motorized vehicles or highly restricted regarding where they can go. For the mountain biker, such a scenario is a rare and happy medium nestled somewhere between wilderness (where mountain bikes aren't permitted) and less restrictively managed forest, where there's sometimes too many ATVers for a lot of mountain bikers' tastes. (Not to dismiss ATVers out of hand; most are fine people, and were it not for funds raised through their activity some of Utah's best trails for mountain biking would never have been built.)

Fish Lake Resort is the current rendition of one of the oldest mountain getaways in Utah, with roots dating back to 1911, when Charles Skougaard built a rudimentary tent camp on the lake's shore. The present lodge is not new by any means; it was built in 1932 of logs cut from Pelican Canyon, the lower portion of which you'll cross on this ride. Fish Lake offers superb fishing and is particularly well known for its monster lake trout. The area's high elevation and top-notch campgrounds make it a popular summer getaway even for nonangling low-country dwellers, and its heralded autumn aspen displays bring in some of Utah's most dedicated leaf peepers.

General location: 45 miles southeast of Richfield.

Elevation change: Lofty Fish Lake is at an elevation of 8,800 feet, and you climb 200 or 300 feet above it on this ride.

Season: June through October.

Services: Meals, accommodations, and some groceries are available at Fish Lake Lodge, the trailhead, and at Bowery Haven Resort, passed at just over a mile into the ride. Drinking water can be found at the resorts and at the many campgrounds in the vicinity. However, if coming in from the northwest, you'll still want to stock up on food in Richfield; if approaching from the southeast, purchase supplies in Torrey or Loa.

Hazards: Take care riding along the highway.

Rescue index: Although much of the ride feels isolated because of the dense forest surroundings, you're never too far from the paved road. Help can be summoned at the resorts on Fish Lake, and there are pay phones at those and at some of the Forest Service campgrounds, including Mackinaw. A Forest Service guard station is located near Fish Lake Resort.

Land status: Fishlake National Forest.

RIDE 45 · Lakeshore Trail West
RIDE 46 · Mytoge Mountain Loop

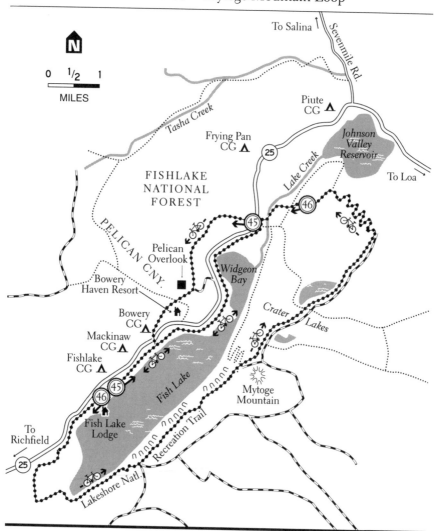

Maps: Fishlake National Forest visitor map.

Finding the trail: The ride starts from the parking lot at Fish Lake Lodge.

Source of additional information:

Fishlake National Forest
115 East 900 North
Richfield, UT 84701
(435) 896-9233

Notes on the trail: From the Fish Lake Lodge parking lot, ride around the northeast side of the lodge and turn left onto the Lakeshore National Recreation Trail, crossing

Twin Creek. The smooth pathway runs between the lake and the highway. Between 1 and 1.5 miles, at Bowery Haven Resort, turn right/northwest onto the pavement. At 4.5 miles, immediately before the Lake Creek Trailhead on the right, turn left off the highway to resume riding on the Lakeshore NRT. Climb for more than 0.5 mile to skirt some private property, then pass through a gate. On the sand-surfaced trail you'll ride across a couple of boardwalks, then climb some more. At 6 miles curve through a broad, grassy swale, earning stupendous views down on the road and the lake. At just under 6.5 miles resume climbing into the woods, then hit a curve in a major gravel road and turn right onto it, arriving at Pelican Overlook at just under 7 miles. From here you're faced with several alternatives. Recommended: Go up-draw through the fence line, then go immediately left where the trail splits. At 7.5 miles you'll make a left toward "Bowery Resort—1 Mile" to pass through an uncommonly beautiful aspen-fir forest. One-quarter of a mile later, bear right along the contouring trail rather than left downhill. At just beyond 8 miles, start steeply down through the aspen, bearing straight at the minor fork in 0.25 mile to enter the aspen rather than riding down through sagebrush. Soon, if you've managed to stay on track, you'll emerge in Site 33 of Bowery Campground. Head down through the campground on pavement, and at 9 miles turn right onto the highway, then immediately left off of it, riding back onto the Lakeshore NRT and closing the loop. At 10 miles you're back at Fish Lake Lodge.

RIDE 46 · Mytoge Mountain Loop

AT A GLANCE

Length/configuration: 20-mile loop

Aerobic difficulty: Difficult, incorporating at least 0.5 mile of climbing, much of it on steep single-track

Technical difficulty: Difficult, due to a combination of excruciatingly steep single-track climbing and exceedingly steep, rock-strewn descending. Other surfaces include lakeside cinder trail, double-track, and pavement.

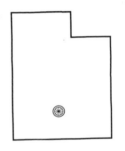

Scenery: From ride's beginning on Fish Lake, you look up at Mytoge Mountain; just a few miles into the ride, you look down from Mytoge Mountain onto glimmering Fish Lake

Special comments: The centerpiece of September's annual Fish Lake in the Fall Mountain Bike Festival

This 20-mile loop begins innocuously enough. Following the cinder-surfaced Lakeshore National Recreation Trail along Fish Lake, you dart in and out of aspen stands—some of them particularly beautiful, underscored by a ground covering of tight little bursts of shrub juniper. Things quickly get more difficult after 4.5 miles, as you face a series of challenging switchbacks. Much of the ensuing climb will be walked by mere mortals. A mile into it you come to a park bench overlook (none too soon), where you can take a load off and enjoy a long gander. Once you get on top the

Gearing up at Fish Lake Lodge before the big climb up Mytoge Mountain.

trail is still signed as the Lakeshore NRT, which is a misnomer of magnificent proportion, since by now you're 1,000 feet above the lake. Relatively new single-track on top feeds into a four-wheel-drive road passing the Crater Lakes, which are followed by a very difficult descent that beats you up en route back to the lower lands.

The "Notes on the trail" section is lengthy and tedious—a necessary evil, as navigation can be tricky. (Note: I rode this trail not long after the new sections of single-track were built on Mytoge Mountain. The signing situation may have changed, but for the better if so.) It's already a long, hard ride, but if you have energy left on hitting the highway at mile 15.5, you can go a short distance southwest, then jump back north off the highway, joining the route of Ride 45 at mile 4.5. This entails an additional four miles of exquisite trail riding and turns Mytoge Mountain into a 21-mile loop almost entirely on trail and double-track.

General location: 45 miles southeast of Richfield.

Elevation change: 8,800 to 9,800 feet, but cumulative climbing is much more than this indicates.

Season: June through October.

Services: Meals, accommodations, and some groceries are available at Fish Lake Lodge, the trailhead; drinking water can be found there and at the many campgrounds in the vicinity. Still, if coming in from the northwest, you'll want to stock up on food in Richfield; if approaching from the southeast, purchase supplies in Torrey or Loa.

Hazards: Steep climbs are common, and there's a memorably radical, rocky descent 12 miles into the ride—probably just about the time you're feeling bushed and letting your guard down.

Rescue index: Most of the ride is fairly remote, although four-wheel-drive vehicles can get on or quite close to the trail in many places. You might also encounter hikers and/or equestrians. Help can be summoned at the resorts on Fish Lake, and there are pay phones at those and at some of the area's Forest Service campgrounds, including Mackinaw. Also, a Forest Service guard station is located near Fish Lake Resort.

Land status: Fishlake National Forest.

Maps: Fishlake National Forest visitor map.

Finding the trail: The ride starts from the parking lot at Fish Lake Lodge.

Source of additional information:

Fishlake National Forest
115 East 900 North
Richfield, UT 84701
(435) 896-9233

Notes on the trail: From the Fish Lake Lodge parking area, ride around the northeast side of the lodge and turn right/southwest onto the Lakeshore National Recreation Trail. At a little over 1 mile pop out in front of the Lakeside Resort, crossing a boat-launch access road and then pedaling through a sagebrush opening. Soon you'll cross a paved road leading down to the lake, where you continue straight uphill on the Lakeshore NRT. At 2.5 miles, about 0.5 mile after passing through a gate, turn onto the rough road, then (just past a cattle-loading chute) turn immediately left back onto the trail. At 3 miles, curve right along the fence line and begin climbing through aspens. At 3.5 miles, back at lake level, turn left to aim eastward and weave through the woods on a rocky section of trail. A mile later begin climbing steeply to confront a series of challenging switchbacks. At 5.5 miles, a little past the viewpoint and bench, go through a fence gap and turn left to follow the fence line on the signed Lakeshore NRT. And you thought the climbing was over! In another 0.75 mile resume climbing on trail newly cut in 1997 (it was rough when I rode it, but it's probably mellowed by now). At just past 6.5 miles, shoot straight through the opening toward a sign marking the Lakeshore NRT. In another mile, cross an unusual, three-dimensional "cattle guard"; 0.25 mile past there, in an opening, go straight ahead on the more gravelly surfaced track, curving left around an aspen grove. You'll then see a Lakeshore NRT trail sign, which you follow into the woods. At 8.5 miles start descending. Important: At 9 miles, in a clearing, rather than veering left to continue along the Lakeshore NRT, bear right onto the double-track, curving through a meadow and staying to the right of some hillside corrals. In about 100 yards, bear right onto the more distinct double-track; then, at the Y in another 100 yards (still in the opening), bear left onto an even more apparent double-track. Just past 9.5 miles you'll see a sign reading "Fish Lake Highway—4 Miles," where you bear straight, passing the first of a pair of Crater Lakes. Climb for about 0.5 mile out of the crater, as the trail becomes a much rougher four-wheel-drive track. At 10.5 miles bear right around North Crater Lake toward "Lake Creek Trailhead—3 Miles." From here you'll climb for a ways, eventually passing through a gate at about 12.5 miles to commence an incredibly gnarly downhill. Feel free to walk, but even then be careful not to twist an ankle. A half-mile later enter a clearing, where the trail becomes quite cruisable for a few tenths. Although it may seem wrong, you'll soon curve southwest up-drainage, away from Johnson Valley Reservoir. At 13.5 miles turn left toward "Porcupine Draw" to meander through an open basin; the trail braids out, but Carsonite signs mark the basic route. Just past 14 miles, bear right at the trail junction toward "Lake Creek Trailhead" and ride into the aspens. In about 0.25 mile, you'll crest a low saddle and start down. Just past 15 miles, go straight at the inverted **Y** toward Lake Creek Trailhead. You'll come into a wetlands area where the trail temporarily disappears; simply head straight to ford the creek and then turn left onto the apparent trail. (There is a bridge a couple of hundred yards to the left before you crossed the creek, but you'd probably get just as wet in the marshes surrounding the bridge as you will fording the creek here.) Pop up into the parking area for the Lake Creek trailhead, then ride up to the highway and turn left. Just beyond the Bowery Haven Resort, at about 18.5 miles, you can leave the highway to the left and ride back onto the Lakeshore NRT. After crossing Twin Creek, turn right at 20 miles into Fish Lake Resort and close the loop. Whew!

RIDE 47 · UM Pass

AT A GLANCE

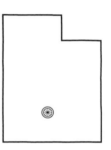

Length/configuration: 18-mile combination with a 0.5-mile spur leading to a 17-mile loop

Aerobic difficulty: Moderately difficult, due to the steep 2.5-mile climb beginning 4 miles into the ride; overall, roughly 2,000 feet are gained

Technical difficulty: Moderately difficult, incorporating pavement, graded two-wheel-drive road, compacted double-track, eroded and muddied ATV trail, rocky stream fords, and a technical downhill with major whoop-de-doos

Scenery: From UM Pass, a saddle separating Mts. Marvine and Terrill, the big, beautiful basin spreading out before you is made up of ponds, meadows, and aspen groves

Special comments: UM Pass and UM Creek were named in honor of the author of this book, who is a University of Montana (UM) graduate

This 18-mile ride is almost a straightaway loop, except for the short, one-half-mile spur at the beginning and end. With 2,000 feet of climbing involved, including a physically challenging 2.5-mile climb to UM Pass, the ride is rated moderately difficult; ditto in regard to technicality, owing to a diversity of riding surfaces that include pavement, graded two-wheel-drive road, dirt double-track, eroded and mucked-out ATV trail, and, most notably, a very fun and quite hazardous descent from the pass that serves up a series of huge humps built to control erosion and/or to preclude large motorized vehicles from accessing the old jeep trail. Lower your saddle before diving off the pass and maintain a light touch on the brakes, particularly the front ones, or you'll chance going ass over over teacups in a big and painful way. Also before descending, take a good look around from UM Pass, which is basically a saddle sitting 1,000 feet below 11,610-foot Mount Marvine to the south and, to the north, 11,537-foot Mount Terrill.

General location: 50 miles southeast of Richfield.

Elevation change: 8,800 to 10,500 feet.

Season: June through October.

Services: Meals, accommodations, and some groceries are available at Fish Lake Lodge (7.5 miles southwest of the trailhead) and Bowery Haven Resort (6 miles southwest); drinking water can be found at the resorts and at the various campgrounds lining Fish Lake. Still, if coming in from the northwest, you'll probably want to stock up on supplies in Richfield; if approaching from the southeast, procure food and camping supplies in Torrey or Loa.

Hazards: Over the first 4 miles of the route you will likely meet a bit of tourist, stock grower, and/or logging traffic in summer, and hunters in October; the same goes for the road sections over the last 9 miles. Go gingerly on the descent from UM Pass, or one of several large earth berms may put you into orbit before you know what hit you. Below that stretch, watch for unexpected holes in the road surface.

Rescue index: Your best strategy in an emergency will be to flag down a passing motorist or to return to Fish Lake Lodge or Bowery Haven Resort. Pay phones are found at the resorts and at some of the area's Forest Service campgrounds, including Mackinaw. There's also a Forest Service guard station located near Fish Lake Resort.

Land status: Fishlake National Forest.

Maps: Fishlake National Forest visitor map.

Finding the trail: From Fish Lake Lodge, drive a little over 7 miles northeast on pavement and turn left toward Piute Campground, situated opposite Johnson Valley Reservoir. Park in the large lower parking area.

Source of additional information:

Fishlake National Forest
115 East 900 North
Richfield, UT 84701
(435) 896-9233

Notes on the trail: From the parking lot, ride northeasterly on pavement, turning left at just under 0.5 mile onto the gravel Sevenmile Road toward Gooseberry and Salina. Start climbing at a fairly gradual but steady grade. At about 1 mile cumulative you'll pass a trail going left to the Fish Lake Hightop Plateau via Tasha Creek; then, 0.5 mile later, cross a cattle guard to enter a broad, grassy basin ringed with aspen groves. Just past 4 miles, turn right off the main road onto the dirt track leading uphill through sagebrush meadow. The ensuing climb is a good test—tough but entirely rideable—over a surface that is quite rutted in places. At UM Pass, gained at just over 6.5 miles cumulative, ride straight toward the corral/fencing (another trail forks right). On the right-hand side of the obvious structure, turn left to go through the gate to start a technical downhill that includes a series of monster earth berms that are equally riotous and hazardous. Toward the bottom, bear right toward "UM Sheep Road—3 Miles," continuing down on double-track ATV trail. At 7.5 miles you should pass a sign reading "Black Flat—1 Mile." About 0.25 mile from there cross a small stream, followed by a very rocky stretch of trail. Less than 0.5 mile later cross the Left Fork of UM Creek and make a short climb to pass through an old log fence line; then, at 8.5 miles cumulative, come to the Right Fork of UM

RIDE 47 · UM Pass

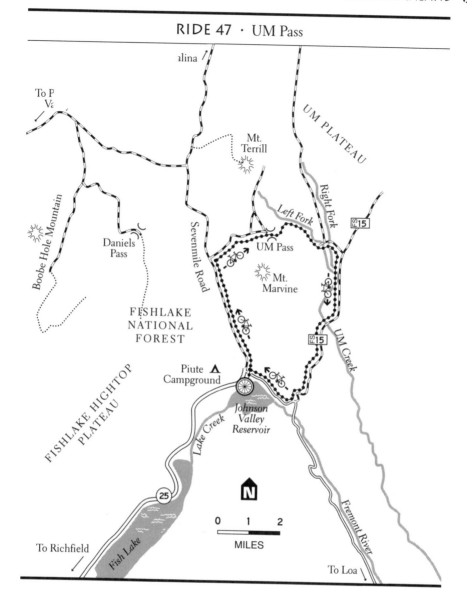

Creek in an area severely mucked up by off-road vehicles. Look around for the best way to cross the creek, then bear right onto a somewhat better four-wheel-drive road. One-half mile beyond the stream crossing, turn right onto the higher-grade road signed "Great Western Trail ATV Route." The road goes up another notch in quality in about 1.5 miles. At 11.5 miles cumulative, go from one side of UM Creek to the other, then ride on the level to 13 miles-plus, where you'll cross a cattle guard and start a 1.5-mile climb to the highway. Turn right onto the pavement at approximately 14.5 miles, and proceed 3.5 miles back to the beginning, skirting Johnson Valley Reservoir as you go.

RIDE 48 · Glenwood Getaway

AT A GLANCE

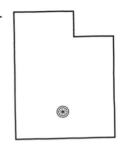

Length/configuration: 14-mile loop

Aerobic difficulty: Easy to moderate, with only about 800 feet of climbing

Technical difficulty: Easy, over pavement and gravel (with some washboard possible)

Scenery: From a badlands setting of scrub brush and piñon-juniper backed by flat-topped Cove Mountain, you descend to floodplain flats to skirt wetlands and alfalfa fields

Special comments: A fun lowlands ride with the spin-off benefit of a visit to historic Glenwood

There's a ton and a half of riding possibilities in the rocky foothills and forested slopes east of Richfield; this ride is a proverbial drop in the bucket. Richfield possesses an ambience that makes it feel rather like a less developed version of Moab, to the extent of red-rock bluffs rising over the west edge of town. The town's original name was Omni, a character from the Book of Mormon, which goes right along with Moab. Considering the riding potential in the area, it could conceivably *become* another Moab. For one thing, Richfield is the primary jumping-off point for the Fish Lake Plateau, which already has gained a degree of notoriety among mountain bikers, largely (1) because it deserves it, and (2) because of September's popular Fish Lake in the Fall Mountain Bike Festival, which has introduced the area to dozens of bikers from afar.

Aerobically, this 14-mile loop is rated easy to moderate; technically, it is easy, as you deal only with paved and well-graded gravel roads. It's a study in contrasts, with piñon, juniper, and scrub predominating at the upper elevations, whereas along the verdant wetland flats you'll see cattails, cows, and Russian olive trees (mmmmm, they smell sooo good!). At about 11 miles into the ride, just past a ragged farmstead, on the right you'll notice an old rock-and-timber corral that blends exquisitely into its surroundings—primarily because it's *constructed* of its surroundings.

Glenwood, where the ride begins and ends, has little in the way of services, but it has substantial appeal for history/architecture buffs. Tour the streets and you'll discover an interesting mix of the new (largely due to the town's role as a "suburb" of Richfield) and the old. Back in the 1870s Glenwood's Mormon settlers experimented with Brigham Young's "United Order," a sort of communal/communistic arrangement under which the local farms and industries were all cooperatively owned, and the cumulative proceeds from them were equally divied out—that is, everyone, regardless of occupation, was paid the same. It didn't work all that well. Several attractive, century-plus-old rock houses are found in town (you'll pass at least a couple of them on the route), along with other historic structures—including the 1879 mercantile located near ride's beginning and the 1874 Joseph Wall Gristmill, a sturdy-looking fortress of brick and volcanic rock.

RIDE 48 · Glenwood Getaway
RIDE 49 · Sevier Grunt

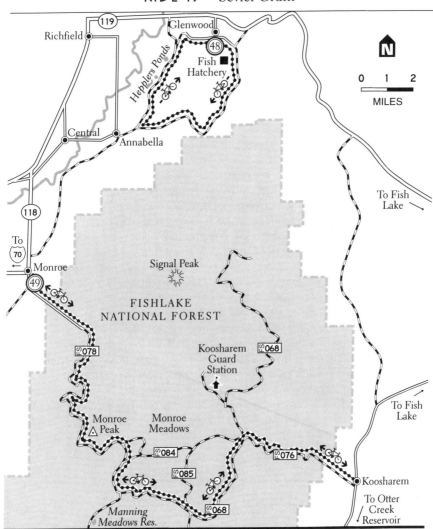

General location: Begins and ends in Glenwood, 5 miles east of Richfield.

Elevation change: Roughly 5,300 to 6,100 feet.

Season: May through October; midday in summer can be very hot.

Services: Richfield is the closest full-service town.

Hazards: There might be some traffic on the roads followed, but not much. All in all, quite a tame outing.

Rescue index: You're never very far from towns and highways on this ride.

Land status: BLM, state, private.

Maps: Fishlake National Forest visitor map.

Finding the trail: From Richfield, drive 5 miles east of town on UT 119, then turn right/south and continue for about a mile into Glenwood. Park in the vicinity of the Town Hall, at the corner of Center and Main.

Source of additional information:

> Richfield District BLM
> 150 East 900 North
> Richfield, UT 84701
> (435) 896-8221

Notes on the trail: From where you parked, ride east on Center Street. Pass the Mormon Church on the left and a gorgeous old rock abode on the right, then begin climbing into desiccated uplands. At about 1 mile go straight toward Cove Mountain, riding onto gravel (a right here goes into the fish hatchery and left goes to the highway). At 2.5 miles-plus, cross a cattle guard; you're now behind the protective confines of a badland barrier ridge, where potential exploratory spurs take off from the main route here and there. At the divide at about 3.5 miles, bear right toward "Anna Bella 5 miles." At 5 miles, at a high point, you'll come around a bend to see Richfield spreading away in the distance, backed by the high Pahvant Range. At just over 6 miles ride from BLM onto state lands; then, a mile later, onto private lands (but on a public-access road). At 8 miles—just after crossing a cattle guard—in the middle of a ranch yard, turn right onto an unsigned gravel road (after turning you should have a board-and-barbed-wire fence on your right and telephone line on the left). This road quickly curves right, then left. At about 9 miles pass under a big power line, then curve left to begin twisting and crawling along the base of Bull Claim Hill, just above the picturesque Hepplers Ponds. Bear right at 12 miles, passing under the power line, to climb through a low notch. In another 0.5 mile swing right around the toe of the ridge to ride along a shelf as you overlook a classically bucolic scene of fields, fences, and horses. At about 13 miles cumulative you'll come down off the hill, taking straight aim at Glenwood. Back on pavement, turn left at the T, then immediately right onto Center Street to pass another historic house. Return to the beginning at just over 14 miles.

RIDE 49 · Sevier Grunt

AT A GLANCE

Length/configuration: 33-mile point-to-point

Aerobic difficulty: Difficult

Technical difficulty: Moderate, over pavement, (steep) graded gravel, and rough dirt

Scenery: Ever changing; all things considered, some of the most amazing views in Panoramaland

Special comments: Physically this is an excruciating ride; one of those you do primarily for the challenge . . . and to be able to say you did it

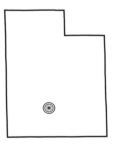

G etting bored with those wimpy rides where you bag only 2,000 or 3,000 feet of climbing? Then try this one, which gains almost a vertical mile over the course of approximately 15 miles—with more than half the elevation accrued in just 6 miles, between mile 2 and mile 8. The 31-mile point-to-point begins in the Sevier River Valley (Sevier is pronounced "severe," and this ride certainly is). Technically it's not bad, since you pedal on surfaces of pavement, graded gravel, and dirt; both scenically and aerobically, however, it's a real killer. Dropping out you don't lose as much elevation as you gain going up, as Koosharem sits more than 1,000 feet higher than Monroe. Be aware that, unless your shuttle driver has high-clearance four-wheel-drive, he or she would be well advised not to follow the same route you're taking. Rather, he should drive north from Monroe to Richfield, then to Koosharem by way of UT 119, UT 24, and UT 62.

Monroe, where the riding begins, is a pleasant little town. If you cannot arrange to be picked up in Koosharem, you could turn this into a 30-mile out-and-back by making the 15-mile, mile-high climb, then backtracking to Monroe. The problem is, much of the descent is so steep and dangerously curving that it won't be a lot of fun, as you work to keep your speed in check. On the other hand, the climb isn't that much fun either, so maybe this would even things out. The good news is that there's a commercial hot springs in Monroe, where at ride's end you could soak your aching hands and the rest of your aching self.

General location: The ride begins in the Sevier River Valley community of Monroe and ends in Koosharem, situated in the Grass Valley.

Elevation change: Approximately 5,400 to 10,400 feet.

Season: June through October.

Services: Monroe and Koosharem are the closest towns with services.

Hazards: Running out of energy, water, food, and/or leg strength; flying off the road on the descent.

Rescue index: You may run into Forest Service personnel on the route, but don't count on it. There's also quite a number of rustic private cabins on high, some of which may contain occupants.

Land status: Fishlake National Forest, along with some BLM and private lands.

Maps: Fishlake National Forest visitor map.

Finding the trail: Begin riding at the junction in Monroe that by now is beginning to sound familiar, regardless of which southern Utah town you're in: the corner of Center and Main. Plenty of parking is located nearby.

Source of additional information:

Fishlake National Forest
115 East 900 North
Richfield, UT 84701
(435) 896-9233

Notes on the trail: Ride south on Main toward "Monrovian Park," curving left in 0.75 mile to remain on pavement. At 2 miles you're gobbled by the jaws of a canyon, as you enter the Fishlake National Forest on FS 078, a paved road that's basically one lane wide. After passing through an exceptionally narrow canyon section, ride onto gravel at 3.5 miles, then bear right steeply uphill toward "Manning Meadows Reservoir/Monroe

Meadows." You'll get a real cliff-hanging sensation in the 5.5-mile range, then skirt Oak Flat in another 0.5 mile, with Signal Peak and Monroe Mountain ahead left. Incredible valley views unfold below in the 6.5-mile range. You'll note that things are getting more "alpiney" the higher you go; at 9 miles the grade mellows some as you get closer to the top. At just under 12 miles pass Devils Dutch Oven; then, at about 13.5 miles, pass a track going left to Monroe Peak. (If you haven't climbed enough, you could try continuing to the top of that 11,227-foot mountain.) In another mile, where a double-track forks left, bear right on the more distinct road. This is approximately the high point of the ride. At 15 miles, go right toward Monroe Mountain Road on FS 078 (left goes into private property). At 16 miles, at a four-way junction, go straight toward Manning Meadows Reservoir, where left goes to Monroe Meadows. By now the route has turned substantially rougher. About a mile from there, bear left toward Squaw Springs and Monroe Mountain Road, where a right leads to Manning Meadows Reservoir and Big Flat. You'll encounter quite a bit of up and down over the next few miles, and the road quality again improves some. At just under 18 miles, where a driveway goes left up to a house, go straight downhill on the main road, entering an area of aspen-regeneration cuts. In another mile cross a cattle guard and come into a setting of broad, rolling sage flats flanked by stands of aspen; it's markedly different from where you've been up to this point. At 21 miles FS 085 comes in on the left (there's also a track going right); continue straight on what is now signed as ATV route "Paiute Trail 01." Just beyond here come to a fork where FS 068 goes both ways; you'll want to turn left toward "Koosharem 13 miles." One-half mile later, bear left on Paiute Trail 01; right goes toward "State Road 62—7 miles." Up and down through drainages you go, on a good road that's rather like an extra-wide, extra-buffed single-track. At 24 miles pass FS 085 on the left again; then, at 26.5 miles, turn right onto the better gravel road toward "Koosharem 7 miles" and start losing elevation rapidly down a mean, twisty, winding run. At just over 33 miles you'll come to Koosharem and ride's end at the corner of— you guessed it—Center and Main. Wow!

RIDE 50 · Lott Creek Trials and Piñon–Juniper Hillclimb

AT A GLANCE

Length/configuration: 5.5-mile double out-and-back (one spur about 1.25 miles long and another that's 1.5 miles long)

Aerobic difficulty: Easy to moderate, due to the short distance of the ride; still, it includes a good 700 feet of climbing

Technical difficulty: Some very tricky moves are necessary/possible on the Lott Creek Trail section of the ride. In addition to single-track, riding surfaces include improved gravel and sandy ATV trail

Scenery: From the high point, there's a terrific look down on the "tent rock" formations of volcanic tuff and the surrounding mountains

RIDE 50 · Lott Creek Trials and Piñon–Juniper Hillclimb
RIDE 51 · Clear Creek–Fish Creek

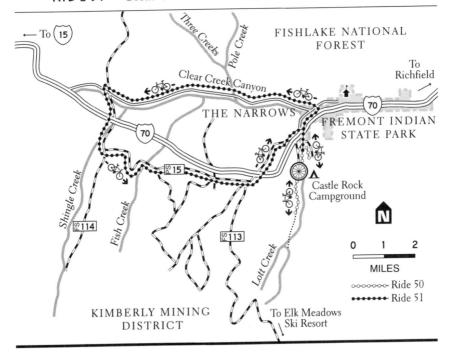

Special comments: A fun little pre- or after-supper outing to do in preparation for tomorrow's more substantial ride. Measurements were taken from Site 20 in Castle Rock Campground

Why do this short ride? Because it's there! After all, distance isn't everything. The brief yet surprisingly varied ride begins and ends at Castle Rock Campground, which is within the Fishlake National Forest but is also associated with nearby Fremont Indian State Park. It's an unusually pleasant campgound, with plenty of shade provided by huge aspens, cottonwoods, and ponderosa pines. Just 5.5 miles in length, the ride consists of two short spurs: a 2.5-mile out-and-back up the interesting and technical Lott Creek Trail 051 (1.25 miles each way, climbing about 300 feet); and a 3-mile out-and-back taking you onto the juniper-piñon benchlands overlooking the campground (1.5 miles each way, climbing 400 feet). Riding surfaces include single-track, improved gravel, and a sandy segment of a side trail of the popular Paiute ATV Trail. The single-track portion is exceptionally pretty, and it dishes up several technical creek crossings and enough exposure to make even that famous bicyclist Peewee Herman give pause. Feel free to ride as far as you can up the trail, but it does get very difficult. It's a pleasant enough setting that you may choose to ditch your bike and take a hike, a mode of travel for which the trail is better suited. The second, rim-top turnaround, reached after four miles of riding, is an exquisite place to watch the sun go down over the Pahvant and Tushar Mountains.

Pull up to the top and watch the sunset over the Pahvant and Tushar Mountains.

While in the area, visit the Fremont Indian State Park Visitor Center/Museum and also consider hiking the trails behind the Visitor Center. Indians of the Fremont culture—whose prehistoric presence was first identified by modern archaeologists in the late 1920s along the Fremont River near Capitol Reef National Park—fashioned distinctive pottery styles and unique pictographs (painted on rock) and petroglyphs (chiseled and etched into the desert varnish veneer of rock surfaces). This state park encompasses one of the most extensive Fremont rock art collections ever identified. Five Finger Ridge Village, the largest Fremont settlement known, was discovered here in 1983 during construction of I-70 through Clear Creek Canyon. Containing more than 100 structures, it's estimated that at its zenith Five Finger Ridge Village was home to more than 200 residents. After excavations were completed, the village was destroyed to make way for the highway, but many of the findings are displayed today in the state park museum. Previous to the Fremonts, hunter-gatherers are thought to have visited the Clear Creek Canyon area at least 7,000 years ago. Even today, the canyon has sacred significance for Paiute Indians.

General location: 25 miles southwest of Richfield.

Elevation change: Approximately 6,000 to 6,400 feet.

Season: March through November.

Services: Richfield is the closest full-service town. Water is available at the campground where the ride begins.

Hazards: The first part of the ride on Lott Creek Trail 051 is quite technical. Novices will enjoy the mellower stretches, but they'll want to walk the stream crossings and precipitous sidehills.

Rescue index: You're never far from the campground. If no one is camping there, help can be procured at the Fremont Indian State Park Visitor Center.

Land status: Fishlake National Forest.

Maps: Fishlake National Forest visitor map.

Finding the trail: 20 miles southwest of Richfield on I-70, take Exit 17 toward Fremont Indian State Park; Castle Rock Campground, the trailhead, is a little over 1 mile south on FS 478 (on the opposite side of the interstate from the state park headquarters).

Source of additional information:

Fremont Indian State Park
11550 West Clear Creek Canyon Road
Sevier, UT 84766
(435) 527-4631

Notes on the trail: Opposite Site 20, ride onto Fishlake Trail 051, heading up Lott Creek. The trail starts off with a shaly and sandy surface. You'll cross the creek four times over the first 0.75 mile, and the suggested turnaround comes at about 1.25 miles. Now, back at the campground, at 2.5 miles cumulative, continue downhill and out of the campground. At 3 miles, turn right uphill onto Paiute Sidetrail 78. In about 0.5 mile turn right away from Paiute Sidetrail 78, which veers left. Immediately curve left, then left again, trending up toward the ridge top. Continue following the main track as spurs go this way and that, attempting to seduce you into exploring off-route. At 4 miles you'll arrive at a rim that provides an outstanding look down on the campground, at the tent rocks of volcanic tuff and down the mountain-shrouded interstate corridor. Turn around here, returning to Site 20 at 5.5 miles.

RIDE 51 · Clear Creek–Fish Creek

AT A GLANCE

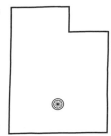

Length/configuration: 20.5-mile combination consisting of a short out-and-back (1.25 miles each way) connecting to an 18-mile loop

Aerobic difficulty: Moderate, with more than 1,000 feet of climbing

Technical difficulty: Moderate, over good gravel, pavement/chipseal, packed sediment, and some gnarly four-wheel-drive track where you toil with Fish Creek and its environs

Scenery: Clear Creek Canyon is a highlight, as are the magnificent views of the volcanic Tushar Mountains, visible to the south once you gain elevation

Pretty little Clear Creek dances alongside the road.

Special comments: This ride has a surprisingly wild feel to it considering that you're rarely out of hearing range of trafficked highways. Follow the mileage log carefully—your intrepid author spent about 5 hours and 30 miles doing this 20.5-mile ride.

Like Ride 50, this 20.5-mile outing—consisting of a 1.25-mile spur connecting to an 18-mile loop—begins at the pleasant Castle Rock Campground. After setting out on gravel, you'll follow pavement for seven miles, passing through the stunning Narrows of Clear Creek Canyon. The route then descends under I-70 before climbing onto the sporadically forested slopes south of the interstate and subsequently getting into some rough four-wheel-drive stuff down around Fish Creek. Route finding can be a challenge, but it shouldn't be too bad if you pay close attention to the detailed and lengthy "Notes on the trail." Overall, the ride is rated moderate in terms of both aerobic and technical difficulty.

General location: 25 miles southwest of Richfield.

Elevation change: Roughly 5,900 to 6,900 feet.

Season: March through November.

Services: Richfield is the closest full-service town. Water is available at the campground where the ride begins.

Hazards: Watch for dogs in pursuit during the first part of the ride, where you pass several rural homes; also, you might encounter some car traffic in Clear Creek Canyon, so ride defensively. Take care descending to Fish Creek and on other technical portions of the route.

Rescue index: You're never really far from I-70, yet parts of the ride are remote and unpeopled. The best place to go for help is Fremont Indian State Park headquarters.

Land status: State, Fishlake National Forest.

Maps: Fishlake National Forest visitor map.

Finding the trail: 20 miles southwest of Richfield on I-70, take Exit 17 toward Fremont Indian State Park. Castle Rock Campground, the trailhead, is a little over 1 mile south on FS 478 (on the opposite side of the interstate from the state park headquarters).

Source of additional information:

Fremont Indian State Park
11550 West Clear Creek Canyon Road
Sevier, UT 84766
(435) 527-4631

Notes on the trail: From Castle Rock Campground, ride for 1 mile downhill on gravel back to I-70. Cross the interstate and turn right onto pavement toward Fremont Indian Museum and Clear Creek Canyon, then turn left up Clear Creek Canyon at the stop sign at 1.5 miles (the museum is 0.75 mile to the right). Pretty little Clear Creek hisses and dances below stands of oak and poplar. At 3 miles enter the Narrows of Clear Creek Canyon, where for about 0.5 mile there's scarcely room for both the creek and the road to squeeze through. At 5 miles pass the mouth of Fish Creek on the left; then, at just over 8 miles, turn left onto FS 114, passing under the monstrous interstate overpasses in another 0.75 mile. Continuing down, 0.25 mile from the interstate you'll ride through a creek on a cement slab; beyond that point, continue curving right uphill through timber rather than turning left onto the fainter track (you may note a Carsonite marker referring to Paiute Sidetrail 15). At 10 miles, turn left off FS 114, following PS 15 into a broad, flat opening. Shortly after turning, be sure to curve right to follow PS 15 downhill, rather than following the fainter track as it continues along the ridge. You'll enjoy a trio of successive piñon-juniper interludes over the next mile, as tremendous Tushar Mountain views erupt to the south. At just under 11 miles, bear right downhill on the main trail. (As I discovered, the fainter track going left rapidly drops 0.5 mile to some cattle tanks.) Just beyond there, continue very steeply down on the main trail, where another faint track drops left (as I likewise discovered, this one descends nearly a mile to the rim of Fish Creek Canyon). The route winds around to cross the head of a draw before dropping radically and rockily to Fish Creek. Ford Fish Creek at just over 12 miles and bear left after crossing a cattle guard; you'll then cross through the creek two more times. After crossing number three, at 12.5 miles, begin climbing, soon to switchback right into the steep-walled wash (still following Paiute Sidetrail 15 signs). After curving left out of the draw, at 13 miles you'll climb to see I-70's high bridges to the left. At a high point at 13.5 miles, with the twin ribbons of the interstate shimmering infinitely eastward, the track becomes more roadlike. In another mile, at another high point, you'll come in alongside the interstate to race east-bound traffic. At 15 miles merge with another road, then continue following Paiute Sidetrail 15 where FS 481 goes left under I-70. In just over another mile, turn left onto FS 113, a good gravel road, and go under the interstate. Close the loop 3 miles later, at 19.5 miles cumulative, and ride the 1 mile-plus back to the campground.

RIDE 52 · Marysvale Flat

AT A GLANCE

Length/configuration: 15.5-mile loop

Aerobic difficulty: Easy to moderate, with roughly 600 feet of cumulative climbing

Technical difficulty: Easy, over good gravel and paved roads

Scenery: A broad expanse of nothingness surrounded by the dark bulks of the hulking Tushar and Sevier Plateaus

Special comments: A nice ride unto itself, or as a warm-up to Ride 53

Marysvale "Flat" might be an overstated name for this ride, since on it you'll gain some 600 feet of elevation. However, relative to Ride 53, Marysvale Not-So-Flat, it really is quite level. The 15.5-mile loop is rated aerobically easy to moderate, but technically it is very easy. Road surfaces include pavement and good gravel, making it excellent for a leisurely (or not so leisurely) cruise. You'll pass a lot of intriguing roads and double-tracks that look like they'd provide excellent exploring and which, if pursued, would up the difficulty level of the adventure. You'll want to keep a close eye on "Notes on the trail," because those ample spurs also provide plenty of opportunities to take a wrong turn (or to go straight when you *should* turn). Incidentally, just north of Marysvale on US 89 is the multihued feature known as Big Rock Candy Mountain, the inspiration for both the song and the Wallace Stegner novel of the same name.

General location: The ride begins in Marysvale.

Elevation change: Approximately 5,950 to 6,450 feet.

Season: March through November.

Services: Marysvale has limited services, possibly including a bed-and-breakfast and an RV park (they appeared to be in a state of transition at this writing); Big Rock Candy Mountain, a few miles north of Marysvale, has a seasonal resort with lodging and some other services. The nearest full-service town is Richfield, 28 miles north.

Hazards: You may encounter auto traffic on the route. Watch out for chasing dogs whenever passing a rural settlement.

Rescue index: There's a good chance you'll share the route with a small amount of vehicle traffic. You also pass some homes later in the ride.

Land status: BLM, private.

Maps: Fishlake National Forest visitor map or DeLorme *Utah Atlas & Gazetteer,* pages 26 and 27.

Finding the trail: The ride begins at the corner of Center and Main in the interesting old mining/agricultural town of Marysvale, located a few miles south of I-70 on US 89. Parking is available along the town's streets.

RIDE 52 · Marysvale Flat
RIDE 53 · Marysvale Not-So-Flat

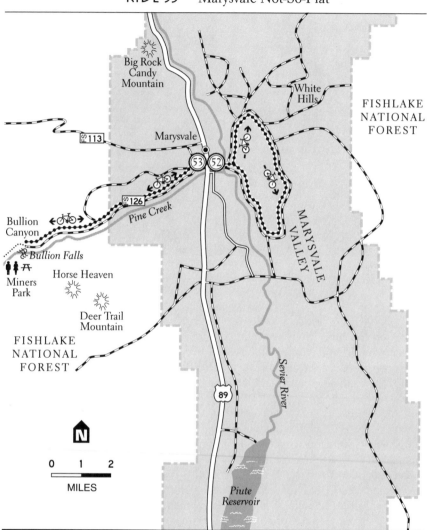

Source of additional information:

Richfield District BLM
150 East 900 North
Richfield, UT 84701
(435) 896-8221

Plenty of double-tracks branch off this main road, inviting off-route exploration.

Notes on the trail: From beautiful "downtown" Marysvale, ride east on Center Street. After 0.5 mile, turn left following a BLM Carsonite marker reading "Marysvale Loop 02." Cross the Sevier River on a new bridge (with a classic old bridge to the right), then continue straight on Marysvale Loop 02 rather than bearing right uphill. You're now on a smooth gravel road. At 2 miles leave the flats to begin climbing into hills. At 2.5 miles continue right uphill on Marysvale Loop 02 rather than going left on the Paiute Sidetrail. In another 0.75 mile, go right following Marysvale Loop 02; immediately past there again bear right on Marysvale Loop 02 where a second road goes left to Willow Spring. At just over 4 miles, pass under some high wires and continue straight on Marysvale Loop 02 as another road goes left. You'll pass some old corrals and the gash of Durkee Creek on the right; the only thing spoiling the view is the power line. At 5.5 miles start a long downhill; then, 2 miles later, begin climbing again. At just past 9 miles you'll come to an important intersection: Go right/backward onto Paiute Sidetrail 35, leaving Marysvale Loop 02, which continues straight (reaching the Elbow Ranch in 1.5 miles). In another 1.5 miles, cross the Sevier River, probably with cattle and sheep looking on. At the four-way junction just past 11 miles, turn right uphill, still following gravel. At approximately 12.5 miles bear right onto pavement in Thompsonville, a most interesting little settlement. Just over 2 miles from there, bear right, staying on pavement amid a setting of houses and, more than likely, dogs. In another 0.75 mile, turn right onto the highway in Marysvale, closing the loop at 15.5 miles.

RIDE 53 · Marysvale Not-So-Flat

AT A GLANCE

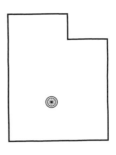

Length/configuration: 13-mile out-and-back (6.5 miles each way)

Aerobic difficulty: Difficult, as it gains nearly 2,000 feet in 6.5 miles

Technical difficulty: Easy to moderate, over good gravel and rough, rock-embedded two-wheel-drive road. The toughest technical challenge is keeping your speed in check on the way out.

Scenery: A narrow, dark, timbered gulley of the sort that seems to typifiy mining country

Special comments: To take your mind off the pain as you inch your way up Bullion Canyon, try singing the Grateful Dead's rendition of "I'd rather live in some dark hollow, where the sun don't ever shine. . ."

This ride, a simple out-and-back of 13 miles (6.5 miles each way), is technically quite easy, but it offers a real test of your aerobic conditioning, as it gains almost 2,000 feet of elevation. Over the early stretches of the ride you'll pass an eclectic array of habitations and yard art. It's a true hill-climb challenge, with history to boot. After about four miles, where you enter the national forest, you'll pass a greeting sign for the "Canyon of Gold Driving Tour." Here you can pick up a self-guiding brochure containing interpretive information keyed to numbered posts seen along the final 2.5 miles. Gold mining took place at least as early as the mid-1860s in Bullion Canyon, and possibly much earlier—as the brochure suggests—during the Spanish conquistador days of the sixteenth and seventeenth centuries. Near the turnaround you'll pass a trailhead from which you can set out on a hike to Bullion Falls thence onward and upward, getting into some God-almighty gorgeous high country.

On the way out of the canyon you'll need to do some serious braking to keep your speed down; consequently, your hands will probably need some major massaging by the time you reclaim Marysvale. Roughly 2.5 miles into the trip down, if you're feeling adventurous, you could take a left onto Paiute Sidetrail 17 and try returning by way of Revenue Gulch, rejoining the main route just half a mile above Marysvale. This route is longer and entails a lot of climbing and descending.

General location: The ride begins in Marysvale.

Elevation change: Approximately 5,950 to 7,900 feet.

Season: April through October.

Services: Marysvale has limited services, possibly including a bed-and-breakfast and an RV park (they appeared to be in a state of transition at this writing); Big Rock

Candy Mountain, a few miles north of Marysvale, has a seasonal resort with lodging and some other services. The nearest full-service town is Richfield, 28 miles north.

Hazards: You might encounter auto traffic on the route; watch for chasing dogs (and peacocks!) when passing rural settlements. Take care on the way out, as you could easily get going too fast on the steep descent.

Rescue index: There's a good chance you'll share the route with car traffic, and you'll probably find campers near the turnaround.

Land status: Private, BLM, Fishlake National Forest.

Maps: Fishlake National Forest visitor map or DeLorme *Utah Atlas & Gazetteer*, page 26.

Finding the trail: The ride begins at the corner of Center and Main in Marysvale, located a few miles south of I-70 on US 89. Parking is available along the town's streets.

Source of additional information:

Fishlake National Forest
115 East 900 North
Richfield, UT 84701
(435) 896-9233

Notes on the trail: From the corner of Center and Main in Marysvale, go west on Center Street/Bullion Canyon Road. In 0.5 mile, go left at the junction toward Bullion Canyon. (Straight goes to Revenue Gulch, which offers an alternative way to come back to Marysvale; see information above. A hard right at the same point heads into the hills on FS 113, eventually meeting I-70 at Fremont Indian State Park by way of the Kimberly mining district. This could make for a very interesting ride.) A little past 1.5 miles bear right uphill on Bullion Canyon Road, where Kennedy Road goes left. The surface is old blacktop reverting to gravel. At 4 miles you'll enter the national forest, where the road narrows and its surface deteriorates into rock-embedded dirt. Continue very steeply up the constricted canyon, through stands of oak, ponderosa pine, and aspen. At 6.5 miles, soon after passing a trailhead and an ATV trail, you'll arrive at Miners Park (administered by the town of Marysvale). Here you'll find a picnic area and good camping, as well as a nice hiking trail visiting a number of old mining artifacts and structures—including an assay-office-turned-outhouse.

COLOR COUNTRY

From summits exceeding 12,000 feet to lowly deserts sprawling at around the 2,000-foot level, Color Country is even bigger from top to bottom than Canyonlands. That lowest corner, defined by the Virgin River basin, is nicknamed "Utah's Dixie" and with good reason—the climate is warm enough for growing cotton, a feat that early Mormon inhabitants did in fact accomplish in and around St. George.

Color Country is a region of startling beauty. You're not permitted to ride off-road in the four distinctly different national parks and monuments found here—Zion, Bryce Canyon, Cedar Breaks, and a portion of Capitol Reef—yet the Forest Service and/or Bureau of Land Management lands typically in close proximity offer scenery that is comparable to that of the parks and has the added advantage of being much less populated. Contrast, for example, Ride 60, Casto Canyon, which lacks almost nothing compared to nearby Bryce Canyon National Park, other than the cars, crowds, and visitor centers. Also within Color Country is a large share of the Glen Canyon National Recreation Area, as well as the new-in-1996 Grand Staircase–Escalante National Monument, which contains some terrific (albeit exceedingly remote) riding.

Even some of Color Country's state parks—Kodachrome Basin, Snow Canyon, and others—feature national park–caliber scenery. They might *be* national parks if they were located in a state more mundane, scenically speaking, than Utah. It's an impossible thing to quantify, but I would argue that there is more spectacular scenery per acre in Color Country than anywhere in the country. That scenery brings in a lot of people and makes tourism a very important industry—good thing, too, because much of the region makes a heck of a hard place to raise a cow.

The small but rapidly growing city of St. George is one of the focal points of mountain biking in Color Country. This retirement center is very popular with "snowbirds" who travel south in winter for warmth and sunshine. The trend was started way back in the early 1870s by none other than Brigham Young, who spent his last few winters here while overseeing the building of the town's Mormon temple and tabernacle.

There's a bunch of rides in the St. George vicinity; about a dozen of them are featured in this guide. Some mountain bikers may feel that the riding is inferior to that of the Moab area; others, though, might find that they like it better. It's very much a personal thing. Similar to Moab, the surrounding terrain is amazingly varied, with some outings that traverse slickrock, others following precipitous canyon rims, and still others that trace dirt single-tracks through scrub-covered desert.

A major advantage St. George enjoys over—make that *under*—Moab is that it's almost a quarter of a mile lower in elevation. This translates to even earlier spring and later fall riding seasons than those typical in Canyonlands. Even winter temperatures in and around St. George can reach into the 60s and higher. Know this, too: If you've thrown your clubs into the back of your rig—some mountain bikers do golf!—you're in luck. As far as Utah goes, what Moab is to mountain bikers, St. George is to golfers. Also like Moab, St. George boasts an outstanding Interagency Visitor Center (located at 345 East Riverside Drive), where you can pick up way more information than you'll need.

One aspect of St. George that is inferior to Moab is its nightlife; parties tend to happen at private homes or in motel rooms and rental condos. However, make the 35-mile drive to Mesquite, Nevada, cutting across the extreme northwest corner of Arizona as you do, and you're in another world, where the nightlife lasts not only all night but all day as well.

Brian Head Resort and the embracing Markugunt Plateau also contain a concentration of top-notch rides. The season is short for the highest of them, typically beginning in June and ending by October. But if you can slip in a trip during that short window of opportunity you will not be disappointed.

Over on the far eastern edge of Color Country, where this chapter begins, you can drive what is possibly the most scenic highway in the state—Utah 12, connecting Boulder and Escalante, two way-out-there settlements. Boulder was the last community in the lower 48 states to have mail delivered by vehicle. As you follow the winding byway you'll wonder how they ever managed to build a road over such an impossible expanse of slickrock canyons and knife-edge ridges—a world of earth-toned Navajo sandstone, swirling, dipping, and contouring toward infinity in every direction. North of Boulder, Highway 12 climbs from desert up and over Boulder Mountain, topping out at 9,200 feet and passing through some of the most expansive aspen stands in the world.

Between St. George and Boulder Mountain there's a whole lot more to be discovered. Have fun finding and riding it!

RIDE 54 · Rosebud Trail

AT A GLANCE

Length/configuration: 7.5-mile loop

Aerobic difficulty: Moderate, with a steady climb of 1,000 feet-plus from Lower Bown's Reservoir back to the trailhead

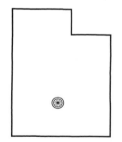

Technical difficulty: Moderate, with churned-up dirt and rocks possible on the rough ATV trail sections. (The trail was new when I rode it and will probably mellow with age.) Other riding surfaces include sand-covered and graded gravel roads.

Scenery: Begins in a forest of ponderosa pine and Douglas fir. As you lose elevation you also lose the timber cover, but you gain long-range views over the Waterpocket Fold and beyond.

Special comments: If you have a shuttle available or are riding self-supported, it is possible to continue down from Lower Bown's Reservoir all the way to the Scenic Drive in Capitol Reef National Park (see Ride 41)

RIDE 54 · Rosebud Trail

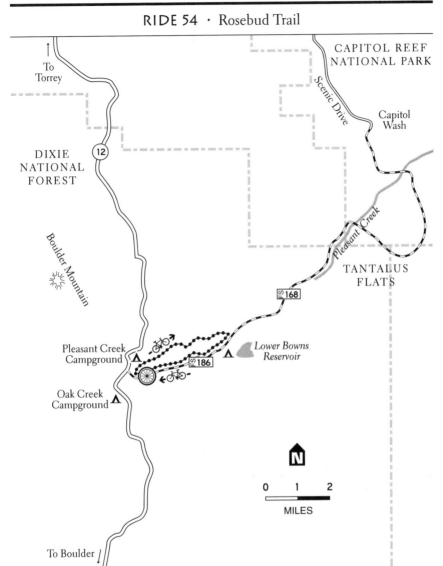

As you leave Torrey heading south on UT 12—a.k.a. the Clem Church Memorial Highway, a.k.a. the Boulder-Grover Road—from the Fremont River bottoms you climb higher, higher, higher. Eventually you reach the heralded aspen forests of Boulder Mountain on the east shoulder of the rugged volcanic highland known as the Aquarius Plateau. Fifteen miles into the drive you come to one of the most all-encompassing views in southern Utah, competing with the likes of Dead Horse Point and Powell Point. Spreading out to the east are the Waterpocket Fold, the Circle Cliffs, the Henry and La Sal Mountains, the San Rafael Swell, and much, much more.

Similar to the situation in a lot of the central and southern Utah highlands, this ride offers evidence that mountain bikers have great reason to retain good relations with ATVers, as a lot of trails built for the machines make excellent mountain bike trails, too. Although only 7.5 miles long, the ride is rated moderate both aerobically and technically; the former because of the 1,000-foot-plus climb over the last three miles, and the latter due to some potentially rough stuff (rocks, churned-up dirt, and sand) on the Rosebud ATV Trail. Nearby Pleasant Creek Campground makes a fine place to overnight, and you can easily begin and end the ride there.

General location: On Boulder Mountain, immediately west of Capitol Reef National Park.

Elevation change: Approximately 8,600 to 7,500 feet.

Season: June through October.

Services: Boulder and Torrey have all services. Water can be obtained at Pleasant Creek Campground, near the ride's beginning.

Hazards: Beware of angular, tire-grabbing rocks on the ATV trail. There may be some truck traffic on the return ride, as Lower Bown's Reservoir is a popular fishing spot.

Rescue index: You're never too far from roads carrying recreational traffic.

Land status: Dixie National Forest.

Maps: Dixie National Forest visitor map, Powell, Escalante and Teasdale Ranger Districts; or DeLorme *Utah Atlas & Gazetteer*, page 28.

Finding the trail: From Torrey, go 18 miles south on UT 12 (or, from Boulder, go 20 miles north on UT 12) and turn east toward Lower Bown's Reservoir. Drive a couple of hundred yards and park at the trailhead for the Rosebud ATV Trail.

Source of additional information:

Dixie National Forest
Teasdale Ranger District
P.O. Box 99
Teasdale, UT 84773
(435) 425-3702

Notes on the trail: From the parking area ride north onto the Rosebud Trail, which climbs briefly before curving eastward through a forest of big Douglas fir and ponderosa pine. In 0.5 mile cross a dirt road, and then pass a track going left to a nice-looking dispersed campsite. At the **Y** at just under 1.5 miles, turn left, following the signed Rosebud Trail (another ATV trail goes right). At 2 miles, after a steep little downhill, cross an elevated cattle guard to exit the forest and ride into the wide open. About 0.25 mile later, continue straight where a sign points left and right toward "Slickrock Trail." At just under 4 miles cumulative, turn right in Slaughter Flat onto unsigned Forest Service Road 168. (Left goes toward Jorgenson Flat/Tantalus Flats, en route to the Scenic Drive in Capitol Reef National Park.) Continue straight where the Rosebud Trail goes left, and at 4.5 miles turn right onto the main road to begin a steepish, 3-mile climb (left at 4.5 miles goes 1 mile to the reservoir). You'll pass several nice dispersed campsites as you climb, some of them replete with fire grates. At 7.5 miles return to the trailhead.

RIDE 55 · Hole-in-the-Rock Road

AT A GLANCE

Length/configuration: 24-mile out-and-back
(12 miles each way)

Aerobic difficulty: Easy

Technical difficulty: Easy, over generally smooth,
graded dirt and gravel

Scenery: A dry, corrugated landscape of subtle pastels,
possibly with the occasional brilliant flash of a
bluebird. The destination, Devil's Garden, holds a
community of whimsical, hoodoo-like sandstone creatures.

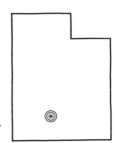

The drive to get to this ride's trailhead from Boulder is unforgettable—surely one of the most scenic drives in the nation. From slickrock-engulfed Boulder, whose irrigated green fields clash magnificently with the surrounding rock, you eventually negotiate a knife-edge ridge road—rather like a petrified brontosaurus backbone—before dropping to the Calf Creek Campground. This site is highly recommended for an overnight, as well as for the hike to Lower Calf Creek Falls.

The easy, 24-mile out-and-back (12 miles each way) takes place within the 1.7-million-acre Grand Staircase–Escalante National Monument. The monument, designated by President Clinton in 1996, is unique in that it is administered by the Bureau of Land Management; all other national monuments are under the jurisdiction of the National Park Service. (You'll find more information on the monument under Ride 56.) Devil's Garden, the suggested turnaround, has picnic tables, a restroom, and a short hiking/nature trail.

This is only a sampler, and a tame one at that . . . a way to get a feel for the loneliness of this infinitely huge country. It will take you past or close to other potentially good rides, including the Cedar Wash Loop, which curves back up to Escalante; and the Egypt ride, starting four miles southeast of this ride's turnaround. Other rides in the Escalante and Boulder areas, as recommended by the Bureau of Land Management, include the Alvey Wash Loop, Wolverine/Circle Cliffs Loop, and Fiftymile Bench. Before setting out on any of these, be sure to swing by the Interagency Visitor Center just west of Escalante, where you can pick up maps and additional information on riding and hiking in the monument.

If you're up for it, a good way to familiarize yourself with the Escalante Canyons portion of the national monument is to drive—or ride self-supported—all 56 miles of the Hole-in-the-Rock Road. Trending southeasterly, the road runs on the plateau between the Escalante Canyons and the Straight Cliffs/Fiftymile Bench. Whether you go by bike or by car, do so equipped with plenty of backup supplies. The first 50 miles are high-grade and, except when wet, typically passable by passenger car. (Rains can make the road impassable, for days at a time on occasion.) The final five or six miles to Hole-in-the-Rock are rougher, requiring high clearance and four-wheel-drive.

As you experience the near-total emptiness of this country, consider what it must have been like 120 years ago. That's when 230 Mormon men, women, and children from southwest Utah answered the call to travel to and settle along the San Juan

RIDE 55 · Hole-in-the-Rock Road

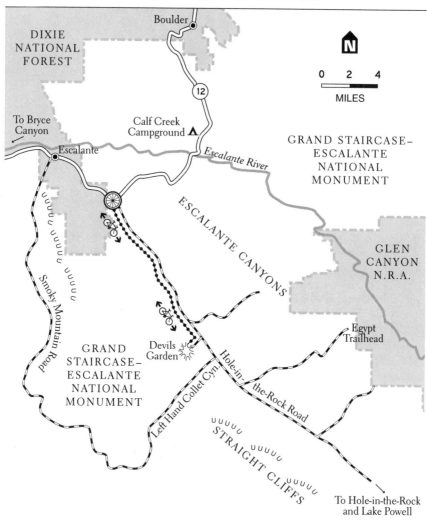

River in the opposite, southeast corner of the state. The church wanted to gain a foothold in that region and establish relations with the Native Americans. The ensuing journey is probably the most often told tale in Utah and Mormon Church history, outside of the original trek to the promised land of Utah. On reaching Escalante, the party learned that ahead lay a very formidable obstacle: the steep walls of Glen Canyon, standing high above the Colorado River. Nevertheless, in November 1879 they pushed on, having little choice: Because of mountain snows it was too late to return to the settlements of central Utah, and there wasn't enough forage in the Escalante area for their 200 horses and more than 1,000 head of cattle. They arrived

While you're riding this desolate country, imagine traversing it in 1879 in a horse-drawn wagon.

at the Colorado River rim with more than 80 wagons and lumber for a ferry boat that they'd carried all the way from Escalante. Here they blasted and enlarged a tight crevice in the vertical canyon walls into a huge slot/wagon passage, known as the Hole-in-the-Rock. The party didn't arrive at the mouth of Cottonwood Creek (the present site of Bluff) until April 1880—and only after accomplishing what may have been an even more grueling feat than getting through the Hole-in-the-Rock: surmounting the steep, unbroken face of Comb Ridge (see Ride 34).

General location: Just southeast of Escalante.

Elevation change: Minimal.

Season: April through May (in May gnats and flies can be a problem) and September through October are best. Know, however, that monsoonal rains can carry over from August into September, making routes impassable.

Services: Escalante has all services.

Hazards: Like almost all of the Grand Staircase–Escalante, you don't want to get stuck out here in a rainstorm. Now that more people are visiting the vast, unpeopled area, more are getting stranded, for days in some cases.

Rescue index: Very remote, although this is one of the relatively heavier traveled roads in the monument.

Land status: Bureau of Land Management.

Maps: Obtain the fold-out map distributed free of charge by the BLM, produced by that agency in partnership with the Southwest Natural and Cultural Heritage Association. Other good maps include the DeLorme *Utah Atlas & Gazetteer,* pages 19 and 20.

Finding the trail: From the corner of Center and Main in Escalante, drive 5 miles southeast on UT 12 and turn south onto Hole-in-the-Rock Road/Route 1862. Park in a wide spot off the road.

Source of additional information:

Escalante Interagency Visitor Center
755 West Main
P.O. Box 225
Escalante, UT 84726
(435) 826-5499

Notes on the trail: Ride southeast on Hole-in-the-Rock Road, Route 1862. At just past 3 miles Cedar Wash Road takes off right (eventually circling back up to Escalante). At 10 miles Harris Wash Road goes left. At just under 12 miles you'll come to the 0.25-mile spur going right to Devil's Garden. After enjoying a lunch with a view, return the way you came.

RIDE 56 · Grand Staircase–Escalante National Monument

AT A GLANCE

Length/configuration: Variable

Aerobic difficulty: From easy to very difficult

Technical difficulty: From easy, over smooth, graded roads, to difficult, over steep, rocky four-wheel-drive tracks

Scenery: A mind-boggling and ever-changing panorama of slot canyons, cliffs, plateaus, and valleys, ranging from low, Sonoran Desert elevations to coniferous forests

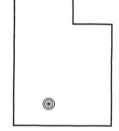

Special comments: The following is a general overview of rides in the monument, as summarized from information provided by the Bureau of Land Management

The huge hunk of the Colorado Plateau encompassed by the Grand Staircase–Escalante National Monument is divided into three physiographic regions, each distinct and extremely scenic: the canyons of the Escalante, which the Hole-in-the-Rock Road (Ride 55) accesses; the mesas and deep canyons of the Kaiparowits Plateau at the center of the monument; and the Grand Staircase, a series of colorful cliffs ascending northward in the west-southwestern part of the monument. The "grand stairway of sequential cliffs and terraces," as the Grand Staircase was described by pioneer geologist Clarence Dutton in the 1880s, climbs through no fewer than five life zones. Beginning with the Chocolate Cliffs south of the monument's boundary, it stair-steps its way to the shocking Pink Cliffs in and around Bryce Canyon National Park. The Chocolate Cliffs are of the Chinle formation (of the Tri-

The sites of the new national monument are diverse and nearly infinite.

assic period); the Pink Cliffs, of the Claron formation (Tertiary). The "risers" and "treads" between include the Vermilion Cliffs (Moenavi and Kayenta formations; Jurassic period), the White Cliffs (Navajo formation; Jurassic), and the Gray Cliffs (Dakota formation; Cretaceous).

Regarding its potential as an outdoor classroom of geological, paleontological, archaeological, and biological significance, the monument has few peers. The mountain biking in Grand Staircase–Escalante National Monument is good, too, ranging from easy outings suited for neophytes to rugged multiday adventures challenging for expert riders and expert route finders alike. Nearly all of the roads within the monument are unsurfaced and will become impassable—by motorized vehicle and by bicycle—during heavy precipitation. So choose your weather very carefully before venturing off the highways. Free backcountry camping permits may be obtained at the three offices listed below, and also at Anasazi Village State Park in Boulder. These help the Bureau of Land Management monitor activity within the monument, as well as the whereabouts of visitors.

General location: Grand Staircase–Escalante National Monument is immense (1.7 million acres), encompassing most of southern Utah between the Colorado River and Bryce Canyon National Park.

Elevation change: 4,500 to 8,300 feet.

Season: Depends on elevation; generally speaking, though, April through May and September into November are best. Note, however, that flies and gnats can be a nagging problem later in May, and the rainy season of late July and August can extend into and sometimes through September.

Services: There are no services within the monument. Bring food and water.

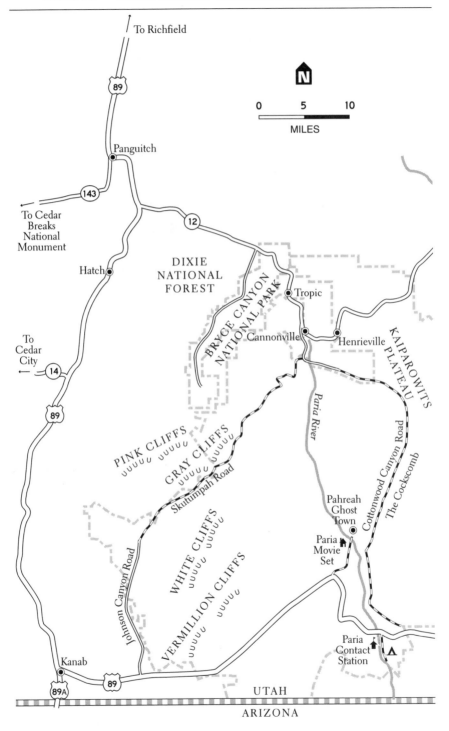

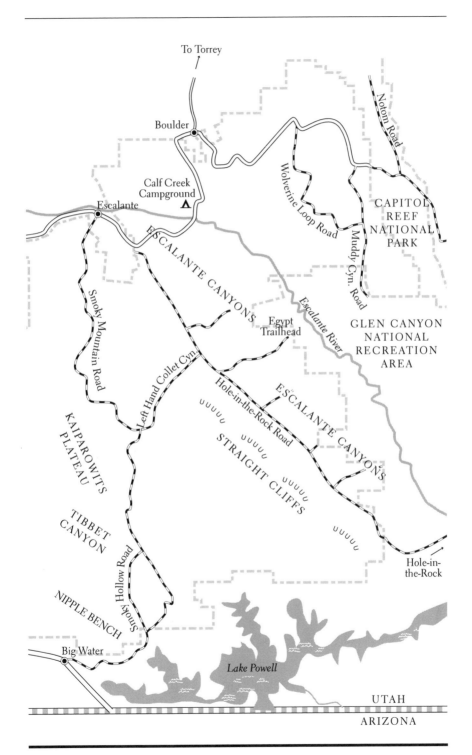

Hazards: The remoteness is probably the biggest hazard—do *not* venture into the outback without plenty of supplies, in case of mechanical breakdown or heavy precipitation. Additional hazards you may encounter include rattlesnakes, scorpions, cacti, and quicksand.

Rescue index: This is one of the most remote areas of southern Utah, which is, in turn, one of the most remote regions of the continent. Be self-reliant and *careful.*

Land status: Bureau of Land Management.

Maps: Obtain the excellent fold-out map distributed free of charge by the BLM, produced by that agency in partnership with the Southwest Natural and Cultural Heritage Association. See information on USGS quads for specific rides under "Notes on the trail."

Finding the trail: Jumping-off points to the north, along UT 12, are Boulder, Escalante, and Cannonville. To the south, along US 89, you can head north into the monument at Big Water, as well as at points west, between Big Water and Kanab, a major town.

Sources of additional information:

Kanab BLM Resource Area Office
318 North 100 East
Kanab, UT 84741
(435) 644-2672

Paria Contact Station
44 miles east of Kanab on US 89

Escalante Interagency Visitor Center
755 West Main
P.O. Box 225
Escalante, UT 84726
(435) 826-5499

Notes on the trail: Following are brief outlines of some of the rides suggested by the BLM. Be sure to obtain more complete information from that agency prior to setting out.

Big Water Area

Nipple Loop: This ride of approximately 26 miles heads up Nipple Creek Wash and down Tibbet Canyon, visiting Nipple Butte and providing views of the Smoky Mountains, lower Kaiparowits Plateau, and Lake Powell. USGS 7.5 minute quads: Nipple Butte and Tibbet Bench.

Smoky Mountain/Smoky Hollow Loop: A long, strenuous spur-with-a-loop ride of more than 60 miles. It begins by entering Glen Canyon National Recreation Area by way of Warm Creek Road. USGS 7.5 minute quads: Smoky Hollow and Sit Down Bench.

Paria Movie Set: 12-mile out-and-back (6 miles each way) beginning at US 89 and leading north to the Paria Movie Set, as well as to the actual Mormon ghost town of Old Pahreah. Steep climb out of Paria River Canyon on the return trip. An alternative way back to the highway is by way of Sand Gulch. USGS 7.5 minute quads: Five Mile Valley, Eight Mile Pass, and Five Mile Pass.

Cannonville Area

Cottonwood Canyon Road: A major road, by the standards of this remote national monument, offering a 50-mile-plus point-to-point beginning at Cannonville and ending at US 12 between Big Water and Kanab. Much of the way the route follows the Cockscomb (East Kaibab Monocline), a major, double-crested fold separating the

Kaiparowits Plateau and the Grand Staircase. The monument map works well for this one, as does the DeLorme *Utah Atlas & Gazetteer*, page 19.

Grosvenor Arch/Long Flat Loop: From Kodachrome Basin State Park (see Ride 58) you take the main road to Grosvenor Arch, then loop back via Long Flat. Approximately 35 miles. USGS 7.5 minute quads: Butler Valley, Horse Flat, 4 Mile Bench.

Johnson Canyon/Skutumpah Roads: These roads connect the Cannonville area on UT 12 with US 89, at a point 11 miles east of Kanab, providing great access to the canyons and plateaus of the Grand Staircase. It's approximately 65 miles from one highway to the other. USGS 7.5 minute quads: Skutumpah Creek, Deer Springs Point, Deer Range Point, Bull Valley Gorge and Cannonville. (Cannonville, by the way, named for pioneer Mormon leader George Q. Cannon, was also known in the past as Gunshot. This was because community members thought it was too small to be named after a cannon.)

RIDE 57 · Alan Canyon–Water Canyon Loop

AT A GLANCE

Length/configuration: 14-mile loop

Aerobic difficulty: Moderate; a test for intermediates and a good "fitness ride" for more advanced riders

Technical difficulty: Easy, over generally hard-surfaced gravel, packed sand with embedded cobbles, and double-track with some mud possible

Scenery: A forested mountain setting with up-close-and-personals of the Bryce Canyon–like hoodoos rimming the high Table Cliff Plateau of the Escalante Mountains

Special comments: If you don't like riding on narrow paved highways— even though it's just 1.8 miles on UT 12—consider having one person in your party shuttle the car to where FS 144 meets the highway

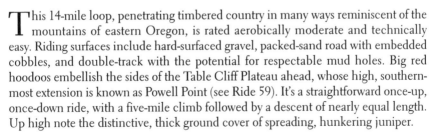

This 14-mile loop, penetrating timbered country in many ways reminiscent of the mountains of eastern Oregon, is rated aerobically moderate and technically easy. Riding surfaces include hard-surfaced gravel, packed-sand road with embedded cobbles, and double-track with the potential for respectable mud holes. Big red hoodoos embellish the sides of the Table Cliff Plateau ahead, whose high, southernmost extension is known as Powell Point (see Ride 59). It's a straightforward once-up, once-down ride, with a five-mile climb followed by a descent of nearly equal length. Up high note the distinctive, thick ground cover of spreading, hunkering juniper.

General location: Twelve miles west of Escalante.

Elevation change: Approximately 7,000 to 8,400 feet.

Season: May through October.

Services: Escalante has all services.

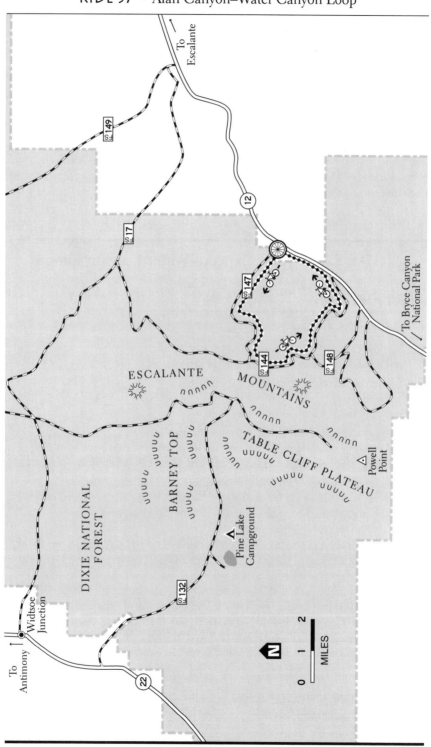

Hazards: The stretch along UT 12 is narrow and can carry quite a bit of traffic. Ride defensively.

Rescue index: There's a good chance of encountering firewood gatherers, hunters (in the fall), and/or Forest Service employees.

Land status: Dixie National Forest, private, BLM.

Maps: Dixie National Forest visitor map, Powell, Escalante, and Teasdale Ranger Districts; or DeLorme *Utah Atlas & Gazetteer*, page 19.

Finding the trail: From Escalante go approximately 12 miles west on UT 12 and turn north onto FS 147. Park at the first wide spot on the right.

Source of additional information:

Dixie National Forest, Escalante Ranger District
755 West Main
P.O. Box 246
Escalante, UT 84726
(435) 826-5400

Notes on the trail: Begin riding up FS 147, through a sandstone canyon decorated with juniper and ponderosa pine. Enter the Dixie National Forest in about 0.5 mile. At just under 1.5 miles continue straight, climbing. At roughly 4 miles, still climbing, swing around the toe of a ridge, where a clear-cut permits inspiring, long-range views onto the desert. In another 0.5 mile round a bend in an old clear-cut and head into and up the next drainage, Left Hand Alan Creek. Shortly past the 5-mile mark, at the ride's high point, turn left downhill onto FS 144 (it also goes up to the right toward Corn Creek). After a long downhill, at approximately 8.5 miles you'll come to a junction. As you break out into a big, beautiful meadow embraced by ponderosa-studded hummocks, ride straight ahead onto the more primitive double-track to stay on designated FS 144, rather than curving right onto the better road, FS 148, which also goes to the highway. (Another hint: Keep the attractive old pole fence line on your right.) One mile past here, continue straight where a decent road dives to the left, then go straight again where another spur goes left. At 11.5 miles, now in the possibly boggy bottomlands, you'll see an old log barn, corrals, and other dilapidated ranching relics on the right. Ride through a forest of sage for the last mile of double-track. At just under 12.5 miles turn left onto UT 12 and return to the beginning at 14 miles.

RIDE 58 · Panorama Trail

AT A GLANCE

Length/configuration: Combination ride consisting of a 2-mile out-and-back (1 mile each way) connecting to a 2-mile loop

Aerobic difficulty: Easy

Technical difficulty: Moderate, over sandy single-track, with a stretch of blacktop leading to and from the trailhead. Some walking of your bike will probably be necessary.

RIDE 58 · Panorama Trail

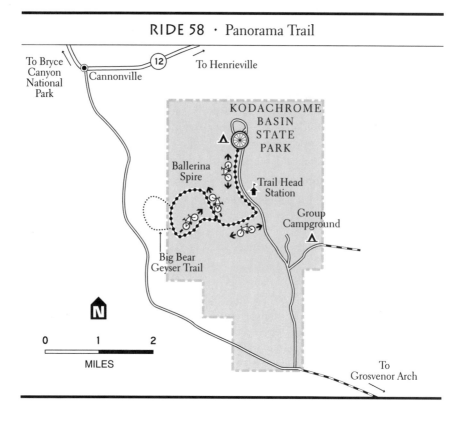

Scenery: Knock-your-socks-off scenery; it was the National Geographic Society that suggested the name Kodachrome Basin, and those folks have shot a lot of Kodachrome in plenty of places

Special comments: This trail, one of several within Kodachrome Basin State Park, is the only one open to bicycles

This four-mile combination ride (two-mile out-and-back connecting to a two-mile loop) is a real kick. It makes a great way to start or end the day when you're camping at the Kodachrome Basin State Park's superlative campground. Technically the ride is rated moderately difficult, but aerobically it is easy. Because of the sand surfaces, it makes a good choice when conditions are wet—and when Cottonwood Canyon Road and other points within the adjacent Grand Staircase–Escalante National Monument will probably not be passable. Take it slow and enjoy the scenery, dismounting now and then to mix hiking with biking. It's the only trail open to bikes in the park, so please respect the rules to ensure that it remains open. Don't ride off-trail onto slickrock or through gardens of spirelike cryptobiotic soil. Consider it a nature bike-hike: It's short but fun enough that you may want to do it again.

It is speculated that Kodachrome Basin's "chimneys," which are composed of different materials than the surrounding rock, formed as geyser plugs. A 1949 article in *National Geographic*, entitled "Motoring the Escalante Land," referred to the area previously called Thorny Pasture as Kodachrome Flat. Likewise, the nearby double arch, Grosvenor Arch, was named in honor of Dr. Gilbert Grosvenor, then president of the National Geographic Society.

General location: Eight miles southeast of Cannonville.

Elevation change: Minimal.

Season: March through May and September through November are best.

Services: Cannonville has a convenience store and motel. You should, however, stock up on major provisions *before* coming to this remote area. Trail Head Station, located within the state park, has supplies such as ice, film, and some food items. Horseback and wagon rides can also be arranged here. The park campground has water and showers.

Hazards: Gnarly wash crossings are best not attempted while still on your bike.

Rescue index: You're never far from help on this ride.

Land status: State.

Maps: A rough, not-to-scale pictorial map of the Panorama and Big Bear Geyser Trail is available at the park headquarters.

Finding the trail: From Cannonville (located on UT 12 between Escalante and Bryce Canyon National Park), turn south onto the road signed for Kodachrome Basin State Park. In 7.5 miles, turn left into the park. (Straight ahead the road leads to Grosvenor Arch and Cottonwood Canyon.)

Source of additional information:

Kodachrome Basin State Park
P.O. Box 238
Cannonville, UT 84718
(435) 679-8562

Notes on the trail: Leave the campground, riding on asphalt toward the park exit. At 0.5 mile pass Trail Head Station on the left; then, a couple of hundred yards farther, go right onto the sandy track, immediately crossing a wash. The trail becomes a double-track. Soon you'll pass Fred Flintstone Spire (a bit of a stretch). Just past there is a green gate; at the top of a rise just beyond that, bear right following the directional arrow as you wind amid sage and piñon-juniper. At just over 1 mile cumulative, bear right to stay on Panorama Trail/Coach Road, taking aim at graceful Ballerina Spire. A couple of hundred yards farther, at a "Keep Bicycles on Trail" sign, now in full view of Ballerina Spire, bear straight/right onto the more single-track–looking trail. (Coach Road drops down to the left.) You'll hit a tough wash crossing, see Secret Passage Trail on the right, then pass the Big Bear Geyser Trail going right (rough country with lots of cryptobiotic crust; better explored by foot). At 2 miles cumulative merge right onto Coach Road. In another 0.1 mile the Big Bear Geyser Trail rejoins on the right. Turn left to stay on the Panorama Trail, which reverts to excellent sand single-track. (Going right here is the Panorama Point Trail, 250 yards of steep walking that reaps terrific views.) At just past 2.5 miles, after descending a low ridge, cross a deep notch wash. Close the loop at just under 3 miles, bearing right downhill. Soon you're back at the trailhead; return to the campground, reached at 4 miles.

RIDE 59 · Powell Point

AT A GLANCE

Length/configuration: 22-mile out-and-back (11 miles each way)

Aerobic difficulty: Moderate to difficult, gaining 2,100 feet of elevation over the first 6 miles at a fairly steep, steady grade

Technical difficulty: Moderate, over graded dirt and gravel roads, as well as stretches holding loose gravel and embedded angulars. The last 4.5 miles are on a four-wheel-drive track with mud holes likely, along with 1 mile of single-track.

Scenery: The destination/turnaround, Powell Point, vies for title of "Best Viewpoint in Utah"

Special comments: Get an alpine start. You don't want to be riding on the Table Cliff Plateau when thunderheads build

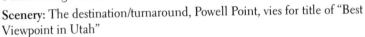

This 22-mile out-and-back (11 miles each way) leads from Pine Lake Campground, a nice place to overnight, to the top of the Table Cliff Plateau, an extension of the massive Aquarius Plateau. The southern tip of the plateau, Powell Point—also known as Powell's Pink Point—provides a staggering view of an impossibly huge hunk of southern Utah, as well as of the surrounding states (on a clear day, anyway). The six-mile climb at ride's beginning is a grind, quite steep in places, but entirely rideable by a reasonably fit cyclist. The ride is rated moderate in both aerobic and technical difficulty. Riding surfaces include graded dirt and gravel, single-track, and four-wheel-drive road twisting through thick woods, with plenty of root drop-offs and, more likely than not, mud holes. To begin you pass through a lush forest of ponderosa pine and spruce; during the later stages, through stands of crooked old bristlecone pine. At 6.5 miles, before turning south onto the four-wheel-drive track, be sure to pedal a couple of tenths up the road to catch the views over the Escalante country. It's quite a different perspective than that enjoyed at Powell Point. There, at the turnaround, you'll probably want to put on a jacket for protection against the winds. It's an unforgettable place to have lunch.

General location: As the raven flies the trailhead is approximately 7 miles northeast of the northeast corner of Bryce Canyon National Park.

Elevation change: 2,100 feet.

Season: June through October.

Services: The closest services are in Tropic and at Ruby's Inn, at the entrance to Bryce Canyon National Park. Pine Lake Campground has drinking water.

Hazards: Winds can be gusty at Powell Point, so don't get too close to the edge! Lightning is also a hazard atop the Table Cliff Plateau. In a couple of places a mishap on the single-track leading down to Powell Point could have serious consequences. On the return trip, the 2,100-foot descent is fast and quite bumpy in places.

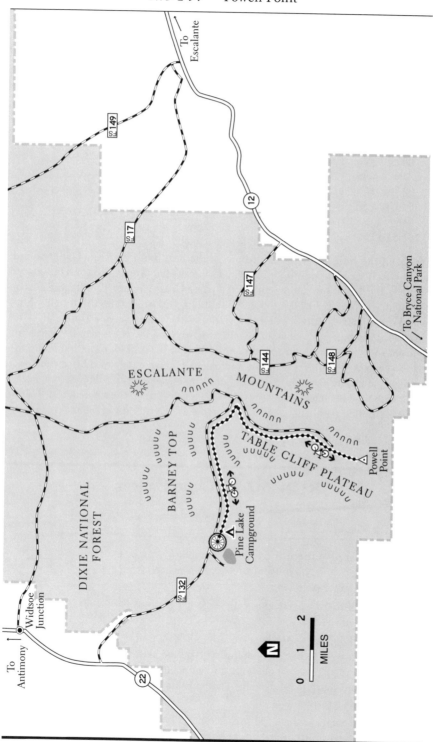

Rescue index: The Great Western Trail skirts Pine Lake, so there's quite a bit of ATV activity in the area. Over the last 4.5 miles of the ride you may not encounter anyone, however.

Land status: Dixie National Forest.

Maps: Dixie National Forest visitor map, Powell, Escalante, and Teasdale Ranger Districts; or DeLorme *Utah Atlas & Gazetteer*, page 19.

Finding the trail: At Bryce Junction, turn north off UT 12 onto UT 22 and go about 11 miles, then turn right onto FS 132. Pine Lake Campground is 5.5 miles from the turn.

Source of additional information:

Dixie National Forest
Powell Ranger District
225 East Center
P.O. Box 80
Panguitch, UT 84759
(435) 676-8815

Notes on the trail: Begin riding easterly at the turn into Pine Lake Campground, immediately heading uphill along Clay Creek on the Great Western Trail toward "Barney Top." At just under 0.5 mile you'll pass a Great Western Trail staging area on the right. At about 6.5 miles, topping out at last, turn right onto the rougher four-wheel-drive track toward "Powell Point Trailhead / Water Canyon Trailhead." (But first, pedal a couple of tenths up the main road to catch the views over the Escalante country.) Up and down you go, remaining at a fairly constant elevation along the plateau's top. At 10 miles ride onto a single-track trail, winding down through a forest of gnarly old bristlecone pine. At just under 11 miles you'll arrive at Powell Point. After soaking up the vista, tackle the testy little climb back out on the single-track. Beware of gravel patches, mud, and overhanging branches on way back to the main road.

RIDE 60 · Casto Canyon

AT A GLANCE

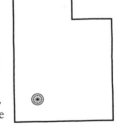

Length/configuration: 15.5-mile combination, consisting of a 7-mile out-and-back (3.5 miles each way) and an 8.5-mile loop

Aerobic difficulty: Moderate, with some semi-serious climbing involved

Technical difficulty: Moderate, over sandy ATV trail, rough four-wheel-drive road littered with potential tire snaggers (angular rocks both loose and embedded), and a couple of miles of dancing—and pushing—in and out of a creek bottom

Scenery: In the canyon depths you wouldn't know you're not in Bryce Canyon; you're surrounded by the same pink cliffs

RIDE 60 · Casto Canyon

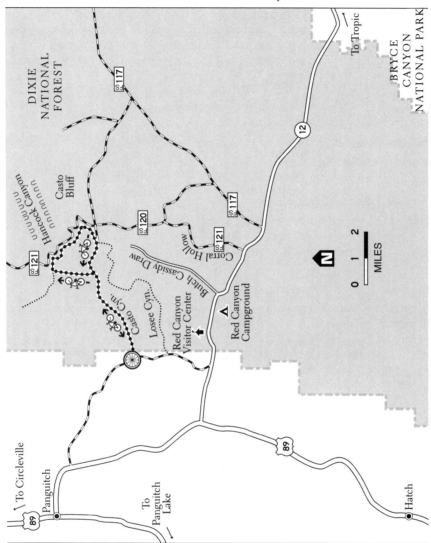

Special comments: An out-and-back along the initial 3.5 miles of excellent ATV trail makes a terrific single-track sampler for neophytes

You're not permitted to ride on the trails of Bryce Canyon National Park—but who cares, with trails like this in the vicinity? The 15.5-mile combination ride includes a 7-mile out-and-back (3.5 miles each way) linking up with a challenging 8.5-mile loop. The first (and last) 3.5 miles of the ride are along an absolutely buffed ATV/single-track trail. Aerobically the ride is moderate in difficulty, with approximately 1,500 feet of cumulative climbing involved. It's also technically moderate, serving up some tricky descents over loose rock, along with a couple of miles of streambed riding and walking. You'll want to watch your cyclocomputer distances particularly closely, because in places the route is easy to lose.

Here in Butch Cassidy's canyon country, after you gain a little elevation, bursts of green needles and rich brown, deeply furrowed bark of lumbering ponderosa pines stand in delicious contrast to the pinkish-red rock and blue sky. Below the ponderosas, scatterings of fallen, blackened needles congregate on brilliant rock surfaces. It's about as pretty a scene as you'll find, and you just may decide to sit under a tree soaking it all in and forget about riding your bike. (If you do make it that far, however, note the abundance of prehistoric chert chippings littering the forest floor when you reach the edge of the burn after climbing out of Casto Canyon.)

General location: Approximately 6 miles southeast of Panguitch.

Elevation change: From around 7,100 to 8,200 feet.

Season: May through October (it may look like desert, but the elevation is quite high).

Services: Panguitch has all services.

Hazards: Large, angular rocks between miles 6 and 10 can cause spills. Take care also over the 2 miles where you go in and out of the streambed.

Rescue index: There's a good chance you'll encounter other mountain bikers and/or ATVers in the vicinity.

Land status: Dixie National Forest.

Maps: Dixie National Forest visitor map, Powell, Escalante, and Teasdale Ranger districts.

Finding the trail: From the Red Canyon Visitor Center (on UT 12 between Bryce Canyon and US 89) drive 1.5 miles west and turn north onto the good gravel road toward Casto Canyon and Losee Canyon. After 2 miles you'll pass the Losee Canyon trailhead, arriving at the Casto Canyon trailhead in another mile. Park in the one of the spaces provided.

Source of additional information:

Dixie National Forest
Powell Ranger District
225 East Center
P.O. Box 80
Panguitch, UT 84759
(435) 676-8815

Notes on the trail: Begin riding up the maintained ATV trail into a juniper- and piñon-studded canyon of multihued limestone walls, spires, and pinnacles. At just past 3.5 miles, veer left toward "Sanford Road" on the ATV trail, climbing (steeply at times) out of Casto Canyon. After 2 miles of ascending, you'll come to a junction at a high point at the edge of a recent forest fire. One-quarter mile past there you'll come to another junction; bear right uphill, where another ATV trail goes down to the left. To verify your whereabouts, you should see signs that point down to Casto Canyon Trail (pointing toward the direction you just came from). Soon you'll ride into an open meadow of sage and juniper; note your trail curving right up the hillside ahead. At just under 7.5 miles, cross a cattle guard and start steeply downhill, watching out for nasty rocks in the way. Cross Hancock Canyon before arriving, at 10 miles cumulative, at your right-hand turn onto the double-track signed "Casto Canyon." Over the next 2 miles you may not see much evidence of a trail as you flirt with the creek bottom, dismounting and pushing your bike on numerous occasions. But simply continue downstream; at 12 miles you'll close the loop to regain the improved ATV trail. From here it's a kaleidoscope of blurring colors as you pedal and coast back to the trailhead, reached at 15.5 miles.

RIDE 61 · Big John Flat

AT A GLANCE

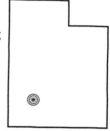

Length/configuration: 7-mile combination consisting of a 2-mile out-and-back (1 mile each way) connecting to a 5-mile loop

Aerobic difficulty: Moderate, with a testy little climb gaining 1,200 feet in 3.5 miles

Technical difficulty: Moderate, over good gravel going up and steep, sometimes rocky and rutted ATV trail heading down

Scenery: The magnificently barren Tushar Mountains are among Utah's highest peaks

Special comments: Great dispersed camping is available on Big John Flat, 3.5 miles into the ride; an alternative plan is to drive there and set up camp, then simply explore the numerous dead-end tracks going this way and that

This ride begins not far from Elk Meadows Ski Area, located in the Tushar Mountains, whose high watershed divide serves as part of the boundary between Panoramaland and Color Country. For an area that's bustling throughout winter with skier activity, it can be surprisingly lonesome in summer. The short, seven-mile outing consists of a one-mile spur connecting to a five-mile loop. It's rated moderately difficult in regard to aerobic challenge, owing to the sustained, 3.5-mile climb gaining 1,200 feet of elevation. Technically it is moderately difficult as well, encompassing a descent over ATV trail that is occasionally steep, rocky, rutted, and/or muddy. The drive to the trailhead from the Sevier River Valley settlement of Junction is memorable in its own right, and after doing it in an uphill direction you probably won't mind going down the other way, on pavement through Beaver Canyon to the town of Beaver. (Beaver, by the way, is home to the Beaver Beavers, mascot of the high school attended by Theodore Cleaver. And you thought he lived in Mayfield.)

When first setting out here, your intrepid author intended to do a loop that rejoins the highway near Puffer Lake, getting there via the heralded Skyline National Recreation Trail. However, your not-always-so-intrepid author had the bejeebers scared out of him by an approaching lightning storm, so he bailed. Unfortunately, he had to be at lower climes the following day. So, you can do the fun little outing as described here, and/or, if you're feeling adventurous, you can explore the Skyline NRT. To find its trailhead from the suggested turnaround, continue uphill for one mile, skirting the eastern fringe of Big John Flat, then bear right uphill for another one-half mile. As the Tushar Road continues running northward, turn right onto the Skyline NRT to

RIDE 61 · Big John Flat

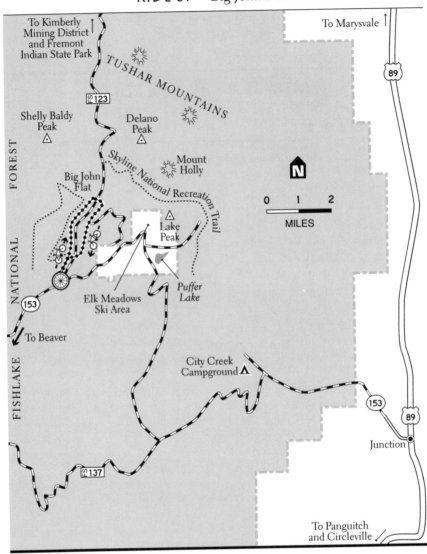

To Kimberly Mining District and Fremont Indian State Park

To Marysvale

TUSHAR MOUNTAINS

FS 123

Shelly Baldy Peak

Delano Peak

Skyline National Recreation Trail

Mount Holly

Big John Flat

N

0   1   2

MILES

FOREST

Lake Peak

NATIONAL

Puffer Lake

153

Elk Meadows Ski Area

To Beaver

FISHLAKE

City Creek Campground

153

89

Junction

FS 137

To Panguitch and Circleville

begin a very steep push and ride up an old jeep road. In about half a mile, you'll wrap around the ridge to look down on the trail as it threads through the splendidly alpine Merchant Creek drainage. (*Blam! Slam!* Lightning! Sorry, that's as far as I'm going.)

FS 123, followed for the first half of this ride, also constitutes the southern leg of a cross-the-Tushars adventure that can take you north all the way to Fremont Indian State Park by way of the Kimberly mining district. More than 30 miles long, it's tough and way out there; careful planning is essential.

General location: Approximately 25 miles northwest of Junction, or 15 miles east of Beaver.

Elevation change: 8,750 to 9,950 feet.

Season: June through October.

Services: Stock up on food and water in one of the Sevier Valley towns to the east (or, if coming from the west, in Beaver) before driving up to the plateau. It's possible that limited services will be found at Elk Meadows Ski Resort and/or Puffer Lake Resort, but don't plan on it.

Hazards: Some car traffic may be encountered on FS 123. Walk the rugged down-hills coming out if your confidence level hints that it would be wise to do so.

Rescue index: You've never far from the road on this ride. Help should be available in one of the private homes or business offices of Elk Meadows Ski Resort.

Land status: Fishlake National Forest.

Maps: Fishlake National Forest visitor map or DeLorme *Utah Atlas & Gazetteer*, page 26.

Finding the trail: From Junction (15 miles south of Marysvale on US 89), turn west onto UT 153 and inch your way up to the Tushar Plateau, over an amazingly twist-ing, switchbacking road that has a gravel surface for most of the way. Eventually, you'll pass the condos and ski runs of Elk Meadows Ski Resort, whose mountainsides can appear rather bombed out when no snow covers them. Park just beyond the resort, off the road at the right-hand turn onto FS 123.

Source of additional information:

Fishlake National Forest
Beaver Ranger District
P.O. Box E
575 South Main
Beaver, UT 84713
(435) 438-2436

Notes on the trail: Pedal up FS 123, rapidly gaining elevation at a sustained and clearly noticeable 6 to 8 percent grade over a good, hard gravel surface. At about 3.5 miles you'll pop into Big John Flat, where the timber cover breaks to reveal stagger-ing views of the high Tushars pushing skyward in the near distance. After exploring the area to your heart's content, turn around at the point mentioned above; at about 0.1 mile back toward the trailhead, turn left/east onto Paiute Sidetrail 26. Immedi-ately bear right where another fork goes left uphill. The trail is very steep and rutted in places, but generally rideable going in this downhill direction. In about a mile, continue straight/right downhill. To stay on the route, simply continue bearing right, keeping as close as possible to the road you came up on, as you hit some clearings and boggy areas. At roughly 6 miles cumulative, ride back onto the main road, turn-ing left and screaming back to the trailhead.

RIDE 62 · Gunlock Loop

AT A GLANCE

Length/configuration: 22.5-mile combination,
consisting of a 4-mile out-and-back (2 miles each way)
connecting to an 18.5-mile loop

Aerobic difficulty: Easy to moderate, with
approximately 1,000 feet of climbing on pavement

Technical difficulty: Easy, over paved and good gravel
roads

Scenery: Gunlock Reservoir, where the ride begins
and ends, has a cove on its far side backed by an extremely colorful, pink-
and-white sandstone expanse; farther into the ride you penetrate a broad
desert landscape of sage and scattered junipers

Special comments: A pretty little loop that can be as windy as Wyoming

This civilized, 22.5-mile ride consists of a short, 2-mile spur connecting to an
18.5-mile loop. Aerobically its difficulty lies somewhere between easy and moderate, with about 1,000 feet of climbing, all of it on pavement. Technically the outing is rated easy, as riding surfaces include only pavement and hardened gravel. A
couple of miles into the ride you spin through Gunlock, named for sharpshooter
"Gunlock Bill" Hamblin. It's a quaint little out-of-the-way community with plenty of
low-slung houses—unpretentious and utilitarian. After climbing to and pedaling
through the busier settlement of Veyo, then ascending the flank of Veyo Volcano, you
drop on gravel past Upper Sand Cove Reservoir—reeds, waters, and cottonwoods
probably whipping southward in the north wind—and then view the big bulk of the
Bull Valley Mountains looming to the distant right and, closer to the left, low desert
mountains. Before dropping back to the main road you zip past the turn to Lower
Sand Cove Reservoir, with its beautiful backing of slickrock. It's definitely worth
dropping down the spur road to explore a bit.

General location: About 20 miles northwest of St. George.

Elevation change: Approximately 3,600 to 4,600 feet.

Season: Spring, fall, and most of winter. Summers in the St. George area are prohibitively hot.

Services: Primitive shoreline camping is available at the trailhead. Veyo, located on
the route, has restaurants, a bakery, a convenience store . . . and a roller rink! St.
George is the closest full-service town.

Hazards: UT 18, followed for 2 miles, carries quite a lot of traffic. It has a narrow
shoulder for riding.

Rescue index: You'll no doubt encounter car traffic even on the gravel portions of
the ride.

Land status: BLM, private.

Maps: Dixie National Forest, the Pine Valley and Cedar City Ranger Districts; or
DeLorme *Utah Atlas & Gazetteer*, page 16.

Finding the trail: From the junction of Sunset Boulevard and Bluff Street at the northwest edge of St. George, head west on Sunset Boulevard. In 12 miles, turn north toward Gunlock. After about 6 miles, turn left into the parking area for Gunlock Reservoir State Beach.

Source of additional information:

Interagency Visitor Center
345 East Riverside Drive
St. George, UT 84790
(435) 688-3246

Notes on the trail: Leave the slickrock-embraced lake, riding north on pavement. In about 2 miles you'll enter Gunlock. A couple of miles later pass Eagle Mountain Ranch, a horse operation surrounded by hundreds of yards of plastic white fence. At 7 miles switchback right and start a steeper climb of about a mile, at the top of which you take straight aim at Veyo. At 9.5 miles, just past a classic old rock residence, turn right onto UT 18. One-half mile later you'll cross a narrow bridge and start a 0.5-mile climb over the flank of Veyo Volcano. At 11.5 miles turn right off the pavement onto the road signed "Sand Cove Reservoir 2, Lower Sand Cove Reservoir 6, Gunlock 9." Just beyond the 13.5-mile mark pass Upper Sand Cove Reservoir on the right. At 16 miles start descending more steeply, amid volcanics toward a desert canyon. At 17 miles, in a slickrock canyon bottom, pass a power substation on the left and, a mile later, a track dropping left to Lower Sand Cove Reservoir. At 19.5 miles you'll commence a very steep downhill, regaining the paved road at 20.5 miles. Turn left and return to Gunlock Reservoir at 22.5 miles.

RIDE 63 · Tobin Ridge

AT A GLANCE

Length/configuration: 10-mile loop

Aerobic difficulty: Moderate, with about 700 feet of elevation gain

Technical difficulty: Moderate, over pavement and gravel, with a few wash crossings and rocky climbs/descents littered with basalt bombs and sandstone cobbles

Scenery: Scrubby desert basin; quite appealing in its own desolate way

Special comments: The ride is short enough that—although it's rated moderately difficult both technically and aerobically—a neophyte could do it by walking the nastier hills

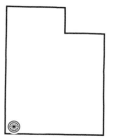

This 10-mile loop is one of those discoveries made by poring over maps; "Hmmm . . . this looks interesting." Interesting it is; not world-class, perhaps, but definitely a fun little loop. Because of some steep hills and 700 feet of elevation gain, the ride is rated moderate in aerobic difficulty; likewise in technical difficulty, owing to

RIDE 62 · Gunlock Loop
RIDE 63 · Tobin Ridge

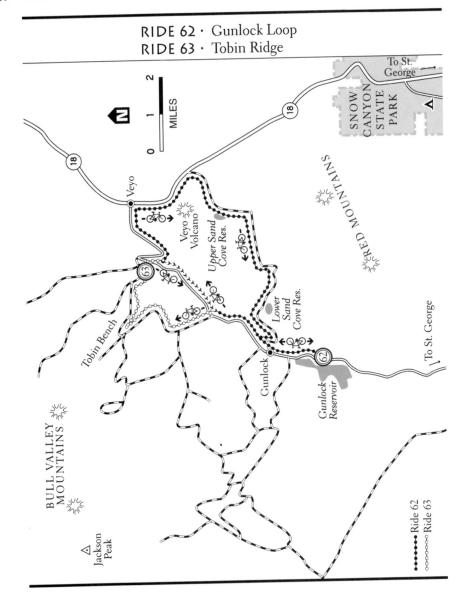

several tough, rocky ascents and descents. This entire desert/mountain basin and those adjacent to it are webbed with roads and could provide days of exploring.

As you drive north from St. George, note the roller-coastering bikeway running beside the highway. It links St. George and Snow Canyon State Park, winding forever northward toward pale and reddish slickrock hills. Snow Canyon is an absolutely gorgeous spot; grassy swales spread below red, pale yellow, and checkerboarded red-and-pale-yellow convergences of sandstone. Definitely pull in to have a look, and maybe even spend the night camping there.

General location: 22 miles northwest of St. George.

Elevation change: Roughly 3,700 to 4,400 feet.

Season: Spring, fall, and most of winter. Summers are exceedingly hot.

Services: Veyo, which you pass through en route to the trailhead, has some services, including a small grocery store. St. George is the closest full-service town.

Hazards: Exercise special caution on the rocky uphills and downhills.

Rescue index: You're never really far from paved roads; however, you may not meet anyone on the off-pavement sections.

Land status: Private, BLM, state.

Maps: Dixie National Forest, the Pine Valley and Cedar City Ranger districts; or DeLorme *Utah Atlas & Gazetteer,* page 16.

Finding the trail: From the junction of Sunset Boulevard and Bluff Street at the northwest edge of St. George, go north on Bluff/UT 18. In about 15 miles, turn left in Veyo onto the paved road going west. The road curves left, then right to descend a hill nearly a mile long. After switchbacking left at the bottom of the hill, pull off on the right and park in the wide area beside the road.

Source of additional information:

Interagency Visitor Center
345 East Riverside Drive
St. George, UT 84790
(435) 688-3246

Notes on the trail: Ride southwesterly downhill on the pavement, attaining speeds in excess of 40 m.p.h. if you're so inclined. At just under 3 miles turn right to pass through lands of the Eagle Mountain Ranch, before crossing a cattle guard onto public lands. Pedal gradually upward on the graded sand/gravel road, toward the deserty Bull Valley Mountains, through a dispersed forest of piñon and juniper. At approximately 4 miles turn right onto the rough four-wheel-drive track (just before a higher-quality road also goes right). Begin climbing steeply toward the ridge, with a piñon-filled draw on your left. Stay on the "main" road where another track goes right. Reach the top of the ridge at around 6 miles, then go left at the Y. Stay on the ridge top where another track goes right and continue climbing, keeping the fence line to your right. At the three-way junction, take the right fork to pass through the gate. At approximately 7 miles, another road comes in on the right. Start down, continuing straight at 8 miles, where a primitive track goes right. You'll pass through a gate at about 8.5 miles, then merge left onto the road coming in from above left. In another 0.75 mile pass through a sandy draw (it may contain water), then turn right onto the wide gravel road to pass between a couple of houses. Cross the creek and come to the highway, closing the loop at 10 miles.

RIDE 64 · St. George to Hurricane

AT A GLANCE

Length/configuration: 28-mile point-to-point

Aerobic difficulty: Easy to moderate. You'll gain about 1,000 feet from St. George to the high point, then lose 400 feet dropping into Hurricane

Technical difficulty: Easy, over surfaces of pavement/chipseal, compacted and graded dirt, a few stretches of sand, and good gravel

Scenery: Early on you'll enjoy a magnificent view of St. George unfolding beneath/beside bright red rimrock cliffs, backed by the quieter hues of the Pine Valley Mountains

Special comments: You'll need to arrange for a shuttle to do this as a point-to-point; if you leave a vehicle in Hurricane, it should be parked along 700 West immediately south of UT 9

This outing makes an excellent introduction to the St. George area, offering a splendid overview of the outlying landscapes. Soon after setting out you'll look down on the mini-city of St. George, which seems to grow larger by the minute, sprawling beneath the brilliantly red Red Hills and other features, all of it backed by the high Pine Valley Mountain Wilderness to the north. Then, about 6.5 miles into the ride, you pass through a low notch to enter a broad, grassy basin rimmed ahead by the distant crinkling of the Hurricane Cliffs; the red, rimrocky bulk of Sand Mountain on the left; and, to the south, the gently sloping, piñon-studded backside of the Warner Ridge hogback. Occasional "For Sale" signs predict imminent change in this area.

At 11 miles on the right a 0.5-mile spur drops down to Fort Pearce Wash and the native-rock ruins of old Fort Pearce. The fort was built way back in 1866–67 by Mormons early on the scene as a defense against raiding Navajos from the far side of the Colorado River who were rustling cattle from the pioneers. From there, where you can almost throw a rock into Arizona, you continue eastward as the high wall of the Hurricane Cliffs gets ever closer. The Hurricane Fault marks the western terminus of the Colorado Plateau.

Aerobically, the 28-mile point-to-point is rated easy to moderate, and technically it is quite easy. Riding surfaces include pavement and chipseal, compacted and graded dirt road holding an occasional wind-whipping of loose sand, and good gravel. If you can't arrange to leave a shuttle vehicle in Hurricane, the outing can just as readily be turned into an out-and-back of just about any distance you'd like. Your destination of Hurricane, by the way, is pronounced HURR-uh-k'n by locals, rather than HURR-uh-kane.

General location: The ride begins in St. George.

Elevation change: Approximately 2,650 to 3,650 feet.

Season: September through May; summers are generally prohibitively hot.

Services: All services are available in St. George and Hurricane; no services are found between the two towns.

RIDE 64 · St. George to Hurricane

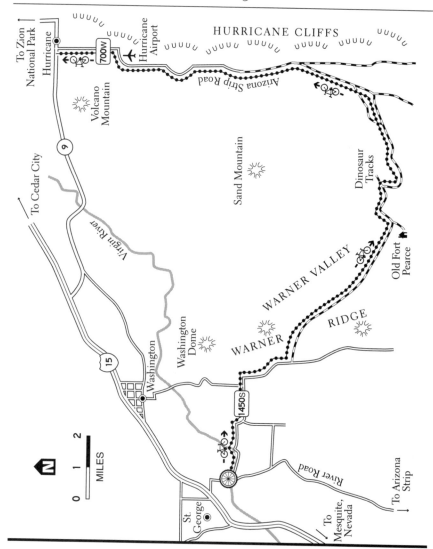

Hazards: Unpaved portions will range from extremely yucky to altogether impassable during/after hard rains.

Rescue index: You will probably meet motorists on this route; still, the ride feels surprisingly remote considering its proximity to burgeoning St. George and Hurricane.

Land status: BLM, private.

Maps: DeLorme *Utah Atlas & Gazetteer*, pages 16 and 17.

Finding the trail: You can start riding anywhere in St. George; for the purposes of the mileage log below, begin your odometer at the southeast edge of town just south of the Virgin River Bridge, at 1450 South and River Road. Parking is available here if you choose to drive to the trailhead.

Source of additional information:

Interagency Visitor Center
345 East Riverside Drive
St. George, UT 84790
(435) 688-3246

Notes on the trail: Ride east on paved 1450 South, a country road of late that shoots through an obviously fast-growing residential area. At just under 2 miles the road curves right and then curves sharply left. You'll pass some big farms at 3.5 miles, then curve right around some fence lines. A mile later, curve left past a new subdivision and golf course. At 5.5 miles, turn left off the pavement onto dirt toward "Warner Valley." Commence a climb of about 200 vertical feet, then, at 6.5 miles, ride through a little notch to enter a wide open, grassy basin. At just over 9 miles, pass through an area of moving pink sand; then, a mile later, begin descending into a more dissected, rugged landscape. At just under 11 miles, you'll see the spur going right to old Fort Pearce. A mile past there, at a four-way junction, turn right and soon you'll drop through a deep wash. (At that four-way junction, going left accesses a short trail leading to some excellent prosauropod and coelurosaur dinosaur tracks.) As you get closer to the wall of the Hurricane Cliffs, green junipers growing on the yucca flats provide quite a contrast. At a little over 17 miles, with a cattle tank on the left, you'll begin hooking around the toe of Sand Mountain. Two miles later, at about 19.5 miles cumulative, turn left onto the good gravel road that's hard to see until you're almost on it. Crest the high point where Sand Mountain and Hurricane Rim converge to begin the long descent into Hurricane, now aiming straight at the Pine Valley Mountains. At 21.5 miles roll onto a chipseal-surfaced road, soon signed as "Arizona Strip Road." You'll pass through a rural subdivision with some beautiful adobe-style residences built atop what appears to be a stark old alkali lake bed. By 23.5 miles, though, you'll be back in the country (at this writing!). At just under 26 miles, turn left opposite the airport entrance at the stop sign onto 700 West. Come into the outskirts of Hurricane at 26.5 miles, and finish the ride at the corner of 700 West and UT 9, reached at 28 miles.

RIDE 65 · Green Valley Toboggan Run

AT A GLANCE

Length/configuration: 10.5-mile loop

Aerobic difficulty: Moderate, with some steep climbing on both pavement and dirt

Technical difficulty: The ride encompasses some very steep descents and a veritable carnival ride of whoop-de-doos. Surfaces include pavement, compacted dirt double-track, sand, slickrock, and wide, braided, and buffed single-track.

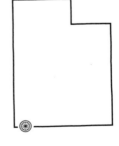

RIDE 65 · Green Valley Toboggan Run

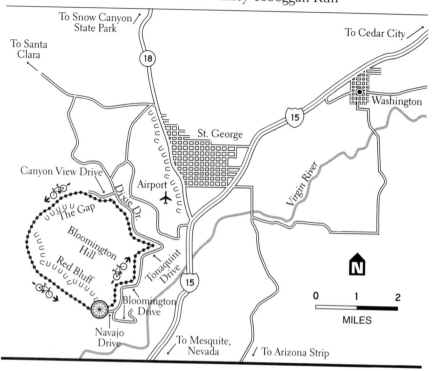

Scenery: Stunning desertscape. Looking back up at the steep trails in the 7-mile range is evocative of Minerva Terrace in Yellowstone; where riders have carved off darker colors, the lighter colors look almost like mineral deposits.

Special comments: This is the classic in-town St. George ride. New construction may modify the trail in the 5-mile range.

This fun, close-to-town spin is both aerobically and technically moderate in difficulty. For such a short outing, a surprising array of surfaces are encountered, including pavement, hard-packed dirt double-track, sand, slickrock, and wide, smooth trails. The first half of the 10.5-mile loop winds through St. George—or, more precisely, through Bloomington, Southgate, and Green Valley—on paved residential streets. After hitting dirt, a steep downhill and an ensuing climb up and through "the Gap" are followed by a dive into a fat-tire playground blazed years ago by motorbikers. More recently the area has been closed to motorized vehicles, in part to protect the endangered bear poppy, which, according to signs posted along the way, is known to occur nowhere in the world outside the St. George area. There's an abundance of side trails in the vicinity, some of them getting into really tough stuff, so you can make the ride about as technically challenging as you choose. (Note: If you're riding from downtown St. George, when following "Finding the trail" you can turn right from Hilton Drive onto Dixie Drive and pick up "Notes on the trail" at 4.5 miles.)

Heading down, then up, toward Hogback Gap.

General location: Adjacent to the southwest edge of St. George.

Elevation change: Approximately 2,600 to 3,000 feet.

Season: February through November, and much of the winter (go at first light if you do it in summer).

Services: All services are available in St. George.

Hazards: Some of the streets ridden on, particularly Tonaquint Drive and Dixie Drive, carry large numbers of cars, so ride defensively. It's a good idea to start very early or at mid-morning to avoid rush-hour traffic. Also, be careful not to get carried away and go too fast on the roller coaster, or you might get carried away to the hospital.

Rescue index: You're never more than a couple of miles from help, and you're likely to meet other mountain bikers on the route.

Land status: BLM, state, city.

Maps: A schematic map of the route is available at the bike shop listed below.

Finding the trail: From St. George, go south on Bluff Street, the main artery running below the bluffs at the west edge of the city. At the south end of town turn right onto Hilton Drive, then continue straight onto Tonaquint Drive where Dixie Drive goes right. Turn right onto Bloomington Drive, then right onto Navajo Drive. Park at the upper end of this street, where undeveloped state lands abut a nice residential neighborhood.

Source of additional information:

Bicycles Unlimited
90 South 100 East
St. George, UT 84770
(435) 673-4492

Notes on the trail: Backtrack the way you drove in by riding down Navajo Drive, turning left in 0.5 mile onto Bloomington Drive West, and then, in another 0.75 mile, going left onto Tonaquint Drive. At just past 2.5 miles cumulative, at the end of the rimrock cliffs, turn left onto Dixie Drive, a primary road. A couple of miles later, turn left toward "Green Valley Spa and Resort" onto Canyon View Drive to begin a steep uphill grunt. Just past the "Las Palmas" condo development on the left, cross onto dirt and drop down a very steep road before crossing a morass of dirt tracks. You want to aim at the gap in the fence and, beyond that, at the road running along the right-hand rim of the hogback gap ahead. At 5.5 miles, pass through the fence line and climb steeply for about a mile over loose dirt, sand, and slickrock. Roads take off here and there; stay close to rim and you can't go wrong. Top out at just under 6.5 miles and curve right, aiming at the gap in the fence about 0.25 mile away. Following a steep, technical downhill, turn left onto the road coming in from below; at 7.5 miles pass through the fence gap to begin riding on wide single-track. You can see your trail below in the distance, wrapping left around the base of Red Bluff/Bloomington Hill. You'll come to an exceedingly steep drop-off where you can take your pick of four or five routes; they look scary, but the runout is pretty good. (Staying far left is probably the best strategy.) Soon you'll ride into the dry streambed, then curve left out of it in about 0.5 mile (a track continues down the draw, too) to enter a braided playground. The main trail tends to be a little wider than the rest. Fun, steep drop-offs just keep coming at you. Bottom out from the hummocky roller coaster and curve left to stay close to the base of the bluff, as you continue meandering up and down, around and about. At about 10.5 miles you'll coast back to the beginning.

RIDE 66 · Live at Leeds

AT A GLANCE

Length/configuration: 26-mile point-to-point

Aerobic difficulty: A moderately tough workout starting off with a 2.5-mile, 1,000-vertical-foot climb. Cumulative gain is roughly 2,800 feet.

Technical difficulty: Easy, over surfaces of hard-packed gravel, packed dirt/clay, brain-rattling volcanic "unslickrock," and pavement

Scenery: Mid-elevation forests of juniper and piñon, impressive sandstone stream cuts, and distant views of Arizona and the Mojave Desert to the south

Special comments: Soften your shocks and/or tires for the ride out, or risk an unplanned visit to the dentist to have fillings replaced

This point-to-point ride of 26 miles gains some 2,500 feet of elevation and loses even more, since St. George is several hundred feet lower than the trailhead. It encompasses both extended climbs and, between 4 and 12 miles, a series of testy little ups and downs that demand constant shifting as you roller-coaster through a repetition

RIDE 66 · Live at Leeds

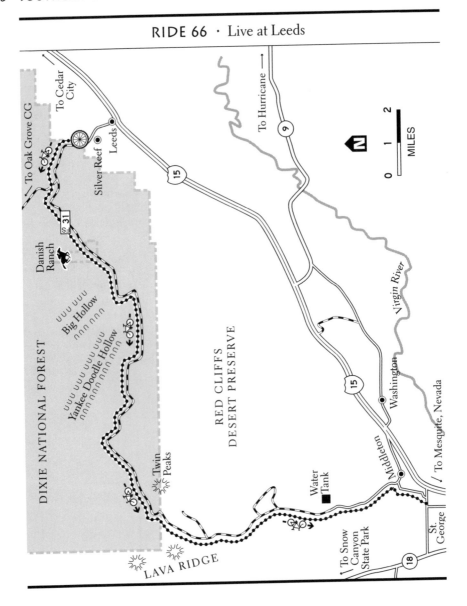

of low ridges and shallow draws (some of which may carry water). Aerobically, the trip is rated somewhere between moderate and difficult; technically, it is easy. Riding surfaces include graded gravel, compacted dirt and clay, annoyingly bumpy spreads of volcanic rock, and pavement. The outing begins just up the hill from the burg of Leeds, near the 19th-century mining town of Silver Reef. Although exclusive homes now grow from the hillsides where mines once emerged, there's enough remaining of an earlier Silver Reef to make it a very interesting detour. The town museum and an art gallery are located in the old Wells Fargo building.

Seven miles from the trailhead you'll round the head of an absolutely mind-boggling sandstone labyrinth, where the earth's slickrock innards have been exposed

Paul Howarth
is precariously
perched above
Yankee Doodle Hollow.

by eons of snowmelt and flash floods storming down Big Hollow and Yankee Doodle Hollow. As you descend from the mountains, you'll pass through the Red Cliffs Desert Reserve, a 60,000-acre preserve set aside in 1996 both to provide unspoiled open space for the human residents of Washington County and to protect unusual and threatened flora and fauna. The reserve is a cooperative project of numerous entities, including the Bureau of Land Management, the local towns and cities, and the U.S. Fish and Wildlife Service. It contains arguably the finest examples of what much of Washington County is: a unique merging of the Mojave Desert, the Great Basin, and the Colorado Plateau.

At ride's end you're spit from the hills into St. George in the vicinity of the Wendy's fast-food restaurant at 120 North 1000 East, close to where St. George Boulevard and Interstate 70 meet. Making a loop of the ride by connecting St. George and Leeds on the interstate/frontage road would add another 16 miles, creating a long-in-the-saddle, 42-mile loop doable by a very fit rider.

General location: The ride runs along the lower southern flanks of the Pine Valley Mountains, north and east of St. George.

Elevation change: Approximately 2,950 to 5,400 feet.

Season: Spring and fall are best.

Services: Procure water and other provisions in St. George, which has all services, including bike shops.

Hazards: This is a long ride in terms of time spent in the saddle, so carry plenty of water or you'll risk dehydration. Watch for rattlesnakes if you go brush-beating.

Rescue index: The entire route is accessible by four-wheel-drive vehicles and/or ATVs, and you may meet others traveling by those modes. Otherwise, the closest help is St. George or Leeds.

Land status: Dixie National Forest, BLM, state, private.

Maps: Dixie National Forest visitor map.

Finding the trail: Drive 12 miles north on I-15 from St. George and take Leeds Exit 22. Cross over the interstate and drive through "downtown" Leeds; 1.5 miles from the interstate turn left toward historic Silver Reef. In another mile bear straight toward Oak Grove Park (Silver Reef is to the left). At 3 miles total, cross the creek and park immediately to the right at the Dixie National Forest boundary.

Source of additional information:

Interagency Visitor Center
345 East Riverside Drive
St. George, UT 84790
(435) 688-3246

Notes on the trail: Begin riding steeply uphill, aiming at a redrock rim, on FS 31, a wide, well-graveled road paralleling Leeds Creek. After a short downhill at 1 mile, venture into the canyon's jaws, with dry, juniper-clad slopes ahead and, to the left, sandstone strata stacked like pancakes. At 1.5 miles, bear straight/left uphill toward "St. George 24" where a fork drops right toward "Oak Grove Campground 6." A little less than a mile from there you'll round a bend and start downhill. Ahead note that curious island of deciduous trees in a sea of piñon-juniper. At just under 4.5 miles, curve around the head of an impressive desert arroyo and enter the Danish Ranch, whose settlers apparently were the ones responsible for that deciduous island. (Off-route travel here is considered trespassing.) Between 7 and 7.5 miles you'll skirt the rim of awesome Big Hollow–Yankee Doodle Hollow, then continue spinning up and zipping down a series of low ridges before commencing a final, mile-long climb at 12 miles. From the top, the ensuing descent is wonderful—perfectly graded so that very little braking is necessary. The only problem is the frozen volcanics that make for some very bumpy going. At just over 16 miles, leave the Dixie National Forest, watching the slot canyon on your right grow as side by side you descend. St. George, front left, is still some 10 miles away. At 20.5 miles, merge right onto the wider gravel road, and then, 2 miles later, ride onto a chipseal surface and pass a water tank on the left. Black igneous rock clashes boldly with the surrounding red sedimentaries. As you drop into town, bear right in the middle of a downhill on Redrock Drive (to the left is Middleton Drive) and turn right at the stop sign onto Industrial Road. In another 0.5 mile, you'll come to Highland Drive and the thick of the city.

RIDE 67 · Race Course Loop

AT A GLANCE

Length/configuration: 8.5-mile loop

Aerobic difficulty: Difficult, with some very steep climbs

Technical difficulty: Advanced, with a little of a lot: slickrock ramps, four-wheel-drive road, ATV trail, gravel, double-track, and steep, winding single-track with plenty of whoop-de-doos

Scenery: Not the most scenically inspiring ride in southern Utah, but you'll be so zoned in on cleaning the route that it really doesn't matter

Special comments: An established NORBA race course used, among other things, as the venue for the World Senior Games mountain bike competitions

This 8.5-mile loop negotiating the Price City Hills, another area of rapid change, is a well-established race (and practice) course. Therefore, the detailed "Notes on the trail" are perhaps superfluous, as you can probably stay on route simply by following others' tracks. Better safe than sorry, however, because the area is an absolute spider's web of dirt tracks and trails. Nearly any level of cyclist will enjoy large parts of this route, so don't let the advanced rating scare you off if you don't have a lot of experience. It's short enough that even if you're reduced to walking substantial portions of the route, it won't be an all-day endeavor. A little of almost everything is encountered along the way, including steep ups and downs on twisty single-track, a memorable stairway of slickrock ledges, four-wheel-drive road, ATV trail, gravel, and double-track.

General location: Four miles south of St. George.

Elevation change: Approximately 2,600 to 2,900 (cumulative gain is substantially more than 300 feet).

Season: September through May; if you go in summer, hit it at the crack of dawn.

Services: All services are available in St. George.

Hazards: This is a race course, after all, so the temptation is to see how fast you can ride it. Be careful, because speed + technically challenging pitches often = crashes. Keep your speed < your discomfort level.

Rescue index: The route is neatly tucked between I-15, a residential area, and the E'Ola distribution center, so you're rarely far from help.

Land status: State.

Maps: A map hand-out is available at the bike shop listed below.

Finding the trail: Go south on River Road, the primary north–south artery on the east side of St. George. Three miles after crossing the Virgin River, continue straight past Brigham Road. Soon you'll pass the E'Ola distribution center on the left and

RIDE 67 · Race Course Loop

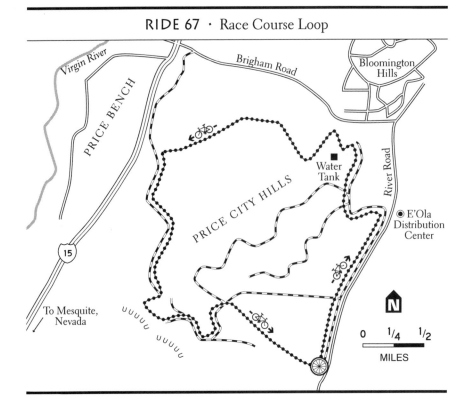

bear right onto a slightly lower-grade hard-surfaced road (left goes to the armory). Just over 1 mile beyond this point, pull off the road to the right and park in the wide flats.

Source of additional information:

Red Rock Bicycle Co.
190 South Main
St. George, UT 84770
(435) 674-3185

Notes on the trail: From the parking area, ride north toward the distant Pine Valley Mountains on the dirt road paralleling the paved road. Pass a trio of spurs going left over the first mile. At just over 1 mile, opposite E'Ola's distribution center, turn left uphill onto the gravel road. Curve left, then back right toward the water tank. In another 0.5 mile, bear right at the fork, trending away from the water tank. In 100 yards go left, aiming back at the water tank; then, within 200 yards of the tank, turn right onto an ATV trail to parallel the power lines as they drop into a canyon toward some houses. At 2 miles cumulative you'll curve left at the fence line, then immediately veer right off the main trail onto single-track, again dropping toward houses. Quickly bear straight/left onto double-track, crossing another track that heads up to the water tank, then continue onto single-track down a steep hill holding a surprise series of ups and downs. At 3 miles cumulative, curve left alongside the power lines, then curve away from the them, traversing a low ridge. With the head of a big draw on your left, continue down toward the interstate; after bottoming out, turn left onto the road passing under the power lines. At 4 miles-plus you'll cross a draw and go uphill, then bear right at the Y at a temporary topping-out point. At just under 5 miles, curve left to ascend an awesomely steep hill. (You're now in a nice little desert canyon, should you bother to look around.) After the steep climb, at a little dip in the road, turn left onto single-track going uphill. After the technical, switchbacking—but fairly smooth—trail climb, continue up the ridge on a wider track. Just before the top, at 5.5 miles, take the single-track going right. It descends, then sidehills around before dropping through a narrow draw. At about 6 miles you'll cross one road and then, roughly 50 yards later, another, more major road, to merge onto a jeep track. Yo-yo back to the road previously crossed and turn left (wrong as it may seem). At 6.5 miles, as you're climbing a hill, turn left onto another single-track that swings left back into the draw to negotiate a technical slickrock "stairway." At just under 7 miles top out, still following serpentine single-track; begin dropping and merge onto a dirt track, then merge onto a more distinct road, quickly turning left off of it onto a slightly lesser road bearing toward a bluff. At 7.5 miles you'll turn right off the road onto single-track, which brings you screamingly to the ride's end at 8.5 miles. That was fun, huh? Now that you know the course, you'd better do it again!

RIDE 68 · Dutchman Loop

AT A GLANCE

Length/configuration: 9-mile combination consisting of an 8-mile loop with a 1-mile out-and-back (0.5 mile each way) spurring off the loop at 2 miles

Aerobic difficulty: Easy, with only about 200 feet of climbing involved

Technical difficulty: Easy to moderate, over narrow roads and tracks of sand, clay, and gravel

Scenery: A desertscape quite unlike other parts of southern Utah you've visited (maybe that's because it's in Arizona!)

Special comments: You're now in the Mojave Desert, rife with goathead and other varieties of ugly vegetation that can readily puncture tires

This nine-mile combination ride consists of an eight-mile loop with a one-mile out-and-back leading to the Little Black Mountain Petroglyph Site. It is easy aerobically, but technically it earns a rating somewhere between easy and moderate. You'll ride over narrow roads and tracks covered with sand and clay, as well as along a short stretch of wider gravel road. This ride and the next (Sunshine Loop) begin at the same trailhead. Both are located in Arizona, but it's that northwest corner of Arizona known as the Arizona Strip, which is cut off from the rest of the state by the Colorado River and the Grand Canyon. As a result, in many ways the area is more like part of Utah; for instance, the lands traversed on these rides are administered by the St. George Bureau of Land Management office. Both rides are BLM-designated mountain bike routes, and they're signed with Carsonite markers. (When I rode them, this ride was much more clearly signed than the next.) The Little Black Mountain Petroglyph Site, the destination of the spur you'll take at two miles, is a developed site with a picnic table, outhouse, and graveled trail winding amid the rock carvings at the base of the mountain. The area is fenced off to prevent vandalism, and you're asked to leave your bicycle outside. An intriguing mix of symbols, ranging from snakes, sheep, and handprints to swirls and circles have led archaeologists to speculate that this was a ceremonial/vision-quest site—particularly in view of what centuries ago was an exceedingly remote, isolated location.

General location: Ten miles south of St. George.

Elevation change: The route meanders up and down around the 3,000-foot level.

Season: September through May.

Services: The closest services are in St. George, 10 miles north.

Hazards: Thorny vegetation off the track can readily insult your tires with multiple puncture wounds. Also, erosional cuts on the road surfaces can take you by surprise.

Rescue index: There's some farming activity just to the north, back in Utah. You may find help there; otherwise, you'll need to head back toward St. George for emergency assistance.

Land status: Bureau of Land Management.

Maps: A map hand-out is available at the Interagency Visitor Center in St. George (see address below).

Finding the trail: From St. George, head south on River Road. Immediately after crossing the Virgin River, turn left onto 1450 South. Stay on the road as it curves right then left in a couple of miles, then, in another 1.5 miles, as it curves right around the fence lines just past some big farms. At 4.5 miles from the Virgin River crossing you'll curve left past the new Red Hawk subdivision/golf course. A little less than 1.5 miles past there the road turns to gravel. At 8.5 miles cumulative, curve left at the three-way intersection. One mile later, just beyond some corrals, bear right to cross a cattle guard and a wash. You'll quickly come to a designated trailhead with sign boards, parking . . . the works.

Source of additional information:

Interagency Visitor Center
345 East Riverside Drive
St. George, UT 84790
(435) 688-3246

Notes on the trail: From the trailhead, ride west on the gravel road paralleling the fence line that marks the Utah–Arizona border. Bear left in about 0.1 mile onto the narrower sand track toward "Little Black Mountain." Cross a wash at about 1 mile cumulative. At 2 miles, where you'll see a double-arrow bike marker, bear right and ride 0.5 mile to the Little Black Mountain Petroglyph Site. After investigating, head back, rejoining the main route—which becomes less traveled beyond the turn to the petroglyphs—at 3 miles cumulative. As you travel south, climbing gradually toward

RIDE 68 · Dutchman Loop
RIDE 69 · Sunshine Loop

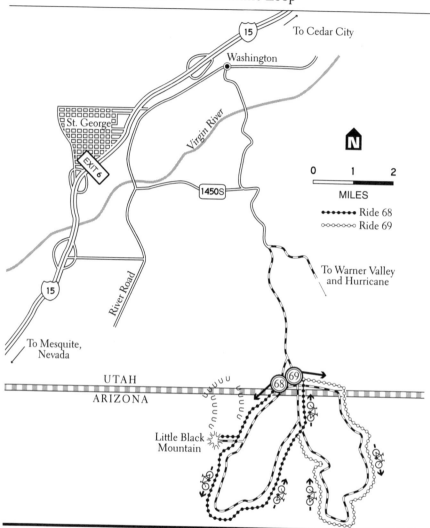

the distant cliffs and power lines, things turn rockier and sandier. At about 5 miles, stay on the lower/left-hand track, then turn left onto the power line road and descend. At 5.5 miles you'll veer left away from power lines to wind along the base of some bluffs. At just under 6.5 miles, bear right on the more distinct track, diving down through a gnarly little wash (you should see a route marker shortly after that). At just over 7 miles, merge left onto a better road; then, at 8.5 miles, merge left onto Road 1035. At 9 miles veer back into the trailhead area.

RIDE 69 · Sunshine Loop

AT A GLANCE

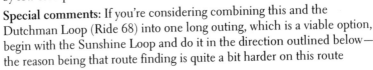

Length/configuration: 9-mile loop

Aerobic difficulty: Moderate, with some tough little climbs

Technical difficulty: Moderate, over clay and sand; angular, tire-popping ankle twisters; and cattle trail and good gravel

Scenery: Radically dissected desert terrain embraced by low escarpments

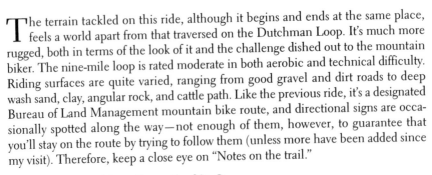

Special comments: If you're considering combining this and the Dutchman Loop (Ride 68) into one long outing, which is a viable option, begin with the Sunshine Loop and do it in the direction outlined below—the reason being that route finding is quite a bit harder on this route

The terrain tackled on this ride, although it begins and ends at the same place, feels a world apart from that traversed on the Dutchman Loop. It's much more rugged, both in terms of the look of it and the challenge dished out to the mountain biker. The nine-mile loop is rated moderate in both aerobic and technical difficulty. Riding surfaces are quite varied, ranging from good gravel and dirt roads to deep wash sand, clay, angular rock, and cattle path. Like the previous ride, it's a designated Bureau of Land Management mountain bike route, and directional signs are occasionally spotted along the way—not enough of them, however, to guarantee that you'll stay on the route by trying to follow them (unless more have been added since my visit). Therefore, keep a close eye on "Notes on the trail."

General location: Ten miles south of St. George.

Elevation change: The route hovers around the 3,000-foot elevation mark.

Season: September through May.

Services: The closest services are in St. George, 10 miles north.

Hazards: Watch for deep sand, potentially sidewall-slicing angular rock, and thorns, particularly along fence lines and in similarly disturbed areas. Flash floods are a very real possibility, too, so don't do this ride if it looks like rain, when some of the road surfaces will turn very muddy, as well.

Rescue index: There's some farming activity just to the north. You may find help there; otherwise, you'll need to head back toward St. George for emergency assistance.

Land status: Bureau of Land Management.

Maps: A map hand-out is available at the Interagency Visitor Center in St. George (see address below).

Finding the trail: From St. George, head south on River Road. Immediately after crossing the Virgin River, turn left onto 1450 South. Stay on the road as it curves right and left in a couple of miles; then, in another 1.5 miles, as it curves right around the fence lines just past some big farms. At 4.5 miles from the Virgin River crossing

The sun often shines on the Sunshine Loop.

you'll curve left past the new Red Hawk subdivision/golf course. A little less than 1.5 miles past there, the road turns to gravel. At 8.5 miles cumulative, curve left at the three-way intersection. One mile later, just beyond some corrals, bear right to cross a cattle guard and a wash. You'll quickly come to a designated trailhead, replete with sign boards and parking.

Source of additional information:

Interagency Visitor Center
345 East Riverside Drive
St. George, UT 84790
(435) 688-3246

Notes on the trail: Ride north the way you drove in, re-entering Utah. In roughly 0.25 mile, cross the wash and cattle guard, then turn right onto the narrow gravel road. In about 0.5 mile the road braids out; stay in the same drainage. Keep the fence line on your right and watch out for thorns. At just under 1 mile cumulative, pass through a juniper-pole fence line, re-entering Arizona. Now ride into and through a nasty, sand-filled draw for a couple of tenths before bearing right, following the bike route sign onto a sand track. Soon you'll again come to a sand draw; "feel" your way through it, and at 1.5 miles pop out to the left side of the draw, where you should see a trail sign. Continue along the sloping sedimentary hummock. It's sometimes hard to tell there's a trail, but you may be able to spot bike tracks. Soon you'll drop down into the draw and ride in it for about 0.75 mile. At 2.5 miles cumulative, you should see another sign directing you to the left, up very difficult, sandy hillside. Climb toward the low watershed divide on the technically challenging trail. Keep your eyes peeled for a trail marker at 3.5 miles, where you'll go straight on the rugged track rather than left on a similarly rough track. A marker then leads you down into the draw, where you remain for a little less than 0.5 mile. Just beyond 4 miles cumulative, follow the marker out of the draw, bearing right onto a gnarly, ugly track. In 0.5 mile you'll top a little rise and soon see a directional marker pointing you left. (Another fork goes right.) Immediately below that is a marker directing you left up the hill. Once atop the knob you should spot another marker pointing you along a very faint track toward the power tower in the distance. At 5 miles-plus, go through the gate in a fence line and turn right to continue tracing the faint trail. About 0.75 mile later, drop into a draw and follow what appears to be a cow trail as it ascends toward a low gap. You should see a reassurance marker at 6 miles. Just beyond that, crest the saddle and start down, looking ahead at the far-off Pine Valley Mountains. Additional markers lead you in a "lefterly" direction toward the main road, onto which you turn right. It's mostly downhill from here. At 8.5 miles merge with the other main road and return to the trailhead at 9 miles.

RIDE 70 · Grafton Ghost Town

AT A GLANCE

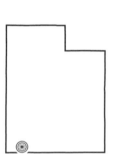

Length/configuration: 7-mile out-and-back (3.5 miles each way)

Aerobic difficulty: Easy, with a moderate amount of climbing involved

Technical difficulty: Easy, over paved and hardened-gravel surfaces

Scenery: Mellow, timbered river bottoms below colorful cliffs

Special comments: Raindrops keep falling on your head

The first settlers to arrive in the Rockville area in 1860 called the settlement Adventure, and an excellent jumping-off place for fat-tire adventures it is. This, the first of five featured rides in the Springdale-Rockville-Virgin vicinity, is very tame, but it offers a good introduction to the area. The 7-mile out-and-back (3.5 miles each way) visits the ghost town of Grafton, noteworthy as the filming site for part of the hit 1968 flick *Butch Cassidy and the Sundance Kid*. The entire short outing, which follows pavement and good gravel, is steeped in history. The Rockville Bridge crossed early on was built by the National Park Service in the early 1920s as a crucial link in the chain of roads connecting Zion National Park and the North Rim of the Grand Canyon. Grafton, settled in the 1860s, once was quite the busy little settlement, but repeated attacks by flooding waters of the Virgin River ultimately convinced the remaining populace to move on in the 1920s. During the three decades following the filming of *Butch Cassidy*, the buildings remaining at the site really went downhill; more recently, however, effort has been going into stabilizing and renovating them.

General location: Immediately southwest of Zion National Park.

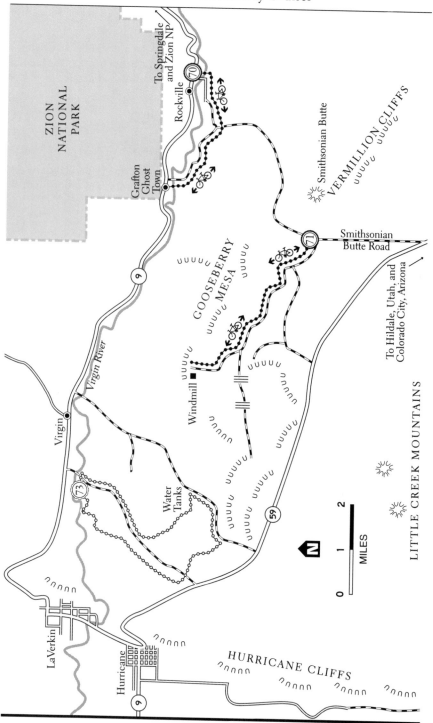

Elevation change: Minimal, as you ride above the Virgin River at around 3,700 feet.

Season: March through May and September through November are best.

Services: A ton of services are available in the tourist-servicing center of Springdale, 3 miles northeast of Rockville.

Hazards: You'll probably share the route with slow-moving auto traffic, as Grafton is a popular tourist stop. It's recommended that you do not attempt to duplicate the tandem ride performed by Paul Newman's and Katherine Ross's characters in *Butch Cassidy and the Sundance Kid.*

Rescue index: You likely will encounter motorists on the ride.

Land status: Private, BLM.

Maps: The DeLorme *Utah Atlas & Gazatteer,* page 17, features a good overview map.

Finding the trail: From St. George, go 10 miles northeast on I-15 and take Exit 16. Follow UT 9 through Hurricane and La Verkin, then continue eastward for another 15 miles to Rockville, where the ride begins. Park near the junction of UT 9 and Bridge Road (200 East).

Source of additional information:

Interagency Visitor Center
345 East Riverside Drive
St. George, UT 84790
(435) 688-3246

Notes on the trail: In Rockville, turn south onto Bridge Road (200 East), crossing the river and following signs toward "Smithsonian Butte Backcountry Byway." (It's also signed as Grafton Road/250 South.) Where an "Impassable When Wet" sign marks the road going straight, go right to stay on pavement. At just under 1 mile cross a cattle guard and start up on a bumpy gravel road. In another 0.75 mile turn right at the T away from the big hill that going left leads to. Just prior to 3 miles you'll cross another cattle guard, beyond which the road narrows some to squeeze through a sandstone notch. In another 0.5 mile, stop to have a look at the Grafton Cemetery on the left. Continue to 3.5 miles cumulative, arriving at Grafton. Look around and then backtrack to Rockville, regained at 7 miles.

RIDE 71 · Gooseberry Cruiser

AT A GLANCE

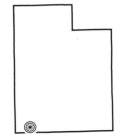

Length/configuration: 10-mile out-and-back (5 miles each way)

Aerobic difficulty: Easy

Technical difficulty: Easy, mostly over a wide, clay-surfaced road

Scenery: Two thumbs up

Special comments: Even if you're not up to the slickrock riding on Gooseberry Mesa (see Ride 72,

The view from Gooseberry Mesa encompasses Zion National Park and much more.

Gooseberry Slickrock Trail), this easy outing gives you an excellent excuse to get on the mesa's top

This ten-mile out-and-back (five miles each way) begins not far from Zion National Park, where everything—even the roadway—turns red. On the ride, rated both technically and aerobically easy, you'll earn startling views of the brilliance of Zion, as well as of the more subdued hues of the Pine Valley Mountains rising in the northwest, and, at the turnaround, a sublime look down on the Virgin River basin. The nearby town of Springdale, tucked between Zion and Rockville, is mighty fancy, with lots of restaurants and lavish accommodations—even an IMAX theater. Rockville, where you leave the highway, is a well-shaded, quieter, and somehow more dignified town. It was originally settled in the early 1860s, with early settlers raising cotton and sugarcane. Look around town and you'll discover some structures that verge on ancient.

General location: Just southwest of Zion National Park.

Elevation change: The top of Gooseberry Mesa is right at the 5,000-foot level; cumulatively you gain roughly 300 feet.

Season: Optimum times of year are March through May and September through November.

Services: All services are available in Springdale, 3 miles northeast of Rockville.

Hazards: Don't get caught in a rainstorm, or you might not get back to your car any time soon; even if you do, you might not get your car down off the mesa.

Rescue index: There may be some vehicle activity on top, but don't count on it. Make like a Boy Scout and be prepared.

Land status: Bureau of Land Management.

Maps: DeLorme *Utah Atlas & Gazetteer*, page 17, offers an overview. Blow-up maps are available at the two bike shops listed below.

Finding the trail: In Rockville, just southwest of Springdale and the entrance to Zion National Park, turn south onto Bridge Road (200 East), crossing the river and following the pavement toward "Smithsonian Butte Backcountry Byway." (The road is also signed as Grafton Road/250 South.) About a mile after leaving the highway cross a cattle guard and start up a bumpy gravel road. Go left at the T then, 0.5 mile later, hit a virtual wall of a road, on which you'll gain more than 500 feet of elevation in 0.5 mile. At 3 miles wend toward Smithsonian Butte at a lower gradient, passing through some potentially gnarly clay areas. A total of 6.5 miles from the highway, pass through the fence line (signed "Gooseberry Mesa") and park.

Sources of additional information:

Red Rock Bicycle Co.
190 South Main
St. George, UT 84770
(435) 674-3185

Bicycles Unlimited
90 South 100 East
St. George, UT 84770
(435) 673-4492

Notes on the trail: Start riding downhill on the smooth, gravel- and dirt-surfaced road. At about 0.5 mile, continue straight where another fork goes left. Climb for a couple of miles; then, at 3 miles cumulative, cross a cattle guard. One-half mile later bear right on the main road. (The less-maintained road forking left leads to Ride 72, Gooseberry Slickrock Trail.) At a little over 4.5 miles you'll pass an old windmill on the left and, at 5 miles, arrive at the end of the road and a marvelous overlook. Soak it in, shoot some photos ("Back up just a little farther . . . okay, just a little farther . . ."), then retrace your tracks to the trailhead, reached at 10 miles.

RIDE 72 · Gooseberry Slickrock Trail

AT A GLANCE

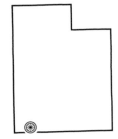

Length/configuration: 10-mile combination ride consisting of a puzzle of spurs and loops marked by green and yellow paint

Aerobic difficulty: Moderate, with plenty of short, steep uphills

Technical difficulty: Moderate to extremely difficult, depending on how tough you choose to make it. Riding surfaces include sandy double-track, slickrock, and dirt single-track

Scenery: The views from the rim defy description

Special comments: Petrified Cowpie City, punctuated with cacti and timber

Despite its relative anonymity, this ride is to the St. George region what the Slick-rock Bike Trail is to Moab. Staying to the "main" route is an exercise in navigational skills and/or frustration. Keep in mind that the large green dots mark the main trail, small green dots mark side loops, and yellow paint marks extremely technical sections. Also watch for cairns. If you can find a local to accompany you, so much the better; check at the bike shops listed below for possible companions. If you can't, you probably won't take advantage of all the great riding, but you'll still have fun. (My riding companion and I missed some of the trail, I'm sure, and I don't think I could repeat exactly what we rode. But we had great fun.) Just keep some paint in sight. If you feel as though you're getting lost, you can always turn around and retrace your tracks as best you can.

General location: Just southwest of Zion National Park.

Elevation change: The elevation at the top of Gooseberry Mesa is around 5,000 feet, and you don't deviate much from that.

Season: Optimum times of year are March through May and September through November.

Services: All services are available in Springdale, 3 miles northeast of Rockville.

Hazards: The marked route out along the rim features a degree of exposure bordering on ridiculous; it's an accident waiting to happen (or maybe by now it has). Walk your bike where prudence suggests it, and even then beware of gusty winds and/or a slip of the foot. Also watch out for overhanging branches and for cacti, which is much more abundant here than on that Slickrock Trail on the other side of the state.

Rescue index: The route is very remote, and much of it is hard to get to. The consequences of a spill and resultant injury could be serious indeed.

Land status: Bureau of Land Management.

Maps: DeLorme *Utah Atlas & Gazetteer*, page 17, offers an overview. Blow-up maps are available at the two bike shops listed below.

Finding the trail: In Rockville, turn south onto Bridge Road (200 East), crossing the river and following the pavement toward "Smithsonian Butte Backcountry Byway." (It's also signed as Grafton Road/250 South.) About a mile after leaving the highway cross a cattle guard and start up on a bumpy gravel road. Go left at the T, and then, 0.5 mile later, navigate 0.5 mile of astoundingly steep uphill. At the top, continue driving upward toward Smithsonian Butte. At 6.5 miles cumulative, take the fork passing through a fence line that's signed "Gooseberry Mesa." One-half mile from there, continue straight where a fork goes left. At 9.5 miles you'll cross a cattle guard, and then, at just past 10 miles, arrive at a fork. Drive onto the less-maintained track going left. In about 1 mile park on the left, just past another cattle guard.

Sources of additional information:

Red Rock Bicycle Co.
190 South Main
St. George, UT 84770
(435) 674-3185

Bicycles Unlimited
90 South 100 East
St. George, UT 84770
(435) 673-4492

Notes on the trail: Ride westerly up the sand track, veering right off of it after about 0.25 mile to follow the green dots into some fabulous slickrocking. Whenever you hit

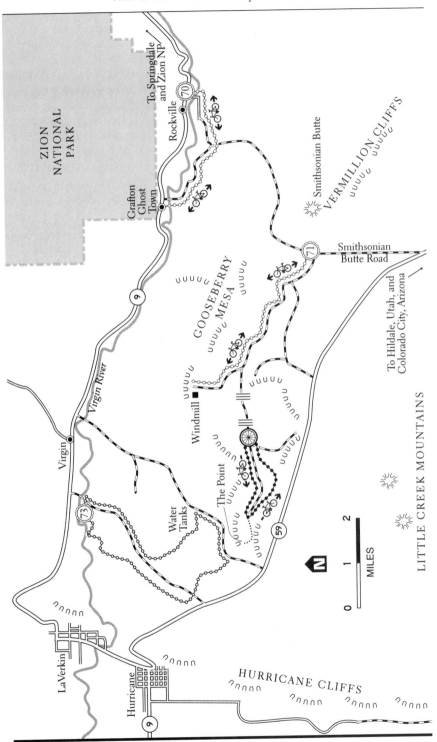

sand or dirt, just watch for tire tracks. At just under 1 mile ride across a double-track, then return to the main four-wheel-drive track. At 2 miles, bear right at the Y. At just past 3 miles you'll come to a sort of jeep cul de sac, although your sand track perseveres straight ahead. At 3.5 miles bear right (left is yellow-dot territory) to ride a very sandy stretch with slickrock ramps. At just past 4 miles you'll hit the north rim and its stupendous views. Bear left and begin a 2-mile stretch directly along the rim, following the green dotted trail. It's technical and threatens great exposure. At 6 miles-plus veer away from the rim, winding mostly on single-track over knobs, through notches, under timber, and around gardens of cacti. Very important: At 7.5 miles cumulative turn left onto the four-wheel-drive road. (Going right, as the author initially did, leads to a serious rim-rocked situation.) At roughly 8 miles you'll close the loop, turning right back onto the main path. At approximately 10 miles return to the trailhead.

RIDE 73 · Gooseberry Gander

AT A GLANCE

Length/configuration: 12.5-mile loop

Aerobic difficulty: Moderate, with a climb of around 600 vertical feet over the first few miles

Technical difficulty: Moderate, over a smorgasbord of surfaces including solid rock, sand, hardened gravel, clay, gravel-like sandstone, and zippity-do-dah single-track

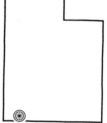

Scenery: Great desert surroundings of sand washes and ledge-rock draws. Early on you'll brush the base of Gooseberry Mesa; later, you'll hold your breath as you negotiate the spectacular and precarious Virgin River rim.

Special comments: This is the numero-uno favorite ride of many locals in the St. George–Springdale area

This ride dishes up a little of everything: Shale, silt, wash crossings, sandstone slabs, sand, hard-packed road, clay, a gravel-like sandstone conconction, and serpentine single-track . . . not to mention outstanding scenery. A favorite of local fat-tire fans, who call it the Jem Loop, the 12.5-mile ride is rated moderate in terms of both aerobic and technical difficulty. If you did Ride 72, Gooseberry Slickrock Trail, you looked down on some of the country traversed on this ride; here you'll have the opportunity to look back up at the bulk of Gooseberry Mesa. Pay very close attention to your mileage, because accidentally getting off the route is a nearly constant possibility—explaining the lengthy "Notes on the trail" section.

General location: Just outside of Virgin, on the other (south) side of the Virgin River.

Elevation change: Approximately 3,500 to 4,100 feet.

Season: The optimum months are March through May and September through November.

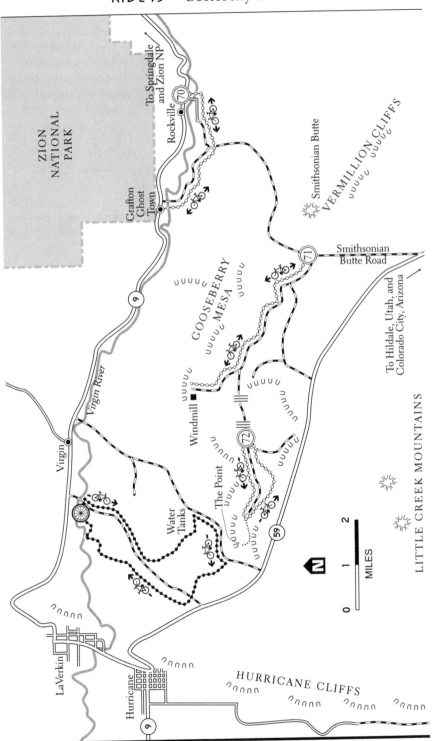

Services: Virgin has minimal services. If coming from the west, stock up in St. George or Hurricane; from the east, in Springdale.

Hazards: Loose-surfaced single-track descents, tire-threatening cacti and thorns, and life-theatening exposure along the Virgin River rim. Be prepared to walk along the rim if heights/exposure freaks you out. Avoid during rains.

Rescue index: Most of the ride takes place in way-out-there country, although you'll possibly encounter a pickup truck or two on the sections following semi-main roads.

Land status: Bureau of Land Management.

Maps: DeLorme *Utah Atlas & Gazetteer,* page 17, offers an overview. A schematic map is included in the pamphlet, "Mountain Biking Guide to Southern Utah," produced by Red Rock Bicycle Co. (see below).

Finding the trail: From St. George, go 10 miles northeast on I-15 and take Exit 16. Follow UT 9 through Hurricane and La Verkin; then take it eastward for another roughly 4 miles to just west of Virgin. A mile before town, immediately east of the 17-mile marker, turn south onto the dirt road that after 0.5 mile crosses the Virgin River notch on a very narrow bridge. You'll soon cross a cattle guard; approximately 100 feet past that turn right onto the dirt track aiming at Hurricane Mesa. Go about 0.25 mile and park at the loop turnaround.

Sources of additional information:

Interagency Visitor Center
345 East Riverside Drive
St. George, UT 84790
(435) 688-3246

Red Rock Bicycle Co.
190 South Main
St. George, UT 84770
(435) 674-3185

Notes on the trail: Ride east back the way you drove in and turn right onto the primary dirt road, setting your sights at a gap on Gooseberry Mesa. Two miles into the ride you'll drop through major wash, then, in a little less than 0.5 mile, arrive at a wide, flat wash, into which you turn left. At 3 miles turn left onto the four-wheel-drive track, leaving the wash and skirting a fenced-off area/corrals to your left (if you come to a fence in the draw you'll need to backtrack a short way). At 4 miles pass some horse-watering tanks, then descend to begin meandering through arroyo-dissected headlands at the base of Gooseberry Mesa. At the fork at just under 4.5 miles go right. At 5 miles you'll encircle the head of a huge cut, curving right, and then ride through a gate as you continue to curve. Up, down, up, down you go, with some testy little steep climbs coming out of the draws. Turn right at 6.5 miles onto the single-track zippering across scrub flats toward the distant Pine Valley Mountains. (There should be a pair of cairns marking this turn. But in case there isn't, watch your odometer as you approach a high point.) At just under 7 miles, cross the barbed-wire fence to find a radical walking trail zig-zagging down into a draw. Keep a close eye out for the trail as it ascends a steep pitch back up the left side of the wash. Then comes a very steep downhill into the wash, which you cross and then begin speeding down through brush. (Note the highway ahead left.) At just past 8 miles, ride straight across the main dirt road, continuing on single-track. In another 0.5 mile cross a sand track road and, at 9 miles, come to a water impoundment that may be dry but still recognizable. Swing left around the head of the pond—don't take the left fork going away from it—while watching out for tire-threatening glass and goathead thorns, and relocate the trail on the other side. Soon you'll merge briefly left onto a double-track, then immediately go right off of it. The trail is good here and quite easy to follow. Just under 10 miles, after a short, technical descent across a wash, aim again at Gooseberry Mesa. At 10 miles even, you'll cross a pair of merging double-tracks as you head straight at the domes of Zion. After crossing another wash, then another pair of washes at 10.5 miles, begin swinging down the left side of a draw, which becomes more pronounced just past 11 miles. Keep heading down-draw on single-track, ignoring side spurs, to just before the canyon digs itself a steep notch deeper. Here you'll cross the draw in a wide, flat area of slickrock. Watch for cairns, which will lead you along the right side of the draw—unnervingly close to the rim in places. At just under 12 miles, swing wide to the right to get around a side wash, then curve left. Continue down along the right side of the main draw. The trail soon swings right, and the draw you've been following merges with the canyon of the Virgin River, which is mightily spectacular. Follow the main track back to the trailhead, reached at 12.5 miles.

RIDE 74 · Rockville Bench

AT A GLANCE

Length/configuration: As described here, a 6-mile combination ride featuring a 4-mile out-and-back (2 miles each way) connected to a 2-mile loop. Realistically, however, in the playgrounds of slickrock you'll probably fashion a custom route.

Aerobic difficulty: Moderate, with some steep uphills

Technical difficulty: Moderate to very difficult, depending on the lines picked. Riding surfaces include blacktop, sandy double-track, single-track, and technical slickrock.

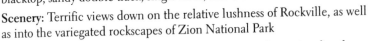

Scenery: Terrific views down on the relative lushness of Rockville, as well as into the variegated rockscapes of Zion National Park

Special comments: Be very careful not to cross into the national park, where riding off the paved roads is illegal. Also, avoid riding through cryptobiotic crusts out on the slickrock.

This ride takes place on a narrow strip of sandy land and moonscape squeezed between UT 9 and Zion National Park. As described below the ride is a six-mile combination, with a two-mile spur leading to a two-mile loop. Aerobically the riding is easy to moderately difficult; technically you can get into some really tough stuff if you choose to. Riding surfaces include blacktop, sand-covered double-track, single-track, and slickrock beds with maneuverability quotients ranging from easy to off the chart. Early on the route passes through an area of current change, with new subdivision roads and who-knows-what-else going in, so it may look different by the time you get there.

If you want, rather than following the black-paint slickrock trail beyond mile two, feel free to simply ride the sandy four-wheel-drive road out and back—or, alternatively, explore the slickrock on your own. Just don't get lost out there! Keep in visual contact with the big red-rock formation to the north. If you'd like to check out Zion's Chinle

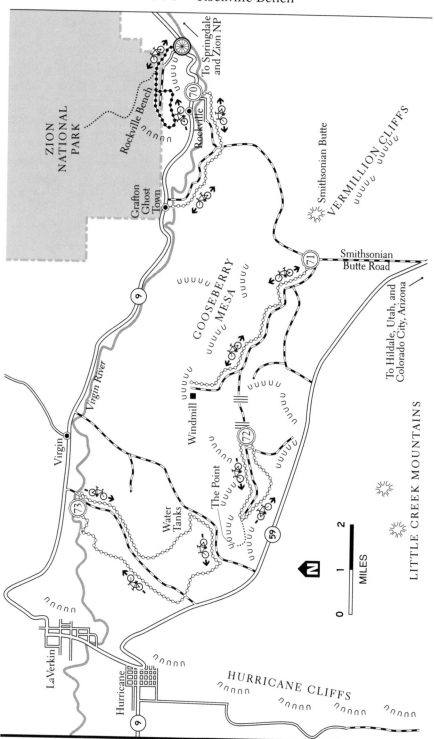

Paul, just before I almost lost him for the night on Rockville Bench.

Trail, go straight at the three-way junction mentioned in "Notes on the trail"; leave your bike at the park boundary, however, and proceed only on foot.

General location: Just north of Rockville and south of Zion National Park.

Elevation change: Approximately 3,700 to 4,000 feet.

Season: March through May and September through November are best, although many days in winter are fine, as well.

Services: All services are available in nearby Springdale.

Hazards: Getting lost, rimrocked, and/or dehydrated.

Rescue index: You're never far from civilization, yet a rescue would be quite difficult out in the slickrock reaches.

Land status: Bureau of Land Management.

Maps: Blow-up maps are available at local bike shops (see below).

Finding the trail: West of Springdale Farms (an orchard just west of Springdale), immediately west of mile marker 29, turn north off UT 9 onto the blacktop access road for Anasazi Plateau Estates. In about 100 yards pull into the parking area for the Chinle Trail. (The "No Mountain Bikes" sign you may see here relates to Zion National Park.)

Sources of additional information:

Red Rock Bicycle Co.
190 South Main
St. George, UT 84770
(435) 674-3185

Bicycles Unlimited
90 South 100 East
St. George, UT 84770
(435) 673-4492

Notes on the trail: Climb from the parking area on blacktop for 0.5 mile (the blacktop ended at this point when I visited); then, at 0.75 mile cumulative you'll come to a sort of three-way junction: A faint four-wheel-drive trail goes right up the wash, and a signed foot trail goes up center (hitting the national park boundary in about 0.25 mile). Left, the way you want to go, climbs for roughly 0.1 mile, then drops down through a draw, before climbing back up to skirt some power lines. Beside the power lines at just past 1 mile, drop right off the new subdivision road onto an obviously older double-track. It's a sandy four-wheel drive road with occasional slickrock patches. At 2 miles pedal onto the slickrock trail marked with black dots and diamonds. At 2.5 miles temporarily leave the slickrock to ride through a sandy, brushy area on single-track, then return to technical slickrock. At 4 miles you'll arrive at at a tremendous overlook above Rockville and the Virgin River Valley. Just beyond here a black arrow points you left, back to the nearby sandy double-track. (Alternatively, black diamonds lead you out onto a peninsula where you'll get rimrocked if you're not careful. Be sure you're able to return by the route you follow out.) Go right onto the road, and you'll return to the trailhead at approximately 6 miles cumulative.

RIDE 75 · Church Rocks

AT A GLANCE

Length/configuration: 11-mile combination consisting of a 4-mile out-and-back (2 miles each way), a 2.5-mile loop, and a second out-and-back spur of 4.5 miles (2.2 miles each way)

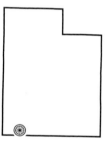

Aerobic difficulty: Moderate, with some testy little uphills

Technical difficulty: Moderate to difficult, including surfaces of good gravel road, primitive double-track, sand, slickrock ranging from smooth to ledgy, and delightful single-track meandering through scrub desert

Scenery: You're rarely, if ever, out of sight of Interstate 15, yet the vistas of the Pine Valley Mountains, the Hurricane Cliffs, and other features are sublime

Special comments: The ride traverses a tortoise protection area, so treat shelled critters with due respect. Also, stay on the trail and don't ride through crypto gardens.

My companions and I did this ride on Easter Sunday; therefore, I was able to report to my mother that, yes, I did go to church on Easter (Church Rocks, that is). It's a great little zip of a ride, incorporating graded gravel (generally good, but occasionally rather deep and unconsolidated), rough double-track, sand, slickrock (sometimes smooth, sometimes ledgy), and a wonderful stretch of single-track teeming with mini S-curves. Aerobically, the ride is rated moderate, while technically, it's

RIDE 75 · Church Rocks

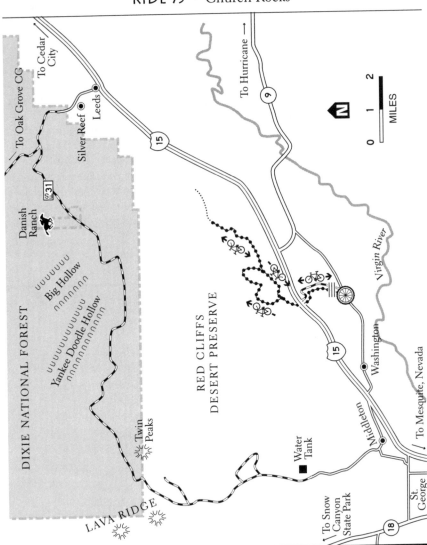

somewhere between moderate and difficult. If you keep your eyes peeled, you may encounter road runners ("ME-MEEP") and huge desert tortoises, which are a real surprise when you first see them. Keep a close watch for marks on the slickrock and for cairns, as well, because parts of the trail are quite challenging to follow.

General location: Two miles northeast of Washington, which is just northeast of St. George.

Elevation change: Approximately 3,000 to 3,400 feet.

Season: March through May and September through November are best, although many days in winter are fine, as well.

Services: All services are available in nearby Washington.

Hazards: A couple of radical drop-offs beg you to dismount and walk; cactus and deep sand are other things to watch for. Don't do this ride if it looks like rain, because part of the route entails riding through a large drainage culvert.

Rescue index: You're never much more than a mile from I-15.

Land Status: State.

Maps: A schematic map is included in the pamphlet, "Mountain Biking Guide to Southern Utah," produced by Red Rock Bicycle Co.

Finding the trail: From the corner of Telegraph Street and 300 East in Washington City, go 2 miles east on paved Telegraph Street/Frontage Road and park on the left side of the road, away from the cattleguard.

Sources of additional information:

Red Rock Bicycle Co.
190 South Main
St. George, UT 84770
(435) 674-3185

Interagency Visitor Center
345 East Riverside Drive
St. George, UT 84790
(435) 688-3246

Notes on the trail: From the parking area, walk gingerly across the cattleguard (there's probably a chain above it, which you'll have to step over). Ride north toward the bulk of the Pine Valley Mountains on good gravel through redrock-surrounded scrub desert. You're heading in the general direction of a flat-topped water storage tank. At just over one mile, turn left off the main road to pass between a pair of wooden posts and drop steeply down a badly rutted road. On reaching the bottom, turn right at the T, ride for 100 yards or so, and, at just under two miles cumulative, turn left to pass under I-15 by way of a huge drainage culvert. (Don't forget to remove your shades—it's dark in there!) At two miles, you'll hit a rugged stretch of sand and rock, where walking is necessary (or prudent, at least). Next, ride onto a single-track trail and pass (on the right) the trail that you'll be looping back on. The route-finding through the subsequent rocky section can be tricky, so watch for cairns and tracks left by previous riders. You'll negotiate a brief stretch of single-track then encounter some more tough stuff in the rocks. At four miles, drop off the main trail and the rock rim onto the single-track bearing eastward. The next couple of miles are generally very good, except for a nasty stretch of sand at about five miles cumulative. At 5.5 miles, you'll pass through a fence line, then arrive at the recommended turnaround at just past 6 miles. Return to the point where you left the main trail at about 8.5 miles; turn left onto the continuation of that trail. A fun stretch of technical slickrock leads back to the junction where you turn left, at nine miles, back onto the original out-and-back segment. Retrace your tracks by riding under I-15, turning right on the other side of the tunnel, then turning left to climb the steep hill toward the "goal posts" at the top, where you'll turn right onto the main road. Regain the trailhead at 11 miles.

GLOSSARY

This short list of terms does not contain all the words used by mountain bike enthusiasts when discussing their sport. But it should serve as an introduction to the lingo you'll hear on the trails.

ATB	all-terrain bike; this, like "fat-tire bike," is another name for a mountain bike
ATV	all-terrain vehicle; this usually refers to the loud, fume-spewing three- or four-wheeled motorized vehicles you will not enjoy meeting on the trail—except, of course, if you crash and have to hitch a ride out on one
blaze	a mark on a tree made by chipping away a piece of the bark, usually done to designate a trail; such trails are sometimes described as "blazed"
blind corner	a curve in the road or trail that conceals bikers, hikers, equestrians, and other traffic
blowdown	see "windfall"
BLM	Bureau of Land Management, an agency of the federal government
bollard	a post (or series of posts) set vertically into the ground that allow pedestrians or cyclists to pass but keep vehicles from entering (wooden bollards are also commonly used to sign intersections)
braided	a braided trail condition results when people attempt to travel around a wet area; networks of interlaced trails can result and are a maintenance headache for trail crews
buffed	used to describe a very smooth trail
Carsonite sign	a small, thin, and flexible fiberglass signpost used extensively by the Forest Service and BLM to mark roads and trails (often dark brown in color)
catching air	taking a jump in such a way that both wheels of the bike are off the ground at the same time

cattle guard	a grate of parallel steel bars or pipes set at ground level and suspended over a ditch; cows can't cross them (their little feet slip through the openings between the pipes), but pedestrians and vehicles can pass over cattle guards with little difficulty
clean	while this may describe what you and your bike won't be after following many trails, the term is most often used as a verb to denote the action of pedaling a tough section of trail successfully
combination	this type of route may combine two or more configurations; for example, a point-to-point route may integrate a scenic loop or an out-and-back spur midway through the ride; likewise, an out-and-back may have a loop at its farthest point (this configuration looks like a cherry with a stem attached; the stem is the out-and-back, the fruit is the terminus loop); or a loop route may have multiple out-and-back spurs and/or loops to the side; mileage for a combination route is for the total distance to complete the ride
cupped	a concave trail; higher on the sides than in the middle; often caused by motorcycles
dab	touching the ground with a foot or hand
deadfall	a tangled mass of fallen trees or branches
decomposed granite	an excellent, fine- to medium-grain, trail and road surface; typically used in native surface road and trail applications (not trucked in); results from the weathering of granite
diversion ditch	a usually narrow, shallow ditch dug across or around a trail; funneling the water in this manner keeps it from destroying the trail
double-track	the dual tracks made by a jeep or other vehicle, with grass, weeds, or rocks between; mountain bikers can ride in either of the tracks, but you will find that whichever one you choose, no matter how many times you change back and forth, the other track will appear to offer smoother travel
dugway	a steep, unpaved, switchbacked descent
endo	flipping end over end
feathering	using a light touch on the brake lever, hitting it lightly many times rather than very hard or locking the brake
four-wheel-drive	this refers to any vehicle with drive-wheel capability on all four wheels (a jeep, for instance, has four-wheel drive as compared with a two-wheel-drive passenger car), or to a rough road or trail that requires four-wheel-drive capability (or a one-wheel-drive mountain bike!) to negotiate it
game trail	the usually narrow trail made by deer, elk, or other game

gated	everyone knows what a gate is, and how many variations exist on this theme; well, if a trail is described as "gated" it simply has a gate across it; don't forget that the rule is if you find a gate closed, close it behind you; if you find one open, leave it that way
Giardia	shorthand for *Giardia lamblia*, and known as the "backpacker's bane" until we mountain bikers expropriated it; a waterborne parasite that begins its life cycle when swallowed, and one to four weeks later has its host (you) bloated, vomiting, shivering with chills, and living in the bathroom; the disease can be avoided by "treating" (purifying) the water you acquire along the trail (see "Hitting the Trail" in the Introduction)
gnarly	a term thankfully used less and less these days, it refers to tough trails
graded	refers to a dirt road that has been smoothed out by the use of a wide blade on earth-moving equipment; "blading" gets rid of the teeth-chattering, much-cursed washboards found on so many dirt roads after heavy vehicle use
hammer	to ride very hard
hammerhead	one who rides hard and fast
hardpack	a trail in which the dirt surface is packed down hard; such trails make for good and fast riding, and very painful landings; bikers most often use "hardpack" as both a noun and adjective, and "hard-packed" as an adjective only (the grammar lesson will help you when diagramming sentences in camp)
hike-a-bike	what you do when the road or trail becomes too steep or rough to remain in the saddle
jeep road, jeep trail	a rough road or trail passable only with four-wheel-drive capability (or a horse or mountain bike)
kamikaze	while this once referred primarily to those Japanese fliers who quaffed a glass of sake, then flew off as human bombs in suicide missions against U.S. naval vessels, it has more recently been applied to the idiot mountain bikers who, far less honorably, scream down hiking trails, endangering the physical and mental safety of the walking, biking, and equestrian traffic they meet; deck guns were necessary to stop the Japanese kamikaze pilots, but a bike pump or walking staff in the spokes is sufficient for the current-day kamikazes who threaten to get us all kicked off the trails
loop	this route configuration is characterized by riding from the designated trailhead to a distant point, then returning to the

trailhead via a different route (or simply continuing on the same in a circle route) without doubling back; you always move forward across new terrain but return to the starting point when finished; mileage is for the entire loop from the trailhead back to trailhead

multipurpose   a BLM designation of land that is open to many uses; mountain biking is allowed

off-camber   a trail that slopes in the opposite direction than one would prefer for safety's sake; for example, on a side-cut trail the slope is away from the hill—the inside of the trail is higher, so it helps you fall downhill if your balance isn't perfect

ORV/OHV   a motorized off-road vehicle (off-highway vehicle)

out-and-back   a ride where you will return on the same trail you pedaled out; while this might sound far more boring than a loop route, many trails look very different when pedaled in the opposite direction

pack stock   horses, mules, llamas, etc., carrying provisions along trails

point-to-point   a vehicle shuttle (or similar assistance) is required for this type of route, which is ridden from the designated trailhead to a distant location, or endpoint, where the route ends; total mileage is for the one-way trip from the trailhead to endpoint

portage   to carry your bike on your person

pummy   soil with high pumice content produced by volcanic activity in the Pacific Northwest and elsewhere; light in consistency and easily pedaled; trails with such soil often become thick with dust

quads   bikers use this term to refer both to the extensor muscle in the front of the thigh (which is separated into four parts) and to USGS maps; the expression "Nice quads!" refers always to the former, however, except in those instances when the speaker is an engineer

runoff   rainwater or snowmelt

scree   an accumulation of loose stones or rocky debris lying on a slope or at the base of a hill or cliff

side-cut trail   a trail cut on the side of a hill

signed   a "signed" trail has signs in place of blazes

single-track   a single, narrow path through grass or brush or over rocky terrain, often created by deer, elk, or backpackers; single-track riding is some of the best fun around

skid road   the path created when loggers drag trees through the forest with heavy equipment

slickrock	the rock-hard, compacted sandstone that is great to ride and even prettier to look at; you'll appreciate it even more if you think of it as a petrified sand dune or seabed (which it is), and if the rider before you hasn't left tire marks (from unnecessary skidding) or granola bar wrappers behind
snowmelt	runoff produced by the melting of snow
snowpack	unmelted snow accumulated over weeks or months of winter—or over years—in high-mountain terrain
spur	a road or trail that intersects the main trail you're following
squid	one who skids
stair-step climb	a climb punctuated by a series of level or near-level sections
switchback	a zigzagging road or trail designed to assist in traversing steep terrain; mountain bikers should not skid through switchbacks
talus	the rocky debris at the base of a cliff, or a slope formed by an accumulation of this rocky debris
tank trap	a steep-sided ditch (or series of ditches) used to block access to a road or trail; often used in conjunction with high mounds of excavated material
technical	terrain that is difficult to ride due not to its grade (steepness) but to its obstacles—rocks, roots, logs, ledges, loose soil.
topo	short for topographical map, the kind that shows both linear distance and elevation gain and loss; "topo" is pronounced with both vowels long
trashed	a trail that has been destroyed (same term used no matter what has destroyed it . . . cattle, horses, or even mountain bikers riding when the ground was too wet)
trialsin	highly technical riding over natural and artificial obstacles at low speeds, with points assessed for putting down a foot, or "dab" (to complete a section without dabbing it is to "clean" it)
two-track	see "double-track"
two-wheel-drive	this refers to any vehicle with drive-wheel capability on only two wheels (a passenger car, for instance, has two-wheel drive); a two-wheel-drive road is a road or trail easily traveled by an ordinary car
waterbar	an earth, rock, or wooden structure that funnels water off trails to reduce erosion
washboarded	a road that is surfaced with many ridges spaced closely together, like the ripples on a washboard; these make for very rough riding, and even worse driving in a car or jeep

whoop-de-doo closely spaced dips or undulations in a trail; these are often encountered in areas traveled heavily by ORVs

wilderness area land that is officially set aside by the federal government to remain natural—pure, pristine, and untrammeled by any vehicle, including mountain bikes; though mountain bikes had not been born in 1964 (when the United States Congress passed the Wilderness Act, establishing the National Wilderness Preservation system), they are considered a "form of mechanical transport" and are thereby excluded; in short, stay out

windchill a reference to the wind's cooling effect on exposed flesh; for example, if the temperature is 10 degrees Fahrenheit and the wind is blowing at 20 miles per hour, the windchill (that is, the actual temperature to which your skin reacts) is minus 32 degrees; if you are riding in wet conditions things are even worse, for the windchill would then be minus 74 degrees!

windfall anything (trees, limbs, brush, fellow bikers . . .) blown down by the wind

INDEX

ABOUT THE AUTHOR

Michael McCoy's combined bicycle trail research and writing career spans a quarter century. His first such job came in 1975, when he helped lay out Bikecentennial's TransAmerica Bicycle Trail. More recently, he spent the summers and falls of 1994 through 1997 researching the Adventure Cycling Association's Great Divide Mountain Bike Route, an off-pavement touring route that runs for 2,470 miles along the Continental Divide from Canada to Mexico.

McCoy is the author of seven other books, including *Mountain Bike Adventures in the Four Corners Region* (The Mountaineers Books), *Montana: Off the Beaten Path* (Globe Pequot Press), and *Journey to the Northern Rockies* (Globe Pequot Press), a general guidebook and travel narrative to the region. His writing on adventure travel has appeared in many magazines, including *Men's Journal, Women Outside, Bicycling,* and *Snow Country.* Today, in addition to his continuing work with Adventure Cycling, he serves as managing editor of *Jackson Hole Magazine* and as western Wyoming–eastern Idaho correspondent for Streetmail.com, an Internet newsletter. He and his wife Nancy live in Teton Valley, Idaho, where they spend the long winters alpine and cross-country skiing. He can be reached via email at mmccoy@emptyhighways.com.